Sharing What I'm Learning:

About Waking Up, Transforming Consciousness, and Undertaking the Spiritual Journey

by Anthony from Granger

Sharing What I'm Learning

Front Cover Photo Credit:
Image: European Space Agency & NASA
http://spacetelescope.org/images/heic0602a/

ISBN-13: 978-1545014332
ISBN: 1545014337

Dedication

This book is dedicated to my nephew, Paul
To my sons, John, Randolph, and Joseph
To my daughters-in-law, Christi and Stefani
And to my grandchildren
Samuel, Thomas, Noah, and Annika

In the hope that at least some of them will read it
And will want to dialogue with me
About the values and beliefs that I have come to accept
And the worldview that I wish to defend
as the best one possible in this day and time

Table of Contents

Preface

I have learned a lot in my 80 years of exploring what being human is all about. The most valuable lesson I have learned is that humans can awaken to a more aware, more awake state of consciousness.

A lot of life's day-to-day hassles are a lot easier to manage if we can occasionally, at least briefly, wake up to this higher state of consciousness.

In this book, I want to share with you some techniques and methods that I have learned for waking up to this state more frequently and for functioning from there for longer periods of time.

The second most valuable lesson I have learned is that there are stages of consciousness and that humans are not all functioning at the same stage of consciousness.

A healthy growth and development process will have us growing up through several of these stages during our lifetime. I have found that learning to differentiate these stages and learning on which stage I am currently operating is very helpful in understanding what is going on in the world. It is possible to transform from one stage of consciousness to the next higher one. I have always found it to be a very joyful occasion every time I managed to transform to the next higher stage.

I want to share with you the transformation strategies that I have found to be most helpful. I have learned these strategies from many sources but most specifically from the Work of George Gurdjieff, the Psychosynthesis of Roberto Assagioli, the Intensive Journaling of Ira Progoff, the Spiral Dynamics of Don Beck, and the Integral Psychology of Ken Wilber.

Gurdjieff's notion of "waking sleep" and his techniques of Self-Observation may just be the key to raising our awareness and attention to a whole new state of consciousness.

Assagioli's concept of Subpersonalities can help us to understand better our many (and often conflicting) drives, needs, and wants, and help us to understand why we behave as we do.

Progoff's Steppingstones provide us with an outline of our life and help us to understand where we have been and where we might be heading.

Beck's descriptions and coloring of the spiraling stages of consciousness as red, blue, orange, green, and yellow have made them easier to understand and to remember the differences among the stages.

Wilber's Integral Psychology synthesizes the work of many developmental psychologists into an evolutionary whole with applications not only for our psychological growth but also for our spiritual development. His descriptions of the stages and states of consciousness I am finding to be a very useful map as I continue on with my inner journey.

If you are not familiar with these 20th century giants of psychological and spiritual growth and development, then this book can serve as a rather gentle introduction to some of their rather profound transformation strategies.

If you occasionally find yourself yearning for something more, something different in your life, this book will help. If your life experiences have caused you to outgrow the life story with which you have been enculturated, then through the exercises in this book you may discover a new story, a story that may be easier to live with and to transmit to your loved ones. You can do the exercises by yourself, in the privacy of your own home and as gradually as you wish.

I believe that it may help you with the exercises if I show you, as examples, how I have used them in my life. This book is also partly an autobiography. You will get to know very well who this is who is giving you this advice. You will come to know that it is joy, enthusiasm, and love that are now encouraging me to share with you what I am learning. I sincerely hope that you will give these exercises a try. And that you will encourage others to do the same. There is a lot of violence, hunger, and injustice in the world today, and I know of no better way to help alleviate this situation, other than to encourage each of us, one by one, to become more aware and awake. Then hopefully, together, we can bring about the cultural changes, which will be needed to bring about a world with less violence, hunger, injustice and lots more joy, enthusiasm, and love.

This book is not yet as perfect as I wanted it to be, but my friends keep telling me, "At some point you have to stop writing and editing and get something out there for the world to see and read, otherwise you will die one day and all that you have learned will die with you, unpublished, unshared."

So here you have what I am calling Version 1.0 (2017). I think it is written well enough by now to be of help just as it is and I hope you will find it useful in your search for a personal transformation. I may have repeated some concepts too many times and some I may not have explained enough. So, I will keep working on it and soon there may be a Version 2.0 (2018). If you are so inclined, you can help me to improve it by suggesting editing changes or by identifying concepts that could use some more clarification. I hope that some of you will write up one of those blurbs that most books have saying how wonderful you have found this book to be. Your suggestions and blurbs will be incorporated into future versions.

"Chapter 1 – Overview" will tell you what personal transformation is all about. I wrote the overview without any notes and references to allow for a quicker reading. The rest of the chapters do have notes documenting my sources in case you wish to read more about any of the concepts. Enjoy.

Anthony from Granger, May 2017

Chapter 1
Overview

What I'm learning and wanting to share with you now, has helped me to cope with the stresses and strains of my life and I am sure that it can help you as well. It has also brought more joy, love, and peace into my life. Most of it has to do with consciousness, our inner world. It's amazing how little most of us know or care about what is going on inside of us.

Socrates is reported to have said that the unexamined life is not worth living. Yet we are not taught at any time just how to go about examining our life. This book will help you do that. We will consider the hard questions, like "Who am I?", "What's going on here?", and "How can I cope a little better?"

As soon as you look inside and ask "Who am I?", you will observe that you are not a single "I" but actually several "I's". You may have a parent role who worries about how the children will turn out and a career role who worries about how to make more money. You may have several subpersonalities like a kid who wants to play all the time, an athlete who wishes she had more time to perfect her tennis serve, or an artist who wishes he had more time to paint. Dealing with the competing demands on our time is the leading cause of stress in our lives. I have learned some wonderful techniques for dealing with the competing demands on my time, and this book demonstrates several of them.

One technique is called self-observation. It is a skill to learn. With it you will be able to take several snapshots of yourself throughout the day, observing what you are doing at the time. This will give you some data with which to determine just exactly how many subpersonalities are competing for your time. But more importantly you will experience that you actually have two modes of awareness.

In one mode, your awareness is focused exclusively on what it is you are doing, say playing tennis. In the other mode of awareness, you can observe yourself playing tennis. Try it right now. Switch from focusing exclusively on reading this book, and think to yourself, "Here I am, reading this book." While you are at it, you can also check on how you are feeling. "Am I hungry? Am I cold? Should I be doing something else right now?"

With some practice, you will soon be able to switch occasionally from functioning exclusively as one of your subpersonalities to functioning as your observing Self. It's called identification. You can choose to identify as one of your subpersonalities or to identify as your observing Self. Without this skill, you switch from one sub to another quite automatically or mechanically, as the situation demands. This is okay, if all is going well in your life. But if you are feeling some stress while trying to time share your one body/mind with a lot of competing interests, learning to identify with your observing Self will allow you to referee among your competing ego-subpersonalities so that "your" best interests are served.

This raises the question of "Who am I?" to a whole new level. On the level of the ego-subpersonalities, who you are is answered with, "I'm a teacher", or "I'm a police officer", or "I'm John's Mom". But who are you when you identify with the observing Self? In most growth psychologies, this observing Self is spelled with a capital "S", and is referred to as your True Self, or Essence, while all the rest of you is simply your "Personality" or Ego, a collection of subpersonalities developed while growing up in a particular culture and a specific home environment. You have been enculturated to behave a certain way initially by your parents, your church, and your relatives, then later by your school teachers, your peers, and your chance encounters with other cultures. This enculturation is often referred to as a "consensus trance", wherein you spend most of your life, living automatically through long established habit patterns. Your behaviors have become very predictable. Again this is okay, if all is going well in your life. But if, on momentarily awakening from this consensus trance, you don't like the way your life is going, the exercises in this book will help you make some changes.

The exercises helped me to make several major changes in my life. In my early twenties, I switched from being in a Catholic seminary studying to be a priest to entering medical school to study to be a physician. In our late thirties, my wife Susan, also a physician, and I, while busily raising our three young sons, were also both heavily involved in academic careers at the UT Health Science Center in the big city of Houston, doing what the consensus trance expects from its physicians in Academia. By "Waking Up" we were able to re-examine our priorities, quit those careers, and move to a farm near my home town in central Texas, where we had more time for parenting and for learning some healthy new skills in homesteading. When I was 44, I "observed" that once again my doctor subpersonalities were taking too much time away from my parent subpersonalities, and was able to reduce my time at work to half-time. Another physician and I were able to job share the director's position at our local health department from 1980 to 1986. In 1986 my kids told me they needed my money more than they needed my time so I went back to work full time. By 1997, I was a very busy Director of a Regional Health Department caring for 30 counties. It was then, at age 61, that I "heard" a plaintive cry from my philosopher/writer subpersonalities wondering when oh when would there be more time for reading and writing. So, I retired and now have more time for sharing what I've been learning all these years about states and stages of human consciousness and the possibilities for personal transformation.

In the Steppingstones exercise you will write up a summary of your life so far in 10 to 12 very short paragraphs. Reading your steppingstones over and over several times will give you a sense of the trajectory of your life. You will begin to understand how, where you have been, has conditioned where you are today and you can almost see how the rest of your life is going to go. Again, if that sounds and looks great to you, fine, continue on as is. But if you don't like what you see coming down the road, the Life-Script Review will help you decide on the changes you would like to make.

But whether or not you can make any changes in a life-script is still an open question. One subpersonality telling another sub to change won't do it. Maybe you have tried to start an exercise program. The sub that wants to exercise can't make the other subs give up the time it would take for you to take up an exercise program. You only added more stress to your life. Only as the more awake, observing Self, can you make some changes in how all the various subpersonalities will spend their time. The chapters on the Morning Sit and Meditation will help you lengthen the time that the Self is awake, self-observing, and directing the whole show.

To help me understand this switching from one mode of awareness to the other, I decided to take on two different names depending on with whom I was identifying. When I am in my more awake and aware state, I think of myself as "Anthony", the rest of the time I am simply one of my "Clarence" ego-subpersonalities. Several of the chapters describe my early efforts at learning how, as Anthony, to make changes in the amount of time each Clarence sub will get.

Throughout the book you will notice several paragraphs indented a little and in italics. These are actual entries I made in a journal that I started in 1984, documenting my initial efforts at writing up my experiences with self-observation, subpersonalities, and steppingstones. I want to share these with you as examples for two reasons: 1) they may help you to understand the exercises you are trying to learn and 2) they may encourage you to write-up similar entries in a journal of your own. All such entries, combined and presented together will form an autobiography of sorts. You can share your autobiography with friends and relatives, in an effort to get to know one another a little bit better. I consider getting to know one another a little bit better to be among the most meaningful of human activities. Hence my desire to share mine with you. You deserve to know exactly who this guy is, who is encouraging you to attempt life-enhancing transformation strategies.

At first, you may be interested in using these strategies to help you make some, relatively simple, healthy and health-enhancing changes, like starting an exercise program, quitting smoking, maintaining your desired weight, or learning how to handle stress better. These are important lifestyle changes and may be all you need to change in order to solve whatever you perceive as sub-optimal in your life. Maybe, but maybe not. What you feel to be "not-right" in your life may be a symptom of something much deeper, and to get at that will require you to re-examine some of the basic values and beliefs by which you are living your life.

It is possible and desirable to outgrow some of the values and beliefs you acquired as a child, but the process of shedding old values and acquiring new ones can be painful. The process can also feel joyful and freeing if understood as a normal process of maturing.

We grow through several stages of consciousness as we mature in life and each stage is characterized as a worldview with its own particular set of values and beliefs. Each of us has been enculturated into one of these worldviews. A worldview is a story, a story you tell yourself and your children about how the world is. Most parents try their best to tell their children a story that they believe will best prepare them for life. This used to be easier to do. One generation simply transmitted to their children the story they got from their parents. Sometimes a story would last for several generations, centuries even. Such stories soon became "the tradition". A lot of different traditions developed around the world. It was easier to maintain a tradition when its people were relatively isolated from other traditions, because a tradition is passed on not only by parents, it also takes relatives, teachers, and peers.

We now live in a time where such isolation is much more difficult. Through books, travels, TV, and the internet we regularly come in contact with cultures and traditions whose values and beliefs may be clashing with ours. It is harder now to come up with a story to tell our children that will successfully carry them through all of their life experiences. So maybe your parents didn't do so great a job of passing on to you a set of values and beliefs to which you could successfully adhere for the rest of your life. One doesn't usually evaluate one's worldview; we just assume that that is the way things are. To automatically and routinely adhere to your "inherited" set of values and beliefs is sometimes called living in a "consensus trance."

"Waking Up" and "Observing" your subpersonalities can be very helpful here. You may observe that not all of your subs are living exactly according to your values and beliefs. This internal conflict can be the cause of some of the stresses and symptoms you may be experiencing. By observing the conflict, you will be shining a light on what, up until now, may well have been an unconscious process.

Scientists who study normal human growth and development identify and describe several stages of consciousness. Some simply number them – 1, 2, 3, 4…; some give the stages names – magical, mythical, rational, authentic…; and some find it useful to refer to them in colors – red, blue, orange, green, yellow. Health and healing, growth towards wholeness, occur through a series of transformations up these stages.

We need to work our way through these stages because sometimes what we feel as not optimal in our life is being caused by a conflict in the values and beliefs of the ego-subpersonalities functioning at different stages. Some of our subpersonalities want to take risks and move on up the stages, while others are still fearful and want to hold back, stay where they are.

Take guilt as an example. Guilt is something you experience when, identified with one of your subpersonalities, you engage in an activity that another sub thinks is sinful. As long as this interaction remains unconscious, you will feel guilt. Experiencing guilt is not healthy. Once you bring this conflict out into the open, you, as True Self, can resolve the issue by carefully examining the two values in conflict. Depending on which value you accept, either you will then stop the "sinful activity" or you will re-define the activity as not sinful. Re-defining an activity as not sinful takes courage, for doing so involves some risk. You could be wrong. There was a reason that that particular value developed in your culture and you will feel pressure from others in your culture insisting that you must adhere to that value.

If the thought of re-defining what is sinful sounds to you like something we should not be doing, then most likely you are operating at the blue stage of consciousness, which is a worldview that says our culture is the best there is and that you must follow all of its values and beliefs, without question. Blue is described as conformist and ethno-centric, and is today probably the stage that has the most people. It can be a wonderful story to live by if all is going well for you in it. But if you are experiencing inner conflict, it may be time to grow up to the orange and green stages, which are said to be more rational, more open to other views, more accepting of other races and cultures, and which encourage doubt and examination of inherited values and beliefs. Transforming from blue to orange is almost always felt as freeing and joyful.

Another example of an inner conflict that has nothing to do with sins is a choice of careers. There are still doctors today who became doctors only because their mothers wanted them to be doctors. Some sons and daughters are carrying on in their father's businesses only because their fathers wanted them to. And they find themselves in conflict with what, as True Self, they really want to be doing.

These unfortunate ones have been enculturated into an overly conformist stage of consciousness. A personal transformation to a higher stage of consciousness will free them from these shackles and allow them to choose how they wish to live the rest of their lives. They may well choose to remain doctors or to stay in their fathers' businesses, but now it will be their choice, freely entered into, knowing that they could choose otherwise.

These are just a couple of examples to show you how one might be constrained by parental and cultural values and beliefs. I'm sure you can find several areas in your life where you are not really living as, deep down inside, your values and beliefs tell you is really you. To continue living this way is said to be inauthentic. Growth towards wholeness is becoming more authentic. Eventually the healthy individual reaches the yellow stage called Authentic Consciousness.

It is reasonable for all of us to aspire to reach this stage. At this stage, we understand the conflicts in values and beliefs among the various stages of consciousness. We have successfully integrated the fragmentation in our lives caused by the largely unconscious interplay among our various ego-subpersonalities. It is called Authentic, because our outward mask, the side of us we are showing to the world, is consistent and in harmony with our inner feelings and beliefs. We have developed a competent, functional ego with which we can achieve our life's goals and dreams. We experience fewer troubling and incapacitating emotions like guilt, fear, and anger. Our lives become increasingly filled with joy, love, and peace.

But you won't get to Authentic just by reading about it and wishing yourself there. It may help to wish yourself there, but it will also take doing some work, i.e. practicing on a regular basis some methods for personal transformation, like self-observation, subpersonalities, steppingstones, waking up, morning sit and meditation. Without working at personal transformation, you may remain stuck on whichever level you are functioning now for the rest of your life.

Because learning how to wake-up, observing the various roles you play, refereeing how much time to give to each, and changing your life-scripts is all pretty serious stuff, I'll also be encouraging you to give your kid subpersonality some time to have fun, and I will share with you some of the things I do to have fun.

It is possible that by the time you reach the stage of Authentic Consciousness and have learned to have some fun along the way, you will have already solved all the problems that were making you unhappy with how things were going in your life. So now may be a good time for you to stop the transformations and stay where you are for a few years. After all, there may be a living to earn, a career to pursue, a family to raise, and/or a work of art to complete. But don't stop waking up, self-observing, and meditating, for there is still more to learn about yourself.

Although you may well enjoy working at this Authentic Stage for years, even decades, at some point in your life, your interest and attention may shift away from a preoccupation with achieving objectives and with re-writing life-scripts. You may begin to wonder, "Is this it? Is this all there is to life?" And a whole new set of worries and unhappiness may set in. This will be the time to set aside your concern about the interests and needs of your various subpersonalities and begin to wonder again about the nature of this Self who has awakened. You may begin to ask, "Who am I, as Self, whenever I function in this higher state of consciousness?"

You may begin to wonder if your worldview really takes into account all that we know about human experiences. There are now several reports from credible, rational people describing either an out-of-body experience, a near-death experience, or a past-life recall. In the out-of-body experience, the Self is able to float free of the body and observe what is happening around the body or even miles away from the body. In the near-death experience, the Self not only has an out-of-body experience, but also encounters other Souls and experiences a loving presence so intensely that it may want to stay. In past-life recalls, the Self remembers having had a previous life as a wholly different personality. If we wish to follow all the evidence in formulating our worldview, their views and experiences will also have to be taken into account.

And you may also begin to wonder if maybe there aren't yet higher states and stages of consciousness to experience. Wilber says that we "grow up" the stages of consciousness but "wake up" to the higher states of consciousness. The higher states of consciousness are said to be Transrational and Transpersonal, so I'll spend a couple of chapters sharing what I am learning about becoming transpersonal and transrational.

Although most scientists who study normal human growth and development today perceive Authentic Consciousness (yellow) as the highest stage to which we can aspire, there are some development researchers, psychologists, and philosophers who do say that there are higher stages yet. But to be able to grow up to these higher stages, we may need to first learn how to wake up to some higher states of consciousness.

There isn't as much known about these higher stages and states. But there are some mystics, yogis, saints, and sages who have awakened to higher states of consciousness and there are some first-person accounts available, describing what it is like to experience these higher states. We, too, can learn to experience these higher states and to attempt to do so is what I am calling, "Undertaking the Spiritual Journey". I'll describe my experiences undertaking the spiritual journey in the remaining chapters.

But that's way off in the future for you. The place to start now is to develop the skill of self-observation. The whole transformational journey starts with, and depends primarily on, your mastering the technique of self-observation. The next chapter will show you how to do it. Go, you can do this.

Chapter 2
Self-Observation

Self-observation is a very powerful practice and the foundation for the rest of the techniques and practices described later on. It is quite easy to learn how to do it; the difficulty comes in remembering to do it often enough.

In the simplest form of self-observation, you simply shift your attention away from whatever you are doing and focus your attention on how you are feeling. Are you tired? Are you hungry? Are you angry? You can do a quick body scan, searching for symptoms. Are there any aches or pains, any areas of tightness?

Next note what it is you are doing. It helps, at first, to silently verbalize to yourself something like, "I'm sitting here reading this book." Tomorrow when you think to do this, you might say, "Here I am sitting in this stupid meeting, bored." Or it might be, "Here I sit, eating my lunch, worrying about my kids." That's all there is to it. Having made your observations, you can go back to paying your full attention to whatever it was you were doing.

The more usual form of self-observation involves splitting your attention in two, keeping part of it focused on whatever it is you are doing and simultaneously focusing the rest on your self-observing routine of noting what it is you are doing and how you are feeling.

I'm sure that already you can see several benefits of doing such self-observations occasionally. If you catch yourself doing a low-priority activity, you can stop and switch to doing something else. If you catch yourself heading for the refrigerator and notice you are angry, but not hungry, you may want to stop and consider doing something else about your anger besides eating.

But let's not worry right now about what we are going to do with these observations. That will come later. For now, just concentrate on getting experience in doing some self-observations.

In order to get some experience, you will need to develop some innovative aids to remind you to do a self-observation. It is easy to shift into this "Observer" mode whenever someone asks you to do it. The skill to learn now is how to shift into it occasionally on your own. When I first started learning how to do this, I would paste several of those little colored circles around the home and the workplace. Then whenever I would notice one, I would quickly run through my self-observation routine. You won't want to use too many colored circles or you will soon get used to seeing them around and learn to ignore them. Paste them so that you spot one just every once in a while. Sometimes I'd set my watch alarm to go off at some key time of day. We all have usual places around the house or office for our keys, our clocks, our purse, our remotes, etc. What works well for me even now is purposefully to place an object not in its usual place. Then in the future when I notice that, I am triggered to self-observe. You can put a small rock in your pocket, and every time you notice it, shift your attention. Sometimes you can use a minor symptom; every time you notice the pain or itch, think to shift attention.

You get the idea. Figure out some way to remind yourself to shift your attention periodically throughout the day from whatever it is you are doing to observing what it is you are doing and how you are feeling.

You need not worry about for how long to stay in this self-observing mode. All too quickly you will automatically snap back into complete absorption with whatever it is you are doing. And only hours later, when you are next triggered to shift your attention, will you remember how briefly you were able to hold your attention on yourself the last time.

For a while I tried to do at least one self-observation session every hour. I would carry around a piece of paper in my pocket and note the time every time I remembered to do one. At first,

I was lucky if I got two or three times written down each day. But over time, the number slowly increased

Self-observation is a method for gathering data about ourselves. Ever since the early Greek philosophers, we have been encouraged to "know thyself." If we are hoping to ever be able to make some changes in our life, we will first need to know ourselves a little bit better right now.

Charles Tart, in his book on Gurdjieff, has this to say about self-observation:

> Self-observation sounds very simple, so simple that you may find a tendency to dismiss it with the idea "I do that anyway." You probably do, but only once in too great a while, and with implicit restrictions on what you apply it to. Try doing it deliberately. All the strings of words in this book are just that, just words, until you use the practice of self-observation to test their reality. If you diligently practice self-observation, you will see much that is painful and much that is joyful, but seeing more of reality will turn out to be highly preferable to living in fantasy. You will begin creating "something" in yourself, a quality, a function, a skill... And you will be pleasantly surprised at how much more there is to life. [1]

Observing our thoughts:

In addition to these occasional, spontaneous, sampling sessions throughout the day where-in we observe what we are doing and how we are feeling, we can learn a lot more about ourselves if we spend some dedicated time observing our thoughts. This thought watching, is an activity designed to give you something else to do while in your self-observing mode so you can begin to stretch the length of time you are able to remain in this state.

You can practice thought watching almost anywhere and in any position, but it is probably best to start off by sitting down quietly where you will not be disturbed and plan to sit there for at least five minutes or so.

In order to do this, you will need to schedule a period of time, say five to ten minutes, every morning or evening, to just sit and observe all the thoughts and worries going on in your mind. To start such a session, sit comfortably in a quiet place, note how you are feeling, do your body scan for symptoms, and then note your breathing; slow it down to a nice and steady rate, and relax. Try to keep your attention focused on the breathing. You are just sitting now, watching each breath slowing coming in and then going out.

You won't have to wait long before some thought will come along and try to capture your whole attention. Note what is happening here. You are trying to keep your attention focused on your breathing and a thought comes along from somewhere and grabs your entire attention for itself. The thought could be about anything -- some worry about one of the kids, a memory of a recent encounter with a loved one, or a brilliant idea for a new project at work. Any thought is usually powerful enough to grab your entire attention and hold it for the full five minutes or longer.

The skill you are trying to learn here is to be able to pull the attention back to yourself. Note what the thought was about; decide when would be a good time to think about that some more and postpone any further thinking until then. Now go back to observing your breathing and wait for the next thought to come along. As soon as you notice that you have been hooked by another thought, repeat the process of noting what it was about and postpone thinking about it until later.

During the first few sessions it is not unusual to spend the whole five minutes on the very first thought that happens to come along. But over time, something about the setting and your position will alert you to the fact that you are trying not to get hooked on thoughts, and you will be able to return more and more quickly to focusing your attention on yourself and your breathing. Soon you will be able to count how many distinctly different thoughts you had watched come and go during a single session.

If you think just sitting and watching your breathing is a big waste of time, you can try observing thoughts while walking, swimming, or bicycling. Yoga and tai chi are good practices of focusing on yourself and what you are doing. There too, if distracting thoughts arise, think to yourself, I can postpone these thoughts and worries until later.

You can also practice doing this several times a day during ordinary activities of daily living. You can practice doing this while washing dishes, or while sitting in a boring meeting, or while standing in line at the checkout counter.

After several days of this practice you will note that several thoughts and worries tend to be frequent repeaters and that these thoughts can be easily grouped into categories. For instance, there will usually be several thoughts relating to work problems or pressures. Some will relate to interactions with loved ones or with problem relatives. If you are a parent, you will notice that several thoughts come up frequently relating to the children. You may also find yourself daydreaming about wishing for more time for some hobby or sport.

It may help to imagine that you have a cabinet full of small pigeonholes, say 100, arranged in 10 rows with 10 pigeonholes in each row. If a thought comes up having to do with some problem at the office, you can say to yourself that you don't wish to think about that right now and file it away in the appropriate pigeonhole to be taken care of later. Then your attention is free to wait and watch for the next thought to come along. Remember that you are still gathering data about your life. Observe the nature, strength, and character of these thoughts. Are they worries? Are they great plans for the future? Are they usually about some person? Do some come up loaded with anger or sadness?

There are several ways that you can label your pigeonholes for filing away the thoughts that come up. Some thoughts will have to do with your children; you can file these in a row labeled, "Parenting," one thought per pigeonhole. Some thoughts will be worries about problems at work; you can file these in a row labeled "Work-related." You can do this for as many interests, responsibilities, and aspirations you may have. These data will be important for you to use in our next exercise dealing with roles and subpersonalities.

So, to summarize this chapter: You are to begin formally practicing self-observation. You will choose some ingenious ways to serve as triggers to remind you to do a self-observation session. At these times, you will note how you are feeling and what you are doing. You will do several of these each day. In addition, you will set aside a few minutes each day to spend observing your thoughts. You will observe the nature, strength, and character of each of these thoughts and then file each of them away into the appropriate pigeonhole. After you have had some experience in doing so, you will be ready to go to the next chapter and begin work on your Sub-personalities.

Chapter 3
Sub-Personalities

As you do your self-observations throughout the day, you notice that you are actually observing quite a few different personalities. When at home with the children, you notice yourself as a different personality than whenever you are playing tennis or interacting with your co-workers at the office. Sometimes you come across as aggressive and demanding, sometimes as very loving, supportive, and caring. Your personality at work may at times appear to be fearful and stressed, but your personality when at a party with friends, may come across as friendly, confident, and in control.

Rather than being one, smoothly functioning, well-integrated personality, most of us still function as a collective of different subpersonalities. Each subpersonality can be described as having certain psychological traits and habit patterns, such as being shy, controlling, brave, aggressive, loving, organized, introverted, extroverted, modest, responsible, spontaneous, etc. All of these traits are common to all humans. While growing up, depending on the forces we were exposed to and the experiences we had, we developed certain of these traits more than others. We learned that a certain set of traits would serve us well to meet a specific need or want. Eventually, each frequently used set of traits evolved into a major subpersonality. Now each of us is going around alternately functioning as one subpersonality and then another.

You have already observed this in others. A co-worker may surprise you by her behavior at a party because it was so different from how you had her pegged. A person may explode in anger at a meeting and then later approach you apologetically saying something to the effect of, "I don't know what came over me." We have all used expressions like, "A part of me wants to go out tonight but another part of me wants to stay home." We often make deals with other parts of ourselves, a favorite of mine while in medical school on Galveston Island was, "If I study for four hours this morning, this afternoon I can go to the beach."

Our subpersonalities are closely identified with the roles we play in life. We can name these roles. The Kid in us wants to play. The Breadwinner uses those subpersonalities that she feels will help her get ahead at work. The Daddy uses the subs that will help him raise his children. The Star is after praise and recognition. The Backpacker is strong, skilled, and adventurous.

You may currently be playing the role of Mother in the morning and evening, role of Teacher during the day, and the role of aspiring Artist whenever you can. Each of these may be exhibiting a major subpersonality of its own, but there could also be some overlap in the traits, say, between the Mother and the Teacher. You may decide you have a major nurturing subpersonality, which you use both in your role as Mother and as Teacher. Each role you play in life is a mix of one or more subpersonalities.

Roberto Assagioli, in his book *Psychosynthesis*, has this to say about roles and subpersonalities:

> William James dealt with this concept of sub-personalities -- which he called "the various selves." The functions of an individual, in whom various psychological traits are not integrated, form what we consider to be sub-personalities. It is probably better to use the word "roles" instead of "functions," to avoid semantic confusion. The patient should be asked to describe himself in his various roles: as a son or daughter, as a husband or wife, as father or mother, as having a professional role of some kind; and in these roles to examine his corresponding attitudes toward subordinates, towards superiors, and towards his peers. Other subpersonalities, or roles, are those played in the different social groups, including his religious group or church, his political group or party, and other roles which he may have or may want to play in life.

The organization of the sub-personalities is very revealing and sometimes surprising, baffling or even frightening. One discovers how very different and often quite antagonistic traits are displayed in the different roles. These differences of traits which are organized around a role justify, in our opinion, the use of the word "sub-personality." Ordinary people shift from one to the other without clear awareness, and only a thin thread of memory connects them; but for all practical purposes they are different beings -- they act differently, they show very different traits. Therefore, one should become clearly aware of these sub-personalities because this evokes a measure of understanding of the meaning of psychosynthesis, and how it is possible to synthesize these sub-personalities into a larger organic whole without repressing any of the useful traits.

Another advantage is that revealing the different roles, traits, etc., emphasizes the reality of the observing self. During and after this assessment of the sub-personalities one realizes that the observing self is none of them, but something or somebody different from each. This is a very important realization and another of the keys for the desired and future psychosynthesis. [2]

The "Who Am I?" Exercise

So, who are you? For this exercise, get a pen and a piece of paper, ask yourself, "Who am I?", and then list all the different ways that you have introduced yourself to someone in the past few weeks. No need to get very profound here just yet. Try to give answers that will more or less fit with what we have discussed in this chapter. I remember clearly the first time I introduced myself as "I'm John's Dad." My wife is a well-known Pediatrician, so often I introduce myself as "I'm Susan's Husband." For a long time, I was, "Dr. Skrovan, the Associate Professor" or "Dr. Skrovan, the County Health Officer." Now I introduce myself as "Anthony, the Philosopher/Writer."

It might be helpful to reflect now on your thought-watching sessions. By now you may have noticed natural groupings of related thoughts and worries. You may already have neatly labeled each row of your pigeonholes with the names of several roles you play throughout the day

Once you have completed your initial list, go over it carefully and scratch out those that appear to be redundant or very similar to another. Now, based on your sampling data of self-observations and thought-watching sessions, start a new list in priority order with the role that is taking up most time at the top. Then pick out the next most frequently experienced role and put it next. Work your way down your list until you have somewhere around six to seven names on your list.

You are going to work with these 6-7 roles for the rest of this book so it is important that you are satisfied with this second list. Take a careful look at the rest of the names on the first list. Is there a role there that you wish had more time to express herself or himself in your life? If there is, add that one to your second list. If your second list is now too long, you can drop the one or two roles that you predict will need less time in the future. Once you have your list down to 6-7, you are ready for the "Pie" exercise.

The Pie Exercise [3]:

On a clear sheet of paper draw a large circle and then a very small one (about one centimeter in diameter) in the center of the large circle. Draw lines from the small circle in the middle out to the circumference of the large circle. Draw as many lines as you need to create as many wedges as you have roles on your list plus one more. Into each section write the name of a role and describe briefly what he or she is like. Into the last wedge write "all the rest".

When I first did the pie exercise in 1985, I described six roles: The Family Man, The Kid, The Doctor, The

Philosopher, The Homesteader, and The Seeker. You will read more about each of these later on but to give you an idea now of how to describe your roles, here is how I described "The Family Man" when I first did this exercise:

> *"He thinks family life is very important, likes to spend time with his wife and children and to help in their growth and development, likes to cook and bake. He is loving, generous, and nurturing, but sometimes gets impatient and angry."*

How you describe yours and in how much detail is up to you, but please take the time to write something down about each of them now. Be sure to include some personality traits like loving, generous, nurturing, impatient, and angry.

One Body/Mind

The problem with having so many subpersonalities is that we only have one body/mind for them to use to express themselves. So, we have to timeshare, but since most of us have more interests and responsibilities then we have time, we get into time crunches a lot, which in most of us, will cause a lot of stress. There is a way to work with our subpersonalities to lessen this stress. The biggest help is in simply understanding what is going on and in learning how to timeshare.

The amount of time each subpersonality is now getting is largely a result of unconscious processes. It just turned out like this; you didn't consciously plan for it to be this way. The purpose of this exercise is to shine some light on this process and re-allocate the time-shares more consciously under your control.

First, take a look at the role that is getting the least percentage of time. Does this role represent an interest or activity that you would like to give more time? Think about the ways that you could arrange that. Maybe you could shave a little bit of time from some of the others. Maybe he or she doesn't need more time every week, maybe this is something you can plan to do more of during the summer. In some cases, you may need to plan, that in five years or so, you will be able to give him or her more time.

Next take a look at the role that is getting most of the time. Why is he or she getting all that time? Sometimes the reason is obvious, for example, you have a 9-5 job and your boss expects you at work 40 hours a week. But if how much overtime you put in at work is under your control, by turning your attention to the process, you may be able to uncover some here-to-fore hidden motivations. Maybe you are staying at work longer because you want to avoid having to spend time at home doing some of your other responsibilities. Or maybe you are spending more time at home because you find the work environment less enjoyable. Regardless of how your time re-allocations work out, the fact that you will now feel a little more in control of the process, usually relieves some of the stress of not having enough time for all of our interests and responsibilities.

If you are now able to do occasional self-observations throughout the day, you may notice that an inappropriate group of subpersonalities is in control at some times. The Breadwinner may be at work with loads of tasks needing to be done, but you notice that The Kid is in charge, daydreaming about next week's vacation or tonight's party. Your spouse may call you at work expecting you to be the kind, loving spouse you usually are at home, only to find that s/he is talking to a stressed, busy subpersonality who does not sound very kind and loving at all.

Your periodic daily self-observations can help tremendously with problems dealing with who is in control of your one body/mind. From now on, whenever you verbalize what it is you are observing yourself doing, you can say something like, "I'm in a restaurant, and there sits 'The Parent', eating lunch and worrying about the kids." Or "I'm at the office, and there sits 'The Kid', daydreaming about tonight. I better call up 'The Breadwinner', so he can get back to work." Usually you switch from one subpersonality to another quite automatically; responding to some external stimulus, but sometimes, if bored or worried, to some internal concern. Which subpersonality you are expressing and for how long are rarely under your conscious control. Doing the self-observation helps to bring this process to your attention. You then have the option of consciously switching roles and subpersonalities should you choose to do so. You may find it helpful to re-draw your pie diagram now with the size of each wedge proportional to the time each is getting to use your body/mind. See how the impact of seeing that affects your re-allocation decisions.

It is now time to look at the little circle in the middle of your pie diagram. In this little circle, write the letter, "I". That is you. That is you, the you who is observing the various role players and subpersonalities who are time-sharing your one body/mind. The you who is re-allocating the amount of time each will get to use your body/mind in the future. So ask yourself again, "Who am I?" No need to write anything down this time, I just want you to start wondering about who you really are.

Let me now share with you a journal entry written way back in 1985 when I was first learning about this exercise. Since I had always intended my journal entries to be used in sharing with others what I was learning, you will notice that even back then I sound as though I were already talking to you. You will also notice some redundancy in this and future journal entries with what I have written in the main text. But rather then editing those out, I decided that a little repetition in slightly different wording may prove helpful.

This journal entry will serve as an example of how you might want to write up your roles and subpersonalities to share with your friends and relatives. In the process your friends will get to know you better, but more importantly, you will get to know yourself better. I'm also sharing it with you now so you can get to know me better and to see how I used this technique in my life.

Who am I?   (5-15-85)

As I observe and get to know myself better, I experience that I am not a single "I" but that there seem to be many "I's". It's as though around each of my major interests and activities, a different subpersonality has formed. I assume and play out many different roles throughout each day. I am a Husband and a Father. I am a Physician and an Administrator. And I am striving to become a nicely balanced integrated mix of Homesteader, Philosopher, and Seeker. I am also a Child, a little Czech-Catholic kid from a small southern town still trying to have fun and to be good at the same time. While playing the role of "Physician" at the office, I exhibit a different set of character traits than I do while playing the role of "Parent" in my home. I experience a different set of moods and I display a different set of emotions. I believe that I can best describe to you, who I am, by defining and describing six major roles that I play throughout the day. I have chosen to name these six: The Doctor, The Family Man, The Philosopher, The Homesteader, The Seeker, and The Kid. I will let each of these speak briefly for himself.

The Doctor: "I am currently serving as this county's Health Officer and am the Director of the Williamson County Health Department. I have the legal responsibility for enforcing certain public health laws of the State of Texas and I have several administrative challenges such as securing the budget, supervising the staff to accomplish our mission, and maintaining staff morale and productivity. Since I have chosen to specialize in Preventive Medicine, I try to do my share to relieve pain and suffering in this world by helping people to prevent certain diseases and disabilities from ever occurring. The major problems in adults today are the chronic diseases and stress-related disabilities such as heart attacks, cancer, strokes, high blood pressure, ulcers, anger, hostility, depression, etc. These diseases and disabilities can be prevented. They are all related to our present lifestyle. So, my main professional interest at this time is to determine the components of a healthy lifestyle and to help others to change over toward such a healthier lifestyle."

The Family Man: "I am married to one Susan Mary Sandstrom and we are now in our 20th year of marriage. We have three strong, healthy, and growing boys. The home is generally a happy place although a bit noisy at times. My highest priority at this time is to nurture and support my family's growth and development. They need me. I try to be responsive to their demands on my time. I cook a lot of meals and wash a lot of dishes. In this role, I alternate between being a lover and companion with Susan and being a parent and friend with the boys."

The Philosopher: "I love to read and think. I would rather sit and read than almost anything else. There is so much to learn, so much to try to understand. My scientific training and the writings of existential philosophers have wreaked havoc with my early belief systems. I am still trying to put together a decent and respectable worldview, which incorporates best, what I have experienced, with what others are proposing. Some of my best highs have come from reading and attempting to integrate Eastern experiences and speculations with Western philosophy and psychology. Someday I will do more of this. I must. I feel driven."

The Homesteader: "I am trying to be a homesteader. In 1974 we bought an old farmhouse and 90 acres of land. I want to be a good steward of the land, to prevent erosion, to enrich the soil, to leave it a little better than we found it. I want to experience a little more directly the seasons, the ecological cycles of our planet, and the evolutionary niche that we humans inhabit. I am trying to learn how to grow some fruits and vegetables, how to raise some animals, how to recycle our wastes, how to utilize alternate sources of energy, how to bake bread and to preserve food, and how to do my own maintenance around the place. This is a new role for me, one that does not come naturally and easily. I have to work at it."

The Seeker: "I am not sure what the best name for this role is. Other names that could possibly fit are Pilgrim, Warrior, Yogi, Ascetic, or Mystic. I am seeking something that is not easily described with words or understood by the intellect. I am being drawn towards becoming I know not what. It is an inner evolutionary journey, exploring new states and stages of consciousness. I am trying to experience what lies beyond the sense of a separate self, to experience a oneness with a greater whole of which I am but a part. I try to stop thinking sometimes, to meditate, to discipline my body and mind, to be more willing to do the wishes of others, to be of service, to love unconditionally."

The Kid: "Somewhere there needs to be time for some fun and games. With all these serious hard working subpersonalities around, it is hard to just want to waste time and have some fun. But I try. I love to play with computers, to program them to do things. I can program for hours and never get tired. I also love to play chess. I love to play in chess tournaments. Someday I would like to be the Texas State Amateur Chess Champion. I like to see movies, to play cards and dominoes, to read science fiction, to go out to eat, and to go hiking and camping."

There may be some other minor grouping of subpersonalities around. I could probably make a case for an artist, a writer, an administrator, a politician, a teacher, and a runner. But to do so seems unnecessarily to complicate matters as each of these can also be viewed as parts of the major six. The main point of this exercise is to help you to realize that you, too, are actually quite a complicated set of characters all trying to find time to express themselves. You might, for instance, be a parent, a schoolteacher, a lover, a tennis player, a gardener and an authority on science fiction. You might also wish you had some time to try out being a musician or an artist. Each of us has several subpersonalities each competing for time to use the one body/mind available to it.

Such a concept is helpful in learning to handle stress in our lives. Most stressful situations have their origin in our feeling that too many demands are being put on our time. It is easier to plan how to manage our time if we know how many subpersonalities or roles are demanding time. Then we can plan to timeshare. Some roles need some time every day; some may need time but once a week. Some roles we may decide we have no time for now, but we can plan that next year or in five years we will give it large chunks of time. Sometimes the cause of psychosomatic symptoms can be traced to a subpersonality that has been repressed and is crying to be allowed some expression. Classic examples of this are the housewife with lots of children also wanting to be an artist or to have a career. Or the busy career woman who would also like to have children. Realizing what is happening and planning some time to allow that role to develop are sometimes all that is needed for the symptoms to go away.

Most of the time I go through the day functioning more or less automatically through well-established habit patterns. Usually I slip out of one role and into another without even noticing that I am doing so. Slowly though, I am learning to become aware of what role I am playing at any given time and to switch roles as appropriate consciously and on purpose. I used to come home from work with The Doctor still fully in control, thinking and worrying about problems at the office. I would greet the kids' excited questions and demands by saying something like, "Don't bother me now, I'm busy." You can imagine what a hit that made. Now I have learned to take off The Doctor hat while I am driving home. I very consciously and deliberately put on The Family Man hat. Then I spend several minutes thinking about the family, wondering what they are doing, and anticipating what their questions and demands might be. Now when I hit the house, communications go a lot better.

Running around frantically timesharing with one's fragmented subpersonalities is clearly not an optimal nor even a healthy way to live a life. It just appears that this is the way it happens to be for most of us most of the time. I think it helps to understand that. It helps to explain why we feel frustrated and time pressured so much of the time. It also explains why

communication with other humans is so difficult at times --
you never really are sure which of your subpersonalities is
talking to which subpersonality in the other person.

One day Susan called me at 11:45 am on one of my at-home
days. The boys were in school. Susan had told me that
morning that she would not be home for lunch because of a
doctors' meeting at the hospital, so I was enjoying a nice solid
block of time from 8:30 to 3:30 doing my things. When the
phone rang, the "Philosopher I" was comfortably seated in
my favorite chair reading Kaufmann's The Portable
Neitzsche. Susan very cheerfully informed me that her noon
meeting had been cancelled. She still had to drive over to the
hospital to see a patient and had called to ask if I would like
to come along and have lunch somewhere together. The
Philosopher I immediately responded with, "No, thank you.
I'm pretty busy right now." Now, can you think of anything
less pressing than reading Nietzsche? Anyway, within five
minutes Susan's message had somehow gotten through to the
"Family Man I." As the Family Man, I had an entirely
different response to Susan's invitation. It had been some time
since Susan and I had gone out to eat and I saw this as a
beautiful opportunity for a lunch date. I called her back, told
her I had changed my mind, and we had a wonderful time
together over lunch. I told her that in the future when she
calls, she should ask "To whom am I speaking?" and then ask
to speak to her spouse and lover.

Clearly the task is one of integration and synthesis. I need to
become one whole healthy personality. The character traits
of each subpersonality need to be available to me all the time.
The love and generosity of the Seeker could serve the Doctor
and Family Man as well. The Kid's humor and search for fun
could enliven the activities of the Philosopher and the
Homesteader tremendously. Writing out the descriptions of
each subpersonality has helped. By highlighting the
fragmentation, by allowing each subpersonality to speak his
mind, and by observing the process, I believe that I have
nurtured along the integration considerably.

Observing the process seems to be the key. Synthesis is hard
work and the progress is slow, mainly because it is hard for

me to remember that I want to work on it. Most of the time I live quite unconsciously, automatically following out one habit pattern after another. I perform as one subpersonality until some stimulus triggers another subpersonality into action. But occasionally I can break out of this automatic behavior. I become more aware and awake and then I remember about subpersonalities. I can then shift the focus of my attention to observing what it is that I am doing, which subpersonality is doing it, and how I am feeling about doing that. Whenever I remember to do this, it becomes easy to switch from one role to a more appropriate one. The trick is in remembering to shift the focus of attention.

Who am I when I shift to the observing mode? Is this just another subpersonality expressing itself? I don't think so. Qualitatively it feels different. Being in this self-observation mode seems almost like functioning on a deeper or higher plane. I feel very much more awake and aware. It feels good to be in this state of heightened awareness. I like myself more. I feel wiser and more at peace. Things are a lot calmer. Gone are the troublesome emotions like anger, fear, guilt, or anomie.

I'll develop each of these roles for you in a lot more detail later on, but now it is time for you to work a little more on each of yours. Write up your various roles in at least as much detail as I did in mine. Doing so will help you do a better job with the next exercise. You will gain further insight into who you really are and how your subpersonalities developed and evolved to the percentage mix you are now enjoying or suffering with, by doing the next exercise on Steppingstones.

Chapter 4
Steppingstones

Ira Progoff described the Steppingstones technique in his book, *At a Journal Workshop* and at various workshops he used to give around the country. In this exercise, you simply divide up your life's journey so far, into 8-12 time periods. The time periods you choose will quite naturally vary in length depending on how long it took for that particular phase of your life to unfold. You can structure your time periods around places you lived, jobs you held, people with whom you lived, or most likely, some combination of the above plus others which may seem particularly important just to you. If you are on your second career, your first career may be considered one time period. The time between your first and second career may have been short but it may deserve listing as a time period of its own. Sometimes such transitions periods are very important to the development of our various subpersonalities and benefit from being explored and written up. You may have lived in two major cities during your first career and might want to split up that length of time into two separate time periods. Or you may have been single for part of it and married for the rest. The time periods during which you were raising small children may be very different from the ones during which they were older. You get the idea, so get out a piece of paper and get ready to do some writing.

Here's a quote from Progoff so you can get a feel for exactly how he taught us to do it:

> To enter the atmosphere in which we can best work with our steppingstones, we close our eyes and sit in silence. In this stillness, we let our breathing become slower, softer, more relaxed. As we are quieted, we let ourselves feel the movement of our lives. We do not think about any specific aspect of our life, but we let ourselves feel the movement of

our life as a whole. In our silence, we let the changing circumstances and situations of our life pass before the mind's eye...

As you do this, it may be that the events of your life will present themselves to you as a flowing and continuous movement, as a river moving through many changes and phases. Or it may be that your life will present itself to you as a kaleidoscope of disconnected events. Whatever the form in which the continuity of your life reflects itself to you now, respond to it, observe it, and let the flow continue...

Sitting in quietness, breathing deeply at a slow and measured pace, let the continuity of your life as a whole move before you. Let yourself feel its movement as a total and unfolding process. Passive receptivity is the best attitude to adopt in doing this. As you sit in silence, let the cycles, the rhythms, the tempos of your life present themselves to you. Let them be free and undirected so that they can shape themselves into whatever form truly reflects their basic qualities; let yourself be free in your quietness to perceive them as they come to you without editing or falsifying them...

After sitting in silence and recording what comes to you, you are ready to make the first listing of your Steppingstones. Since they are the most significant points in the movement of your life, the list should be limited in number. Spontaneous selectivity is the essence of marking off our Steppingstones. No matter how old we are and how long our life, the best practice is to place eight or ten Steppingstones on our list, but in any case, not more than a dozen. [4]

These events or milestones will then become the steppingstone periods in your life that got you to where you are today. Make a brief list of these and read them aloud to yourself or to a friend to get a feel for how your life sounds when described in this way. The last steppingstone is the present period and the ending date should be left open, since you don't know how long this one will last.

At his workshops, Progoff would have us read out our steppingstone periods to the others in the group. I was amazed at how much you could learn about the others just by hearing them read their steppingstones. Next you may want to do some editing on your list. Preface each brief description of a time period with the calendar years it covers and your age at the beginning and at the end of that period.

You want to be able to read through all of the periods very quickly so you can get a sense of the flow of your life. How's it going? Are there several ups and downs emotionally? Have there been any major catastrophes? Can you determine during which steppingstone periods your major subpersonalities got started? Can you detect any subs that got squeezed out during one or another of your steppingstone periods? Can you pick out any patterns? Given where you have been, can you project where you might be in the future, say 10 years from now, 20 years from now?

Now as you observe what you are thinking and doing, note how often your thoughts are dwelling on something that happened in the past, or on something you hope will happen in the future. The experience of writing out your steppingstone periods gives you more data with which to work in deciding how to re-allocate your percentages of time-shares among your various roles and subpersonalities. The experience of trying to re-allocate the time among your roles, will help you decide on how you want to live the rest of your life.

Here now, for you to see as an example of how I first wrote up my steppingstone periods, is another entry from my journal:

Where Have I Been?   (5-20-85)

I believe that the key to studying and understanding our life story is to organize it into several small-time intervals. As we look over these intervals we get a sense of the flow of our life. We see the continuity of it. We see how certain early time periods have influenced later time periods. Looked at in this way, each of these time periods can be thought of as a steppingstone along the path our life has taken. Listing, reviewing, and sharing our steppingstones can help us to know ourselves better. The steppingstones also form an outline or table of contents for the telling of our life story. Here then, in quick summary, is an overview of my steppingstones:

I. 1936-42 PRESCHOOL YEARS: (Age 0- 5) Born into a happy, stable; Czech-Catholic family. Dad is 48, Mom 37, and big sister is 5. Pleasant memories.

II. 1942-50 ELEMENTARY GRADES: (Age 6-13) At a Catholic School under heavy influence of nuns and priests. I love it. I want to be a good boy.

III. 1950-55 HIGH SCHOOL AND COLLEGE: (Age 14-18) Growing up, asking questions, wondering what to be. Scientist, engineer, teacher, or priest?

IV. 1955-58 SEMINARY YEARS: (Age 19-21) Greek, Latin, Aristotle, Aquinas. I try hard to become a priest, but the enthusiasm isn't there. Turmoil.

V. 1958-60 TRANSITION NO. 1: (Age 22-23) "Now what do I do?" Renew my interest in girls, science, and math. Joy again. Enter medical school.

VI. 1960-66 MEDICAL TRAINING: (Age 24-29) Earn my M.D. and M.P.H.; Under heavy influence of doctors and research scientists. I love it and thrive.

VII. 1966-71 EARLY MARRIAGE AND CAREER: (Age 30-34) Adjusting to. demands of both. Study Preventive Medicine. Three sons are born. Some joy, some strife.

VIII. 1971-76 EARLY SUCCESS: (Age 35-39) Faculty position, Government -- grants, healthy growing family, beautiful home, many friends, but something is not right.

IX. 1976-77 TRANSITION NO. 2; (Age 40-41) Resign my position, move to hometown, reexamine my values, "Now what do I do?" Turmoil, confusion.

X. 1977- A NEW BEGINNING: (Age 42-) Putting down roots, working close to home, nurturing the family, understanding self, being, becoming....

I have done this exercise many times. What you have just read is but the latest version. I find it very useful when comparing life stories with someone over a cup of coffee. With such an outline of someone's life, you can direct the discussion into areas of interest to you. Do you want to hear more about the Seminary Years? Or maybe you would rather hear more about some of the joy and strife of those Early Marriage Years? Nothing is more discouraging to me than to listen to someone launch right into the middle of her life story and talk on and on. I have no idea where she is coming from and worse yet, no idea when she will stop. What she is saying would be more interesting if I had some context into which to fit that particular part of her story. I like Steppingstones for the same reason I like a Table of Contents, they help me to see where you are and where you have yet to go.

I want to encourage you to try the exercise. Lots of people will enjoy reading your Steppingstones. With such an outline of your life, we could discuss how our lives were similar and how they were different. We could compare certain time periods, like our preschool influences and enculturation. We could speculate on how certain accidents of life determined future time periods. Since you are not here talking to me over a cup of coffee, I will continue my end of the discussion now by elaborating a little on each of my Steppingstone Periods. Along the way I will introduce you to each of my Subpersonalities during the period in which they came into being.

I. I was born on September 10, 1936 into a Czech-Catholic family and culture in a small (pop. 1300) southern town in central Texas. The family constellation -- Father (48), Mother (37), and a big sister (5), was stable and loving. We all spoke Czech. I learned English as a second language when I started to school. My father and mother ran a small cleaning and pressing shop with Mom doing all of the sewing repairs. I had good friends in the neighborhood and remember the entire environment as a loving, nurturing one. Obviously, the Kid subpersonality got its start here and stays with me, more or less, from now on. In many ways, I still think of myself as a little Czech-Catholic kid from Granger, Texas trying to make good in the big world.

II. I entered Ss. Cyril and Methodius Catholic School at the age of six. We read the Bible a lot and went to church every day. We said our prayers before and after almost everything. Lunch was the big meal of the day and we all walked home for it. Serving Mass as an altar boy and receiving communion made me feel very good. I wanted to be just like Father George. At age 12 I started working after school and on Saturdays at a local grocery store for 25 cents an hour. Life was very exciting. I thought I would simply burst with all the enthusiasm and energy I felt within me.

III. The next five years were spent at "public" schools -- four years at Granger High and one year at Texas A&M. I ran into a lot of new ideas about life and on how one should live it. I enjoyed being around girls. Father Arthur replaced Father George and we did a lot of things together. I enjoyed science and math and began to speculate that I might want to be an engineer. I remember one especially exciting moment. I had put together a crystal radio set. I could not get it to work for several days. Then one day I tried it, it worked, and I experienced an indescribable surge of joy and happiness. I entered A&M with Electronic Engineering on my mind. Once there, however, many other choices presented themselves. I finally decided on math with the idea that I would teach kids in high school like Coach Algood did. But I wasn't happy with this decision. Father Charles at the Catholic Student Center suggested that maybe I can't settle on a major because God is calling me to the Priesthood.

IV. The decision to enter the Seminary felt right. My family and the whole parish thought it was a great idea. The church needed priests, especially Czech ones. And it had been so long since the Granger Parish had sent one of her sons to the Priesthood. I spent my sophomore year at St. Mary's in Houston and my junior and senior years at the Catholic University of America at Wash. D.C. At first, things went very well. Both Seminaries provided a safe, secure, and nurturing environment. I made many new friends. We prayed and chanted daily in the chapel. We took long meditative walks through wooded parks. I studied Latin and Greek and majored in the Philosophy of Aristotle and St. Thomas

Aquinas. Somewhere during my three years in the Seminary, my Seeker and Philosopher subpersonalities were born. I tried my best to fit in, but eventually, it became obvious that something was not right. I began to have doubts as to whether or not I really wanted to be a priest. What kept me there was the thought that it did not matter what I wanted; what mattered was what God wanted. I believed that I was one of God's chosen ones and that I should practice saying, "Not my will but Thine be done, O Lord!" Finally, I decided I couldn't say that any more. It was as if something in me had awakened for the first time and shouted, "I exist. What I want is important, too. And I want out." The surge of joy, enthusiasm, and power that I experienced on walking out of that seminary was enlightening.

V. I moved to Austin, entered the University of Texas, and got a job washing dishes at the Toddle House. In general, this was a happy, joyful period, marred only slightly by occasional guilt feelings for having left the seminary. I enjoyed the freedom of living on my own without all those meal and sleep schedules. I had a lot to learn about dating girls again and, except for a minor embarrassment here and there, I enjoyed the process very much. My biggest preoccupation was trying to decide what to do with my life. My Seeker subpersonality wanted to go to a foreign country to serve God and society as a Catholic Missionary. This would help with the guilt feelings. The Philosopher, however, was thriving in the University and wanted to go on to get a Ph.D. degree in physics, computer science, or mathematics. I finally decided to go to medical school because it seemed like a good compromise. I could combine my desire to serve mankind with my interests and abilities in science and math. And besides, I could always go to the missions later, as a physician. Occasionally, The Kid would urge me to do something wild, irresponsible, and fun like running off and hitting the road with the Dharma Bums and the Beat Generation. But the wiser subpersonalities persisted and I entered the UT Medical Branch in Galveston.

VI. This six-year period includes four years of medical school, one year of internship in Baltimore, and a year at Johns Hopkins University getting a Master Degree in Public Health. An intense enculturation into the academic, scientific and research community characterize this period. My philosophic readings at this time were primarily into Existentialism with all of its scary nihilistic voids and I found the scientific worldview a welcome relief and safe refuge. It was so precise, so logical, so certain of itself. When I started Medical School, my heroes were Dr. Schweitzer and Dr. Dooley. I wanted to go to foreign lands and treat the poor and the sick like they did. During Medical School my perspective on how best to help improve health in poor countries shifted toward more organized population-based programs like the Public Health Service was running in malaria eradication, tuberculosis control, and smallpox immunization. I did a couple of electives in Tropical Medicine -- one for eight weeks in Costa Rica and one for two weeks each in Puerto Rico, Venezuela, Colombia, and Panama. Along the way I got rid of any remaining guilt feelings and by the time this period ended, I felt free to forget about the Catholic missions and to plan for a career in Preventive Medicine and Public Health. I joined the United States Public Health Service and was assigned to the Tuberculosis Control Program among the Cuban refugees in Miami, Florida. The Doctor had firmly replaced The Seeker as the dominant sub-personality. And also during this period I met and fell in love with a young doctor named Susan. She too, had a Catholic background; had considered joining the Medical Mission Sisters; and shared some of my interests and values about helping the poor in foreign countries. The courtship was not a smooth one and spread itself out over several years and a couple of continents. It had many ups and downs, with many misunderstandings and miscommunications. But the chemistry was right, the care and concern for one another were there, and eventually, it all worked out and we were married in June of 1966. After a brief honeymoon in Mexico, we headed for Miami.

VII. We spent two years in Miami and then moved to Columbia, Missouri for three years where I completed my residency training in Preventive Medicine and joined the University of Missouri faculty as an Assistant Professor. Susan and I had considered going abroad to work with the World Health Organization, the Public Health Service, or the Peace Corps; but finally, I decided that there was enough of a challenge for me in Preventive Medicine and Public Health right here in the United States. There was no longer any need in me that had to be satisfied by going off to foreign lands. Besides, the Doctor-Scientist was not yet ready to give up the University environment. The U. of Missouri had just received five million dollars to set up a Regional Medical Program and was attracting top talent and promising young professionals in Medicine, Electrical Engineering, Information and Computer Sciences, and Operations Research to work together in trying to prevent and to improve the treatment of the major chronic diseases of our time -- Heart Disease, Cancer, and Stroke. It was a very exciting environment in which to work. There were a lot of evening meetings and many trips to various parts of the country to keep up with what others were doing. Meanwhile, our family was beginning to grow. Our first son, John, had been born in Miami in 1967; Randy and Joseph were born in Missouri in 1968 and 1970. Susan kept her career going with fellowships and occasional part time work but she was bearing the brunt of raising the kids and maintaining the home. Obviously, somewhere in here, my Family Man subpersonality got his start. It took me a while to grow into this role. After so many years of living alone, it was hard to adjust to living with others and to accept their demands on my time. Susan and I had some hard times, times of misunderstanding and miscommunication, times of stress while trying to develop two careers and raise a family at the same time. There were also a lot of happy times. We made several good, lasting friendships; we enjoyed our first home; and we shared many happy moments in watching the boys grow. We were not happy with the services at our parish church so we started going to Sunday Mass at the Newman Center. Somehow we felt more comfortable there. The priests and nuns seemed more open, more loving, and less dogmatic. I grew a beard, went to a few protest marches, and began to wonder if all the adults in charge of things really knew what they were doing. Even though I enjoyed working in multi-disciplinary groups in developing computer applications in medicine, again I got the feeling that something was not right. Was this the kind of work that had attracted me to public health? I decided not, and started looking around for other work opportunities and soon accepted an offer to join the U of Texas School of Public Health in Houston as an Associate Professor.

VIII. We were very happy about being back in Texas. The move put us closer to both of our parents to whom we were regularly making long trips to visit. We bought a nice large home in one of the older suburbs with a nice large back yard for the boys to play in. At the School of Public Health, I was teaching graduate students about public health, health planning, epidemiology, and human ecology. I was directing a couple of government grants in the training of nurse practitioners and health planners. And I started and directed the Health Maintenance Laboratory where, with colleagues and students, I began to explore the relationship among our present health status, our future risk of disease, and our current health affecting habits and practices. This too, was an exciting time, with lots of night and weekend meetings and many trips. We were not happy with the services at our parish church here either, so we looked around Houston until we found a folk mass held in a gym at St. Anne's. The priests and the people here were very supportive and interested in our experiences, our needs, our desires for a church. Soon Susan joined the faculty at the UT School of Medicine in the Department of Pediatrics. She, too, found the academic scene exciting. It was a new medical school, many new faculties were being recruited, and many new programs were being started. She was put on the Admissions Committee and soon, became the Assistant Dean for Student Affairs. At first she worked only half time; then it became three quarters time, and finally, full-time. She, too, had many meetings and trips, and brought a lot of work home to do at night. We made many new friends, were making lots of money, and the boys were doing fine. But the euphoria did not last. Something was not right. We were trying to do too many things and there was not enough time to do them all. Too much time was going into our careers and not enough time into parenting or any of our other subpersonalities. And worst of all, the careers were beginning to seem meaningless. We asked ourselves, "Is this success? Is this what we want to be doing the rest of our lives?" We decided that it was not. Academia had lost its charm. Houston had gotten too big. And in the air, was all that talk of "energy conservation", "small is beautiful", "back to the land", "living simply", and "alternate lifestyles". We resigned from our positions, packed up all our belongings, and headed for a farm just outside of my hometown of Granger.

IX. Moving to Granger meant coming home again and the move greatly extended our family. My mother, my sister, her husband, and their three children were all living in Granger. Susan's father came to live with us. Father George was back in Granger as pastor now. We enrolled the boys into the first, second, and fourth grade at Ss. Cyril and Methodius School. We all spent a lot of time fixing up the old farmhouse. Everything needed work -- the electricity, the plumbing, the windows, the roof, the floors. We were very much into solar energy then and made the attic into a solar collector with a clear plastic roof and then added underground rock storage. We planted a garden and got some animals. Here the Homesteader got his start. Emotionally, this was a mixed time. There was the enthusiasm and excitement of a new venture. There was also a lot of stress. Susan and I were both unemployed; we were with each other all day long; and we each had a different set of priorities for what we should be doing. And so again, we had a lot of arguments and miscommunications. Underneath all this I was continuing my midlife, existential crisis. I got down to the basic questions -- "Who am I? What's the purpose of life? What ought I to do?" I read a lot. I began to give my Seeker subpersonality a little more time. I started going to a lot of "Holistic Health" workshops. I took up meditation, yoga, and tai chi. I started jogging again. We stayed "retired" for a full year. During that time Susan decided to go into the private practice of Pediatrics and built herself a small office in Granger. The Texas Department of Health and the Williamson County Commissioners Court agreed that our county was big enough for a full-time Director for its Health Department and accepted me into that position. We both started back to work in September of 1977.

X. This time period by all measures continues to be the best one yet. Even though we occasionally miss some of the advantages and excitements of the big city, we have never regretted the move to Granger. We worry a little occasionally if putting the boys into the Catholic school had been a good idea. And we worry if attending such a small high school is not compromising in some major way their future educational potentials. But they seem to be doing okay. They are cheerful, noisy, lift weights, play a lot of Dungeons and Dragons, read a lot, and don't drink or smoke. As Susan's practice was building up, it did not demand her full-time attention. She had time to devote to taking care of the home, to parenting, and to caring for her elderly father. As her practice built up, I reduced my involvement at the Health Department to half time so that I had time to help in a major way with the parenting and the householder chores at home. Susan and I are better at communicating now and our relationship continues to deepen. I have not answered all of life's major questions but seem to have worked out a method to work on them without letting the doubt and uncertainty affect my mood too drastically. I have grown out of the need to travel all over the country looking for answers and now search for them in reading, in meditation and in discussion with friends. We have put down some roots and have formed some deep and meaningful relationships. And the period appears to be drawing to a close. The phase of intense need for parenting is over. My mother has died; Susan's father has died. The boys have grown up and will soon be leaving home. So, we have started looking forward to what lies ahead. Which subpersonalities need more time for their expression? Wonder what the next steppingstone period will be like?

There you have it, my life in 10 steppingstone periods, from birth to May 20, 1985 when that journal entry was written. A lot more living, learning, and sharing have occurred since then. We'll get around to what the next steppingstone periods were like a little later. Take some time now to write up each of your steppingstone periods in a little more detail, maybe 200-300 words at most. As you write up each steppingstone period, describe what you did and where you lived. Mention the names of people who were very significant in your life. Mention whether this was a happy time or a sad time. Was there a major decision you made during this period, like whom to marry or where to live? Be careful not to get stuck in any one time-period for too long. Once you get going there is a temptation just to write on and on as if you were writing your autobiography. You may well wish to do that someday, but now is not the time. The experience of elaborating on your steppingstones will help you to understand better the next chapter on Waking Up.

Chapter 5
Waking Up

This may well be the most important chapter of this book. The concept of "waking up" is profound and its implications are exciting. If I had tried to tell you about it at the start, you may have found it too preposterous to believe. But now, if you have been doing your self-observations and if you have written up your subpersonalities and steppingstones, you have had the experiences on which "waking up" is based. It is now no longer a question of belief; your experiences will tell you it is so.

When you are doing your self-observations, who is observing whom? Who are you when you are observing your body/mind and all of his or her subpersonalities doing things and worrying about stuff? When you were writing up your steppingstones, you described different time periods during which different subpersonalities came into prominence and during which some faded out of prominence. But throughout the life span you had a sense that you were there. Who are you, really?

I first read about "waking up" in the Gurdjieff, Ouspensky, and deRopp literature, but there are hints of it present throughout history. The basic concept is that most of the time we are living automatically and mechanically, functioning through long established habit patterns, following a script that was enculturated into us early in life by our parents, our church, our community, differing throughout the world depending on country, ethnicity, and religion. It is as though the enculturation process hypnotized us and so we eat what our culture eats, we behave as our culture expects us to behave, and we believe what our culture believes. We are living as though in a trance, a consensus trance. Everyone agrees that this is the way things are around here. In response to these enculturating forces, our one body/mind develops a unique set of self-functioning subpersonalities and it is these subpersonalities which then carry out the scripts we have been handed.

The deRopp literature describes four states of consciousness that we can experience. The first state is when we are asleep and not dreaming. State 2 is when we are asleep and having dreams. The third state is when we think we are awake but are actually in a "waking trance" living our lives automatically and mechanically. The fourth state of consciousness is when we truly "wake up" to whom we really are and can then live our lives consciously, with a heightened awareness, focusing our attention wherever we choose.

Here now is a quote from Robert S. de Ropp, in his book, *The Master Game*, writing about self-observation and waking up. He sometimes refers to the third and fourth states of consciousness as the third and fourth room:

The third state of consciousness is experienced when man awakens from physical sleep and plunges at once into the condition called "identification." Identification is the essence of the third state of consciousness. In this state, man has no separate awareness. He is lost in whatever he happens to be doing, feeling, thinking. Because he is lost, immersed, not present in himself, this condition, the third state of consciousness, is referred to in the Gurdjieffian system as the state of "waking sleep." Man in this state is described not as the real man but as a machine, without inner unity, real will or permanent I, acted upon and manipulated by external forces as a puppet is activated by the puppeteer.

For many people, this concept of waking sleep makes no sense at all. They firmly maintain that, once they "wake up" (from physical sleep), they are responsible beings, masters of themselves, fully conscious, and that anyone who tells them that they are not is a fool or a liar. It is almost impossible to convince such people that they are deceiving themselves because, when a man is told that he is not really conscious, a mechanism is activated within him which awakens him for a moment. He replies, indignantly, "But I am fully conscious," and because of this "trick of Nature" as Ouspensky used to call it, he does become conscious for a moment. He moves from the third room to the threshold of the fourth room, answers the challenge, and at once goes to sleep again, firmly convinced that he is a fully awakened being.

A man's chance of attaining the fourth state of consciousness depends on whether or not he has experienced this state. If he does not even know it exists, he will not long for it any more than a bird born and raised in captivity can know what freedom is like or long for freedom. Man can, and from time to time does, experience the fourth state as a result of some religious emotion, under the influence of a work of art, in the rapture of sexual love or in situations of great danger and difficulty. In these circumstances, it is said that he "remembers himself." This term is not entirely descriptive of the fourth state but it is the best available. Self-remembering is a certain separation of awareness from whatever a man happens to be doing, thinking, feeling. It is symbolized by a two-headed arrow suggesting double awareness. There is actor and observer, there is an objective awareness of self. There is a feeling of being outside of, separated from, the confines of the physical body; there is a sense of detachment, a state of nonidentification. For identification and self-remembering can no more exist together than a room can simultaneously be illuminated and dark. One excludes the other. [5]

Our life task, then, is one of waking up to this fourth state of consciousness and our life journey is to find out who we really are. You and I will deal with "finding out who we really are" later on in the book, for now let us concentrate on how to wake up.

Let's reflect again on your self-observation sessions. What is actually going on in such a session? I told you in Chapter 2 that it is easy to shift into this "Observer" mode whenever someone asks you to do it, and the skill to learn now is how to shift into it occasionally on your own. What is this observer mode? Who is the "Observer"?

We met the Observer again in Chapter 3. While doing the pie exercise, I asked you to draw the pie with a little circle in the center and to place the letter "I" into it. I told you that that "I" is you, the you who is observing the various role players and subpersonalities who are time-sharing your one body/mind. The "I" in the little circle is the "Observer."

In doing your steppingstone periods you also functioned as the "Observer", this time observing the history of your life, noting the various ups and downs, noting which subpersonalities were most active in each time period, and finally deciding how to organize all of that material into 8-12 steppingstone periods.

Whenever you are functioning as the "Observer", you are more alert, more aware, more awake. You have momentarily awakened from your usual mode of functioning, which is through automatic habit patterns, in a kind of consensus trance. You, no doubt, have managed to wake up occasionally throughout your life. In doing your steppingstones you may have noticed that some periods went very smoothly, the time seems to have passed quickly, you knew what you had to do, there didn't seem to be any question about it. These were the time periods during which you were most likely "asleep" and happily following your script. Turmoil and indecision as to what to do may have characterized other time periods. My steppingstone period #V, after I left the Seminary and before I entered Medical School, and #IX, after I resigned from my faculty position with the School of Public Health and before I joined the Texas Department of Health, which I have described as transitions, were such. They were brief periods, lasting only one or two years but they were periods during which I spontaneously "awoke" several times and consciously considered who I was and what I wished to do.

You may have noted several such periods in your life. It is not like you are being asked to do something you have never done before. I'm just calling attention to the fact that you may already be alternating between states of consciousness 3 and 4, only not aware that this is what is happening. Understanding the difference between state one (deep sleep, no dreaming) and state two (dreams and nightmares) is easy and straightforward. We know that sometimes when we sleep, we have dreams and at times we don't. We know that whenever we are having a nightmare (state 2), it's a relief to wake up (to state 3) and realize that it was only our dream that has frightened us. The difference between states two and three, is also easy to detect.

The point of this chapter is to inform you that there is a fourth state, that you have already experienced it, and that now we need to learn to notice how it feels to be in this fourth state.

Charles T. Tart, in his essay, "The Dynamics of Waking Sleep", has this to say about the third state of consciousness:

One of Gurdjieff's principal themes is that "man is asleep." In my own vocabulary, I would say that the ordinary state of consciousness of man, "consensus consciousness," is like a trance, which pejoratively implies a loss of vitality and a lack of initiative, accompanied by highly mechanical thought. The adjective consensus signifies that this particular form of trance is induced by the kind of culture in which we grew up. It is a consensus -- implicit and explicit -- concerning not only what is socially important but even the nature of reality itself.

Gurdjieff's assertion that "man lives in sleep" is fundamentally provocative; it is bound to arouse a reaction. But, if one accepts it, this reaction can lead to self-observation, to "self-remembering" and thus to the possibility of action that is more effective, more awake. [6]

If we could wake up, what could we not do? [7]

Arthur J. Deikman, in his book, *The Observing Self*, has this to say about alternating between the third and fourth state of consciousness:

We have learned to interpret the thinking, feeling, and functioning selves as expressions of an object self. Thus, their activity supports and strengthens the object self and the mode of consciousness organized to serve it. But in considering the fourth domain, the observing self, we come to a phenomenon of a different order. The observing self is the transparent center, that which is aware. This fourth self is most personal of all, prior to thought, feeling, and action, it experiences these functions. No matter what takes place, no matter what we experience, nothing is as central as the self that observes. In the face of this phenomenon, Descartes starting point, "I think; therefore, I am," must yield to the more basic position, "I am aware; therefore, I am." [8]

We can view the network of fantasies that influence our actions as hypnotic suggestions to which we comply. Thus, depending on the force of the fantasy that is active, we are likely to conduct most of our lives in a state of trance of varying depth, broken by interludes of relatively awake consciousness.

As habitual is the trance of ordinary life that one could say that human beings are a race that sleeps and awakens, but does not awaken fully. Because half-awake is sufficient for tasks we customarily do, few of us are aware of the dysfunction of our condition. Moments of more complete awakening do occur, but the consensus of the group and the automatic functioning of the object self-make such phenomena transient curiosities rather than urgent signals that something is wrong with the normal state. [9]

The difference between the third and fourth state of consciousness is subtle and at first, you may not feel any difference, but over time, as you continue to purposefully shift from the third state to the fourth, you will begin to notice several differences. The best way that I know of for you to get the necessary experiences is to continue your self-observations and thought watching sessions, but this time with the notion clearly in mind that you are waking up to a higher state of awareness or consciousness.

It may help if you compose a short phrase for yourself to use when you remember to start a self-observation session, something like, "Hello, World. Here I am again, a human being functioning on the Planet Earth, fully awake in a higher state of consciousness." What follows is another entry from my journal with some of my observations on waking up.

On Waking Up   (9-10-85)

Now I try coupling the saying of the "Hello, World" message to things that happen occasionally throughout the day, like answering the phone or getting into the car. Gradually I'm getting a little better at it. Now when the phone rings, I try to wake up so I could be ready to respond with whichever subpersonality is being called. Or when I get into the car, I try to take off whichever hat I've been wearing and switch into whoever is the subpersonality needed when I get to my destination.

This has been fun to experiment with. To be in that so-called fourth state of consciousness is almost always more pleasant that to be functioning mechanically and automatically half asleep. I have had enough experience now in doing this that I have come to believe that there may be something positive to be gained by pursuing it further. I have let my family in on what I am trying to do and they have been a big help. I still get angry with the boys every once in a while, and then I rant and rave like the worst of parents. I have explained to them that parents have been programmed to behave this way by our culture and that I am simply carrying out my role automatically and mechanically. So now whenever I begin to rant and rave, the boys simply wave their hand in the air and say something like, "Wake up, Dad. You're stuck on automatic again." It works. As soon as they say that, the focus of my attention shifts, away from them and their behavior, to me and my behavior. And the anger fades away. Then all together we can look at what it was that they did that triggered the anger and we can discuss what we can do to prevent the anger trigger in the future. It is easy to be angry when you're stuck in the half-asleep third state of consciousness but it is hard to stay angry once you switch into the fourth state of self-observation.

Whenever I am fully awake, I already feel that I am one whole healthy personality. It is only when I stay in deRopp's third state of "waking sleep" that my subpersonalities can carry on their fragmenting and stress producing automatic behavior patterns. So, my goal for the future is to learn to stay fully awake for longer periods of time, to have available to me at all times all the various character traits of my subpersonalities, and to be able to exercise a little more conscious choice in my life, rather than simply playing out a script that has been programmed into me at some time in the past.

Finally, I will quote from P.D. Ouspensky's *In Search of the Miraculous*, a humorous account of himself trying to self-remember, or to keep his attention on the fact that he is trying to stay in self-observation, while going to a tobacco shop in Moscow. Don't let the Russian words confuse you, they simply refer to streets and parts of town. All the italics are Ouspensky's:

I was once walking along the Liteiny towards the Nevsky, and in spite of all my efforts I was unable to keep my attention on self-remembering. *The noise, movement, everything* distracted me. Every minute I lost the thread of attention, found it again, and then lost it again. At last I felt a kind of ridiculous irritation with myself and I turned into the street on the left having firmly decided to keep my attention on the fact that I would remember myself at least for some time, at any rate until I reached the following street. I reached the Nadejdinskaya without losing the thread of attention except, perhaps, for short moments. Then I again turned towards the Nevsky realizing that, in quiet streets, it was easier for me not to lose the line of thought and wishing therefore to test myself in more noisy streets. I reached the Nevsky still remembering myself, and was already beginning to experience the strange emotional state of inner peace and confidence which comes after great efforts of this kind. Just around the corner on the Nevsky was a tobacconist's shop where they made my cigarettes. Still remembering myself I thought I would call there and order some cigarettes.

Two hours later I woke up in the Tavricheskaya, that is, far away. I was going by izvostchik to the printers. The sensation of awakening was extraordinarily vivid. I can almost say that I came to. I remembered everything at once. How I had been walking along the Nadejdinskaya, how I had been remembering myself, how I had thought about cigarettes, and how at this thought I seemed all at once to fall and disappear into a deep sleep.

At the same time, while immersed in this sleep, I had continued to perform consistent and expedient actions. I left the tobacconist, called at my flat in the Liteiny, telephoned to the printers. I wrote two letters. Then again I went out of the house. I walked on the left side of the Nevsky up to the Gostinoy Dvor intending to go to the Offitzerskaya. Then I had changed my mind as it was getting late. I had taken an izvostchik and was driving to the Kavalergardskaya to my printers. And on the way, while driving along the Tavricheskaya, I began to feel a strange uneasiness, as though I had forgotten something. -- And suddenly I remembered that I had forgotten to remember myself. [10]

That's probably enough quotes for now, you get the idea. Remember that your task now is to experience on your own how it feels to shift from "waking sleep" or "consensus trance" to the more awake, more aware state of consciousness. So, continue with your self-observation sessions, but now as you verbalize your "wake-up message", pay attention to any feeling tone differences you experience in shifting into the "observer" mode. You may be able to stay in your observer mode for longer periods of time if you write up your subpersonalities in greater detail. The next chapter has another journal entry as an example of how I wrote up my Philosopher sub.

Chapter 6
The Philosopher Subpersonality

Although I have given the ideas of Gurdjieff, Assagioli, and Progoff top billing so far, there are several other authors who have influenced, in a major way, my psychological growth and development. In order to share with you who these are, and to tell you a little more about one of my subpersonalities, here is another entry from my journal. It is my Philosopher subpersonality speaking:

The Philosopher: (6-2-85)

I need more time to read. I have this library full of books and so little time to read them. And more great stuff is being published every day. Worse yet I have discovered that I can go back and reread a good book and still get a lot out of it the second time. I get a really good and joyous feeling inside as I sit there and engage some author and grapple with his or her ideas. It is a real natural high and understanding this joy is a key defining characteristic in understanding who I am.

Let me tell you about some of the books and authors that have shaped, molded, and continue to influence my thinking and my beliefs. A prominent place on my bookshelves is reserved for the books of Walter Kaufmann. His Faith of a Heretic and From Shakespeare to Existentialism, which I read during the early 1960's, introduced me to the existential literature and provided the stimulus to grow past some of my childish notions of who God is and what life on earth was really about. Kaufmanns's books hit home, planted doubt, and created confusion in what till then, I thought, had been a pretty consistent worldview. The books challenged me. Here was a writer who was saying, in a clear, logical, believable manner, things that simply could not be true. I read on, not only his books but also the authors' books he wrote about. I was vaguely anxious that maybe I was placing myself in an occasion of sin but someone, I felt, had to answer this man. So, in trying to answer Kaufmann, I was forced to think on my own, to form my own arguments, and to learn to accept doubt as one of the conditions of life. Keep in mind that by this time I was 27 years old and in the middle of my Medical School years. One has to wonder how I could have made it through college with a BA in Philosophy without having encountered the Existentialists. I guess it was some combination of my not being ready for them and Catholic U. not really thinking it was necessary to emphasize them in the training of priests. Very soon I stopped fighting Kaufmann and began to like him.

Right next to Kaufmann, I keep two books by William Barrett – Irrational Man and Time of Need. Barrett did a good job of helping me understand how existentialist thought and the history of the twentieth century have intertwined and defined our time as a time of need. The existentialist literature describes the experiencing of doubt, of meaninglessness, of nothingness. Reading the existentialists and rereading them helps me in understanding and surviving my own bouts with the nihilistic voids.

Another major influence on disturbing my early beliefs and values was, of course, the scientific literature. Labwork in scientific methodology introduced me to a way of arriving at certitude that I found refreshing and invigorating. Courses in Physics, Astronomy, Biology, Ecology, Genetics, and Evolution really extended the worldview of this little Czech-Catholic kid from Granger. I remember with some embarrassment and upset one particular question I had on an entrance exam when I first hit college. The question was, 'For approximately how many years have humans been on earth?' Included among the choices were: a. 6000 and b. one million. I answered 6000, reasoning that it was about 2000 to Jesus' birth, 2000 from then to the flood, and then 2000 more to Adam. Right? Wrong!!! My profs tried to tell me as gently as they could that even respected priests in

Rome now accepted the evidence that humans have been around for over one million years. (For a wonderfully written novelized version of what happened approximately 30,000 years ago just as Neanderthal man was dying out and Cro-Magnon was emerging, you can read Jean Auel's Clan of the Cave Bear, Valley of Horses, and Mammouth Hunters.)

How could I, in 1954, after 12 years of education, which included several science courses, not know that man has been around for longer than 6000 years? Or that our solar system is at least 5 billion years old? Or that there are approximately 100 billion stars in our galaxy and that there are approximately 100 billion other galaxies? Such vastness of space and time puts the question of who we are and what are we to do each day into a whole new context and perspective.

If I give Walter Kaufmann most of the credit for disturbing my early peaceful worldview and for getting me started on the road to disillusionment, confusion, doubt, and despair, then I need to give Robert S. deRopp the major credit for helping me to turn things around and getting me started on the road again towards hope and psychological well-being. His books, The Master Game and The Church of the Earth, introduced me to the rich traditions of Gurdjieff and Ouspensky and to the key concept that we live mostly in a state of 'waking sleep' from which we can awaken and live in a more aware state of consciousness.

The next biggest help probably came from Abraham Maslow and Roberto Assagioli, whose psychology focuses on the healthy personality and on how we can integrate psychological growth with spiritual growth and development. Their works – The Farther Reaches of Human Nature and Psychosynthesis led me to the field of Transpersonal Psychology where my continued growth gets most of its nurturance today.

Other major influences were the books of Teilhard de Chardin and Sri Aurobindo. I can remember very well the surge of joy that flowed through me as I read Teilhard's

Phenomenon of Man. Here was a Catholic priest and a competent, respected scientist describing with excitement the evolution of man and documenting the evolution with archeological findings he himself had participated in. He then continues the evolution into the future speculating along the way and weaving into the theme a thoroughly Christian perspective with union as Christ, our endpoint. Teilhard's efforts at integrating his scientific findings with his spiritual beliefs and experiences have helped me to do the same with mine.

Sri Aurobindo, from a thoroughly Eastern perspective and tradition, develops some of the same themes as Teilhard on the evolution of humanity and as Assagioli on the nature of the self and a Higher Self. Other writers helping me to understand the Eastern perspective were Alan Watts, Ram Dass, and Herman Hesse. These writers introduced me to a literature, a psychology, and a spirituality that filled in nicely some of the gaps I was beginning to experience in our Western perspective on science and religion.

And then, there is Ken Wilber. His worldview is truly integral and cosmological. He integrates well the Eastern and Western perspectives on psychology and spirituality. His ideas are probably best put forth in the Atman Project and Up from Eden. Reading Wilber sends the same kind of shivers up and down my spine as does reading Kaufmann, deRopp, and Teilhard. Any metaphysics that I may yet develop will have to either incorporate or refute the tenets of Ken Wilber.

Also I have read practically everything ever published by Colin Wilson, Lawrence LeShan, Sheldon Kopp, John Lilly, and Carlos Castaneda. Major current influences from workshops and books are Willis Harmon, Roger Walsh, Frances Vaughn, Kathleen Speech, and James Fadiman. I am really looking forward to reading Charles Tart's new book on Gurdjieff.

But what's the point of all this reading and intellectual speculation? Wouldn't all this time be better spent caulking the windows, baking bread, programming the computer, meditating, or making more money? I think not. To look at the stars and to speculate on what's the meaning of it all, just has to be one of the noblest of human endeavors.

So I read, think, and write. I try to integrate and synthesize the ideas of others with my own experiences and beliefs. I do it to understand myself better and to understand better humanity's role in the grand scheme of things. And as this understanding grows, it is becoming easier for me to decide what it is that I am to do each day. And with increasing frequency, I am able to do what needs to be done that day with at least a modicum of grace, joy, and nobility. This has to be worth something."

Most of the authors mentioned above have continued to write during the years since the above was written and I continue to be guided and nurtured by them. Ken Wilber has emerged as the leading spokesperson for a Transpersonal Integral Psychology. Today I would say that the best introduction to his writings are probably *A Brief History of Everything* and *A Theory of Everything.* I'll have more to say about some of Wilber's ideas later on.

Another major influence since the above was written was my meeting with Don Beck. At one of his workshops on Spiral Dynamics, he introduced me to the stages of consciousness up which humans grow on our way to maturity. His coloring of the stages as red, blue, orange, green and yellow have made it easier to understand and to remember the differences among them. I'll have a lot more to say about these stages later on also.

But for now, I want you to let one of your subpersonalities write-up in greater detail what it is that excites him or her about life. Doing so will give you some more experience in shifting your sense of "I", your sense of who you are, back and forth from a complete identification with the subpersonality and identification with your more awake Self who knows that the subpersonality is not who you really are, but simply a part of a role you are temporarily playing.

This experience will supplement the experience you are getting with your self-observations and your morning efforts at watching your thoughts. What follows will make a lot more sense if you have truly experienced that felt shift which comes on waking-up from your consensus trance.

Chapter 7
The Self and The Personal Ego

Most of the authors mentioned in the proceeding chapter have struggled with the question of how to refer to these two different states of awareness. The more aware state is usually referred to as our Higher Self or True Self. The Gurdjieff literature refers to it as our "Essence". Our usual mode of awareness, while behaving in our automatic, habitual mode, is usually referred to simply as a self (with a small "s") or sometimes as a false self. Assagioli uses the term Self (with a capital S) for our True Self and uses the term "personal ego" whenever he is referring to the "I" with which we usually identify.

The term "personal ego" or just "ego" will work fine for us here and I will use this term from now on to identify us whenever we are functioning in our usual automatic, half-asleep, trance-like behavior patterns, identifying with our various ego-subpersonalities. We will explore further the nature of your True Self a little later on, but for now just keep in mind, that from your own experience, you already know that as soon as you wake up and shift your sense of "I" to your Self, one of your capabilities is to function as an Observer of your ego activities.

What you, as Self, are observing is your personal ego at work and at play. Your ego has developed over your lifetime and is basically the "I" you think of as being in charge of directing all of your day-to-day activities. Your ego was formed by all the influences it encountered while growing up, with the major influences being your parents, your siblings, your church, your culture, your peers, and the environment in which you grew up. Of all the possible human personality traits that you could have adopted, you adopted those that served you best while interacting with those in your immediate environment. The set of subpersonalities and roles, which your ego developed, was the set best suited to cope with the challenges you faced while growing up, given the support you were receiving.

Pause for a moment now to consider all of the possible variations in a home environment. It could have been a very loving one or one with various degrees of verbal, physical, or emotional abuse. It could have been a peaceful time or the middle of some war or terror. It could have been an isolated existence with foster parents or a very gregarious one with loads of friends and relatives. You may have developed a strong and domineering ego, and others may criticize you as being egotistical or egocentric. You may have an ego described by others as weak, one easily controlled by others. You may have an ego with a few neurotic hang-ups or crutches. Or hopefully, you may be functioning with a fairly normal, healthy ego.

Do not be too critical of your personal ego's values, beliefs, and actions. Those values, beliefs, and actions have worked. They were responsible for the development of successful coping strategies. You are alive today primarily because your ego has been able to cope successfully with the various challenges encountered in life so far. For better or for worse, your ego is your creation. And on waking-up, and observing and understanding your ego, the most natural and appropriate stance to take toward it, is to love it.

But even while loving it, you may still find yourself wanting to change some of your ego's activities. On reviewing your subpersonalities, you may wish to give one of them more time at the expense of another or you may wish that one subpersonality stop being so angry or critical all the time. On reviewing your steppingstone periods, you may decide that the time has come to move to another city or to start a new career. You may wish to lose some weight, or to stop smoking, or to exercise more. But can we actually make changes of any meaningful magnitude? Hasn't our ego's life script been written by the age of five, and are we now not doomed to simply observe as our life plays itself out?

Obviously, the whole premise of this book is that we can change, but it will not be easy. Your newly awakened Self will have to not be content with simply observing, but will need to strive to become the Director as well, the Director of your usual day-to-day ego-subpersonalities' activities.

Gurdjieff was fond of comparing our life with a horse-drawn stagecoach. Picture a stagecoach being pulled by six powerful horses controlled by a strong driver. There seems to be someone asleep inside of the stagecoach but we are not really sure if there actually is anyone in there. Who is deciding where the stagecoach will go? The horses? The driver? Or the sleeping passenger inside?

Think of the horses as your subpersonalities, each wanting the stagecoach to go its own way. Think of the driver as your ego, who has over the course of the trip so far, learned to coordinate the drives of each of your subpersonalities in order to make some progress in the best compromise direction. In Gurdjieff's story the passenger inside is the Self, actually the Master, who owns the horses, and who has hired the driver to take him to a specific destination. But since the Master has fallen asleep, the driver has forgotten that he is in there. The driver thinks that he is on his own and free to go wherever he wishes. Imagine the Master's dilemma when he awakens and tries to assert his preference for the stagecoach's direction. The driver thinks that he is doing the best job possible in controlling the horses and is firmly convinced that the direction the coach is headed now is the best compromise course. He hopes the Master will soon fall asleep again.

Your ego faces exactly the same dilemma, when you, as Self, try to assert some control over its activity. You have experienced that as your awake Self, you are capable of observing your ego's feelings and actions. Your next step will be to see if you are also capable of directing and influencing some of your ego's feelings and actions.

It may help at this point to introduce some of Assagioli's affirmations into your morning review. He advocated the use of an Identification exercise, throughout which we are encouraged to identify with our Self, a center of pure Self-consciousness and to realize its permanency and its energy. Note especially his reference to "directing" and being a "director." You might try copying the following onto a card and reading it as part of your morning exercise. See if it works for you.

Identification Exercise:

I have a body, but I am not my body.

I have emotions, but I am not my emotions.

I have a mind, but I am not my mind.

What am I then? What remains after having disidentified myself from my body, my sensations, my feelings, my desires, my mind, my actions? It is the essence of myself – a center of pure Self-consciousness. It is the permanent factor in the ever-varying flow of my personal life. It is that which gives me a sense of being, of permanence, of inner balance. I affirm my identity with this center and realize its permanency and its energy.

I recognize and affirm myself as a center of pure Self-awareness and of creative, dynamic energy. I realize that from this center of true identity I can learn to observe, direct, and harmonize all the psychological processes and the physical body. I will to achieve a constant awareness of this fact in the midst of my everyday life, and to use it to help and give increasing meaning and direction to my life. [11]

Finally, the following affirmation summarizes nicely our progress so far. All the italics are Assagioli's:

I engage in various activities and play many roles in life. I must play these roles and I willingly play them as well as possible, be it the role of son or father, wife or husband, teacher or student, artist or executive. But I am more than the son, the father, the artist. These are roles, specific but partial roles, which I, myself, am playing, agree to play, can watch and observe myself playing. Therefore, I am not any of them.

I am Self-identified, and I am not only the actor, but also the director of the acting. [12]

To become the Director of your ego activities, the Self will need to begin exerting its will. But the will is weak, it has been so rarely exercised. To be helpful to you, your will must be strengthened. And the way to do this, will be for you to try training it on baby steps before you attempt to make any major changes in your life.

One exercise that Assagioli had me do, was to stand on a chair, take a piece of newspaper, and tear off little one-inch strips. Normally, no one's ego has been programmed to occasionally stand up on a chair and tear off little one-inch strips of newspapers. If you can will yourself to do this, then you have successfully demonstrated that you, as Self, can indeed direct at least some of your ego activities.

You can very quickly come up with some better ideas for things to do to train your will besides tearing up newspapers. Be careful though, that one of your subpersonalities doesn't take over here and have your body/mind do things that it wants done. One idea might be to willfully change slightly some of your automatic routines. If you always start shaving on the right side of your face, switch to starting on the left side. If you always eat your cereal in the morning before eating toast, try eating your toast first. After you have been secretly demonstrating to yourself for a while, that as Self, you can will that the ego undertakes some activity that it does not normally do, you are ready to give "Unpredictability" a try.

The notion of predictability in our behavior is a key defining characteristic of living solely under the influence of the consensus trance. Given a certain stimulus, you get a predictable response. You know this. You have witnessed the predictable behavior of lots of people you know. You may not, however, have noticed that most of your actions and comments are equally predictable. There is a joke going around about an elderly couple, married forty years, sitting in a restaurant eating their meal without saying a word. The waitress comments on this. The woman replies that she had thought to say something several times, but each time decided there was no point in doing so because she already knew exactly what he would say in response.

Here again is an entry from my journal, when I first wrote about practicing unpredictability.

Unpredictability (3-30-85)

I also kid our sons about how predictable their behavior is. If I ask them to burn the trash, I always get the same predictable response.   Ask them to go to bed, same predictable response. I know that they understand this issue because they have learned to use it very effectively on me. Whenever they want my permission to do something and they are afraid that the answer will be a "No!", they start off by saying something like, "Now Dad, here comes another chance for you to show off how unpredictable you can be." And this works too, because when I do wake up and look at their request with heightened awareness, sometimes I do see it their way and say, "Yes!" Sometimes I say "Yes!" even if I don't see it their way, just to practice unpredictability.

Practicing unpredictability is the next step after self-observation. What is the point of breaking free into another state of consciousness if all you can do is observe your old automatic and mechanical behavior patterns? I would like to think that I could make some changes in my behavior if I would like to.   This is actually quite a challenge.   Do you think it is possible for you to perform an unpredictable act? To qualify as an unpredictable act, it has to be something you do in front of family, friends, or coworkers and one of them has to spontaneously exclaim something like, "How uncharacteristic of you to do this." It is fun to try this. It's good exercise.   It's like developing a new set of muscles. Assagioli calls it "training your will." There is obviously some danger here.   After all, our family, friends, and coworkers have defined who we are by our particular set of predictable behaviors. It can become quite disconcerting to them if we, all of a sudden, begin behaving "strangely". I suggest you start off slowly and with loving and considerate behaviors. If you are not in the habit of doing housework, try mopping the kitchen floor. If you have never baked a loaf of bread, buy yourself some yeast and a cookbook and try it tomorrow. Such gentle and considerate behavior changes, I have found, are easier to take by family, friends, and coworkers. But be forewarned. There is no predicting where you will stop once you experience the freedom of not having to continue behaving as you always have and begin experimenting with new patterns of behavior. Who knows, you might decide to do some strange and wonderful things for the first time -- like moving to San Francisco, adopting a kid, or writing a book. Or you might decide to start doing again some things you've done before -- like cooking meals, saying your prayers, or enjoying sex.

The danger of too much change is considerably minimized by our proclivity to fall back asleep and to continue acting in our usual automatic ways. This gives everybody around us time to get used to it and to slowly redefine us as someone who occasionally does something unpredictable. So far, I think that my dabbling in this fourth state of consciousness business has had a positive effect on those around me. Susan says that I have become more loving, less angry, and in general easier to live with, since learning about self-observation and direction.

Over the years I have also used growing a beard and then shaving it off, or letting my hair grow long and then cutting it short, as a way of demonstrating to myself that I could direct changes in my usual day-to-day activity patterns. One day the idea hit me that shaving off all the hair on my head would really be a neat unpredictable stunt. But for several years I couldn't will myself to do it. Once, I actually told my barber to shave it all off, but then I let him talk me out of it. He said, "Oh, Dr. Skrovan, that would not look good on you at all. It would be too much of a shock to all the people around here. Let's cut it shorter and shorter each month for a while. Let the people get used to it." Finally, on March 28, 1998, the barber shaved it all off.

That was quite a willful act. I know that, nowadays, you do see a lot of men with their heads shaved off, but not old men in Central TX. Here was Dr. Skrovan, a pillar of sorts in the community, and his head was shaved off. Most people assumed I must be on chemotherapy. When asked, I would tell people that I was trying to prove to myself that we actually do have a free will. That gave me the opportunity to tell them about doing unpredictable acts.

I won't ask you to do anything this drastic but I hope you get the idea. Now go on and try doing an unpredictable act, like maybe writing up another one of your subpersonalities right now.

Chapter 8
The Homesteader Subpersonality

When we moved, in 1976, from our city jobs in Houston, to a farm in Central Texas, I was suddenly faced with needing to do many tasks that I had never done before. Clearly these were tasks my ego had not been enculturated to do and daily I had opportunities to practice training my will to direct ego activities. In a sense, I had to create a new role, whom I called the Homesteader. Here is an entry from my journal written by him:

The Homesteader: (9-20-85)

I really shouldn't be writing this right now, there are a lot of things outside which need doing. The pasture needs shredding; the electric fence is shorting out somewhere; the watering trough needs a new float cutoff; the corral needs a new wooden post; it's time to get the cows out of the oat field; the gray water grease trap needs cleaning out; the composting toilet needs to have some liquid pumped out and some compost removed; the leak, in the new plumbing I put in, still has not gone away; the garden is a mess; the peaches need to be picked and preserved or dried; the list goes on and on.

I have 25 acres of pasture on which I am trying to keep one bull, five cows, and four calves. I have 12 acres of land in cultivation on which I am trying to grow alternately oats for hay, clover for the nitrogen, and wheat for flour and cash. I maintain my own electric fences. I am doing a fairly good job maintaining our water system of well, pump, tower and tank, and associated plumbing. I do best at maintaining our electric system. I spend some time helping Susan with the garden and with the preserving.

Every once in a while, I ask myself, 'Why am I doing all this?' Do I have time and energy available to continue to nourish this activity with all of my other subpersonalities each still clamoring for more time? My neighbor would love to take over and rent the 25 acres of pasture. My cousin would love to take over the 12 cultivated acres. We could hire a plumber and an electrician. We could buy our beef, vegetables, fruits, and preserves. We could simply live here in our house much like one lives in an apartment or house in the city and all the time and energy saved could go into my other interests and roles.

Those are times when my other subpersonalities are breaking through and complaining. As 'the Homesteader', I would find that very sad. I feel as though I would be losing something very important if I stopped the homesteading. It's a value in me that has developed over the past few years. I believe the impetus for developing 'the Homesteader' first came while still in Houston on reading Robert deRopp's Master Game *and* The Church of the Earth. *Somewhere in these two books, deRopp develops the theme that humans need to devote some time to the following three areas -- the Temple, the University, and the Garden.*

In the Temple we satisfy the needs of our Spirit. We pray. We meditate. We develop communication channels with God. We nourish our inner growth. In the University, we nourish our minds. We read. We study. We think. We compare ideas and concepts. We philosophize. We try to understand the Universe and our place in it. In the Garden, we can ground ourselves to Mother Earth. By working in the garden, we are reminded of our place in the natural order of things. We become more aware of the cyclic nature of life sustaining processes. We understand the true costs of our food, our clothes, and our shelter. We find our niche. We become connected to a time and to a place. We are no longer separated and isolated. We become grounded.

This theme of deRopp's struck a very responsive chord in me. I felt that I had spent a lot of time in the Temple, was now spending most of my time in the University and had not ever, spent much time in the Garden. Most importantly, I was feeling the symptoms deRopp implied went with such a pattern -- a sense of airiness, head-up-in-the-clouds.

A part of my motivation for returning to Granger was to go back to the last place where I had felt connected to something outside of myself. Granger was where I had grown up. The community still thought of me as a natural part of it. Moving to a farm gave me the opportunity to give working in the Garden a try. I have prayed in the Temple; I have studied in the University; now I have a chance to, as deRopp so crudely puts it, 'shovel shit in the garden'.

Actually, as it turned out, I have done a lot of shit shoveling over the past nine years. When we first arrived here, we often gathered cow chips for roto-tilling into the garden. The old farmhouse we moved into had no indoor bathroom, so the first thing we had installed was a composting toilet, the Clivus Multrum. The Clivus is a large fiberglass tank, 8x7x4ft, which sits under the house. It accepts human wastes into one compartment, food scraps into another, and after suitably composting it all, slides it into a third compartment. It is this third compartment which needs to be emptied periodically. I assumed that it would be nice, dry compost, like you buy in a bag. Actually, it's always very wet in this compartment. First the liquid needs to be pumped out and then the solids need to be scooped out with a small bucket into a larger garbage can. Try to picture this: I am stooped in a small hole about four feet under a small trapdoor in the floor so I need to hand the small bucket up to someone. Since I have just used the bucket to scoop out the sludge, it has wet sludge all over it. As I hand it up, big drops fall, into my hair, onto my glasses, and all over my face. It is at times like these that I try to remember to utter a silent prayer of gratitude to Robert S. deRopp for pointing out to me all the wonderful benefits to be gained in shoveling shit. The fruit trees love it.

Let me tell you about a few other projects Susan and I have tried over the past nine years. One is solar heating. We put a clear plastic roof over our house thereby turning the entire attic into a solar collector. Next we built a rock storage area near to the house -- 8x8x16 ft. Then we connected attic to house to rock storage with a series of ducts and fans. The idea was to blow hot attic air over the rocks and store heat during the day and then to blow house air through the rocks at night to warm the house. The attic does get hot enough to warm the house during the day on cold but sunny days. However, there just is not enough heat transferred to the rocks to make it worthwhile to run house air through it at night.

We used to rely a lot on wood heating during those first few years. The boys and I have a lot of memories of going out to cut the firewood. We had a wood burning stove in the boys' bedroom and a fireplace in the living room. I remember many a cold morning getting up to start the fires. To keep myself from complaining, I tried to think of, and feel kinship with, all the humans throughout the ages and around the world who have gotten up each morning in the cold and have started fires for their loved ones. The fireplace was sending a lot of our heat up the chimney so we eventually had it sealed up and placed a wood burning stove in front of it. The stove has a see-through glass front, so we can still enjoy watching the logs burn. We have a propane burning space heater in one bathroom and an electric heater in the other. For a while I kept a portable kerosene heater going and moved it from room to room depending on who was the coldest. There is a kind of security in knowing you can heat your house in so many different ways. Finally, in 1983 we had installed a central heating unit and now all we have to do is argue about the thermostat setting.

We have had a garden each year since we have been here although the size of the plot has been shrinking each year. We have learned a lot about gardening. We have learned how much work it is to keep it up but we have also learned how good the vegetables taste fresh from the garden. We kept a flock of chickens for a while, even hatched a brood of chicks once. We slaughtered and cleaned several chickens and rabbits for the dinner table. Once we even trapped, killed, skinned, and ate a possum. We are not very good at slaughtering animals and we don't do any of that any more.

I guess my best success story as a homesteader is about what happened with the cows. I undertook the prime responsibility for the cattle operation reluctantly. Susan strongly felt that with all that pasture around we should graze cows. My cousin had five-registered Black Angus, which he wanted to sell me. My brother-in-law had one old cow with calf, which he wanted to keep out here. My neighbor had a big white Brahma bull, which he needed to get rid of. In short, I got talked into it. At first I grumbled a little. It seemed as though the cows always needed something done and right then. I was anxious and scared that I would not be able to keep them confined to our place and that they would not follow me back home if they ever did wander away. It all worked out well, however. We developed a nice relationship. They seem to like me. They seem to know what I want. Whenever the fence breaks down and they do wander away, I simply go find them, fuss at them a little, tell them to follow me home, and they do. Whenever I want them to come in from the pasture, all I have to do is to holler, and here they come. I like being around them. They bring me joy.

Reading John and Nancy Todd and the New Alchemists, Wendell Berry, Gene Logsdon, Organic Gardening, and New Farm magazines has helped a lot. I have good friends and neighbors who are always available when I need them. They have been my teachers, my helpers, and my cheering section. I would like to be more like them.

Susan and I have developed a real sense of place. We are putting down some roots. We would like to keep this as home for the duration. We would like to develop some more homesteading skills. Maybe we will grow some more of our own food. Maybe we'll raise some more animals -- some pigs maybe, and goats, and chickens. Maybe.

Now I am not suggesting that you quit your job in the City and move to a farm. But if you are not gardening already, you might give some thought to deRopp's encouragement to spend some time in the garden. The essence of gardening is to prepare some soil, plant something, water it, encourage it to grow, enjoy how it looks, eat it if edible, then compost what is left over, and return it to the soil. It doesn't have to be a big garden. If you have a yard, two feet by six feet will be enough for starters. If you live in an apartment, a one foot by two feet box in a window will do. You could plant some flowers, some herbs, and some lettuce and spinach. Each day you could nibble on some leaf and then be able to say you eat some things from your garden every day. And if you have not been enculturated to normally do this, it will qualify as an unpredictable act, a training of the will, a demonstration that you, as Self, are able to direct at least some of your ego's activities. Go, you can do this.

Chapter 9
The Morning Sit

We are still talking about training your will. It doesn't matter whether you take up gardening or not. Doesn't matter if you cut off all of your hair. But by now, you should have been able to do something unpredictable, something to indicate that you, as Self, can direct your ego's activities.

Ever since the second chapter, I have been encouraging you to set aside a few minutes every morning or evening to do a "thought observing" session. Maybe you are doing it and maybe not, but in any case, it is now time to give it a little more structure and some added emphasis.

Here's what I want you to do. Starting tomorrow morning schedule at least 15 minutes for what we will call your Morning Sit, when you will simply sit and observe which thoughts pop up. Your first reaction to this may be that you don't have 15 minutes to spare in the morning. Well, of course you don't, as long as you identify as ego. As ego, you have developed a set of habit patterns that take you from morning to bedtime, with no time to spare and with each subpersonality still clamoring for more time. What will most likely happen tomorrow, is that you will forget, no matter how seriously you intend not to forget at this time.

What you need to do now is to put something by your bedside that will remind you tomorrow morning that you have decided to set aside 15 minutes for a Morning Sit. Once you notice that something new by your bedside tomorrow, you will need to "wake-up" a second time, and shift into your higher state of awareness. Move your sense of "I", the who-I-am feeling, away from your personal ego and your earliest-rising subpersonality, and move it to your Self. Become the Observer, and as you observe the situation, decide if you have trained your will enough yet to be able to also become a Director of Ego Activity. If you are skilled enough now to be a Director, you will calmly, lovingly, find a place to sit and begin your Morning Sit. The important crisis you are facing here, is the "who is in charge?" question. Of course, there is no need to be a fanatic about this just yet. If a kid wakes up and needs you, stop and go take care of her. If the phone rings, answer it. If it's possible to go back to your Sit, do so. If not, that's okay too. That's life, still going on while we are busy making other plans. But if you are persistent, eventually you will have 15 uninterrupted minutes every morning to practice your Morning Sit.

Probably it is best to start with your usual "wake-up" routine, shifting your sense of "I" to you as the more awake, more aware Self. You've done this before, hopefully many times, but usually just for brief periods of time. But this time you will try to keep this sense of Self for most of the 15 minutes. Your Self is literally a newborn; you will need to stay awake for longer and longer periods of time in order to discover who you really are. You know the routine, observe how you are feeling, are you cold, are you hungry, any aches or pains? Relax. Focus your attention on your breathing. Watch it coming in, going out. Coming in, going out.

You are trying to avoid getting hooked by your very first thought and then spending the full 15 minutes just thinking about that. Try to stay in your more awake Self mode. See if you can let go of that first thought and return to just paying attention to your breathing. See how many completely different thoughts come up during your 15-minute session.

That's really all there is to it. Just to be able to sit still for 15 minutes and watch your thoughts come and go. The intention here is to watch the random spontaneous arising of thoughts. It is not in the spirit of things here to decide ahead of time that you will use these 15 minutes to plan your next project or to think about improving a relationship.

There's no need to grade yourself or try to evaluate how good a session you just had. It is not better to have had only 10 thoughts instead of 20. It doesn't matter how long you have gotten hooked by one thought. You just keep trying, trying to experience your Self and not let an ego subpersonality take over and use this 15-minute session for its own purposes. The main objective here at this time is simply to establish a practice of doing this for 15 minutes every day.

So, why are you doing this? For four reasons – 1) you will continue to gather data about your personal ego and its various subpersonalities, 2) you will learn some more about the nature of thoughts and emotions, 3) you will begin to experience what it feels like to function as Self, and 4) you will be getting more experience directing as Self.

As for number 1), you already have some experience in matching up your various thoughts and worries with the ego subpersonality who is having them. On any given day, different subpersonalities will be feeling the most stress or urgency for getting things done. By sitting there observing these thoughts come up, but not sticking with any of them, you are giving each subpersonality a chance to be heard. By the content of the thoughts that come up, you are getting a preview of how your day is most likely to go.

As for reason number 2), you can learn a lot about the nature of thoughts and emotions as you sit there calmly observing them come and go. You will notice that some thoughts come along prepackaged with a strong emotion – with some thoughts comes anger, with some, joy, and with some, sadness.

Picture this. You are sitting in your Morning Sit and a thought arises prepackaged with anger. An unskilled response would be to immediately identify with the subpersonality having this thought and begin to feel angry. You might even go so far as to quit your Morning Sit, storm out of that room, and start yelling at your spouse or your child, or you might call someone up on the phone and begin yelling at him.

The skill you are trying to learn is to be able to stop the identification with the subpersonality having this thought and stay identified as Self. As Self, you are not getting angry, you are merely observing anger arising together with a thought that one of your subpersonalities is having. Even if you can stay identified as Self, the temptation will be to start analyzing why anger came with this thought, at whom is it directed, whose fault is it? While getting hooked on analysis is better than getting angry, analysis is not the task of the Morning Sit. The skill is to let go of the thought and the anger, return to observing your breathing and waiting for the next thought. This will be hard to do at first. Analyzing the anger seems like such a worthwhile thing to do. Promise yourself that you will give it some time later on during the day, but for now, return to just observing your breathing and waiting for the next thought.

Now on to reason number 3) -- experiencing what it feels like to function as Self. There is a definite feeling tone that comes with identifying with Self. I have mentioned this before, but now I want to give you a few more details. It may take a while to experience this feeling clearly, but once you experience it, you will always be able to tell when you are really identifying with Self.

The biggest danger to look out for while doing your Morning Sit, is that it will be taken over by one of your more critical and judgmental subpersonalities. We all have one or two of these. Eric Berne told us in his book *Games People Play* that we each carry with us. The Critical Parent subpersonality Sigmund Freud referred to it as our Super Ego. This is a subpersonality that has incorporated into its character a critical attitude towards enforcing the RULES of our parents and of the culture in which we were raised. This subpersonality is always with us, sometimes quietly in the background, and at times openly criticizing us to tears. The Morning Sit is an ideal setup for its operations. From its point of view, this is an idle time, during which you aren't really doing anything useful. This subpersonality will feel that it is its duty to take over and make a better use of this time.

You can tell that it has taken over if you notice that most of the thoughts that come up are criticizing you for something you have either done or not done. Or else are exhorting you to do better. Several sessions may go by before you notice this. But eventually you will "wake-up", you will "observe" what is going on, and you will be able to let these thoughts and emotions go and return simply to observing your breathing and waiting for the next thought to come along. Even after you have let a thought go, its emotion may linger. It is a little harder to also let go of an emotion. But once you learn to let go of the emotions as well as the thoughts, you will eventually be left a pleasant, calm, peaceful feeling, a feeling of being OK.

The feeling is subtle, it's fleeting, but it is definitely there. During those brief moments of silence, in between the constant flow of thoughts, worries, and plans, you will suddenly realize that you are feeling good, really good. The longer that you are able to stay identified with your Self mode, the stronger the feeling will become. Soon you will be able to say, "I want to do this for 15 minutes."

And finally, reason number 4, you will be getting more experience directing as Self. After your Morning Sit is over, as you return to your daily routine of responsibilities, try to stay identified as Self for at least a few more minutes, at least long enough to review the content of the thoughts that came up during the Sit. This content will alert you to which subs are most likely to want to dominate your one body/mind for most of that day. But, as Self, you should now be capable of setting some priorities as to which subpersonalities will get time that day. This is the important part. You are getting the experience and the confidence that you, as Self, can set these priorities and not let your ego subpersonalities fight it out on their own as to how you will spend your time that day. You will also need to "wake-up" periodically during the day and "self-observe" in order to remember the priorities that you, as Self, had set. You can do this!

Okay, it's possible that you really can't take the time to do the Morning Sit immediately upon arising. If you wake up each morning to the sound of urgent demands from your loved ones, then try to work it in as soon as things quiet down a bit. Maybe after you have gotten the kids off to school or gotten yourself to work. Yes, it is okay to do this at work. If your boss really understood what you were doing and why, he would be most happy to let you do your Morning Sit on company time. You will be a more effective worker throughout the rest of the day.

I'll have a lot more to say about this Morning Sit as we progress, but this may be enough to get you started. Maybe tomorrow after your Morning Sit you could direct one of your subpersonalities to write up in a little more detail the role in which it plays a dominant part. Good luck!

Chapter 10
The Doctor Subpersonalities

My Doctor subpersonalities made good use of some of these exercises in helping students, patients, and colleagues make changes in their health affecting habit patterns, first as an associate professor at the UT School of Public Health, then as the Director of a local health department, and later as a Regional Health Director for the Texas Department of Health. The following entry from my journal written by me in my Doctor role is another example of how I would like for you to write up another one of your roles.

The Doctor: (6-5-85)

I am enjoying very much my present position as the Director of the Williamson County Health Department. It's a nice mix of experiences and challenges. Securing the budget involves me in negotiations with the Texas Department of Health, the County Commissioners, several City Managers, and several Superintendents of Schools. Enforcing county regulations on construction of private sewage facilities and development in the flood plain involves me with many stressed developers, builders, septic tank installers and homeowners. Providing public health services to the poor involves me in dealings with patients, other physicians, hospitals, and many support agencies. Supervising a staff of 30 involves me in many issues concerning staff development, morale, and productivity. And I am learning the trials and tribulations of being occasionally quoted in the papers or on the radio and TV. I am enjoying the challenge of being an executive, of managing people and resources effectively and efficiently, to bring about organizational goals and objectives. One can accomplish so much more with an organization of people than one can working all alone. Someday, I may want to direct a larger Local Health Department, a Regional Health Department, a State Health Department, or maybe even the World Health Organization.

Health Departments are in the business of preventing disease and improving the health of the public. Our biggest accomplishments to date have been the sanitation of the environment and immunizations against communicable diseases. When I first got started in this field, my interests were strictly in physical health. I wanted to do physical things -- immunize people, kill mosquitoes, sanitize the environment, put fluoride into the water. For a couple of years, I concentrated solely on eradicating tuberculosis within the Cuban community in Miami. I was not at all interested in anything having to do with mental health. That was someone else's job. I built a wall between physical and mental. I read only the journals dealing with the physical. When I first ran across the word 'psychosomatic', it was used derisively, implying that there was really nothing wrong with the patient, that whatever he was complaining of was simply in his head. I didn't worry myself about preventing psychosomatic illnesses; these too were mental.

That worked fine for a while, as long as I confined my interests to simple relationships like fluoride and tooth decay or vaccination and smallpox. But as soon as I turned my attention and efforts to some of our more complex problems like heart disease, cancer, stroke, and the stress-related conditions, it became obvious that if I wanted to have an impact in preventing these, the wall between physical and mental had to come down. These were all conditions with complex cause and effect relationships with strong psychosomatic interactions.

Slowly over time my relationship with the word, 'psychosomatic', changed. It went from avoidance to tolerance, to neutrality, and finally developed into a positive love affair. I began reading the psychological literature more and more. I began to understand better the body-mind interaction. I found it exciting. Soon I started going to national meetings of Psychological Associations as well as medical meetings dealing with Psychosomatic Medicine.

I now consider myself equally comfortable and competent in dealing with both the physical and psychological components in the prevention of these chronic and stress-related diseases and disabilities. I believe that the key to preventing these conditions is in modifying our lifestyle, our day to day health-affecting habits and behavior patterns. What are the key components of a healthier lifestyle? How does one modify one's own behavior? How does one help someone else change to a healthier lifestyle? These are the questions that excite me today and attempting to answer them is where I put most of my professional energies.

Together with some of my staff I have developed the 'Williamson County Program for the Improvement and Maintenance of Your Health and Well-Being.' Through this program we counsel any and all who care to come by and listen. We are now in the process of developing an index called 'The Personal Health Profile', which will measure a client's present health status and will assess his or her lifestyle with regards to several health affecting behaviors. The Personal Health Profile serves as an outline for the counseling points we wish to make with our clients and helps them to clarify their objectives and priorities. The clients' Health Profile scores will be used over time to measure their progress and will also serve as an evaluation tool to measure the effectiveness of our counseling.

The Personal Health Profile currently has sixteen components. Eight are used in determining the present health status and eight are used in assessing the healthiness of the lifestyle. Most of the components of our definition of a healthy lifestyle are fairly traditional, time-honored ones such as eating habits, exercise patterns, alcohol and tobacco usage, rest, relaxation and leisure time activities, self-care, and psychological growth and development. Some components we are including as experiments, as hypotheses to be tested, to see if we cannot gather some new evidence either for or against there being advocated as appropriate components of a healthy lifestyle.

One such component we are calling 'Establishing and Nurturing Relationships.' I believe that the evidence is fairly conclusive that those with a strong social support network do better health-wise than those who feel isolated and alone. Also, those who have to work and live in very hostile and stressful environments have more health problems than those do who live and work in a friendly and supportive environment. Now the question we are asking in our hypothesis is whether there is something one can do as an activity each week which will bring about a stronger social support network and a friendlier and more supportive living environment.

Another hypothesis we are proposing to study is whether activities directed towards 'Spiritual Growth and Development' should be included as a component of a healthy lifestyle. One hears a lot these days about Holistic Health and its prime thesis that humans are composed of body, mind, AND SPIRIT. For a long time, I had a problem talking about Spirit. As Doctor-Scientist it seemed to me that Spirit was something I should leave to the priests and ministers and that I should stick with good solid physical-mental stuff. I tried to build another wall and to put Spirit into a separate compartment for someone else to worry about. It didn't work. If humans truly are composed of Body-Mind-Spirit, then we are not treating a whole human very wisely if we insist on always dividing him up and having one specialist treat only the physical, another specialist treat only the mental, and ignore completely the spiritual. Empowered by my experience at integrating successfully the body-mind interactions, I decided to likewise tear down the wall separating me from including spirit in my prevention armamentarium.

So I am studying Spirit, through reading, through spiritual exercises, and through meetings and workshops. I am beginning to feel comfortable in talking about Spirit with clients, but as Doctor-Scientist I still would like to see a little more evidence. Hence the reason for including Spiritual Growth and Development on the Personal Health Profile. I am hoping that we can define a set of spirit enhancing activities and test them out by comparing the health outcomes between those who practice them and those who don't.

I occasionally give a workshop or seminar on the Personal Health Profile and the components of a healthy lifestyle. I try to keep one group or class meeting at least monthly. And I continue to experiment with changing my own lifestyle. I think that it has been the experience in seeing how much better I feel when living a healthier lifestyle, that has provided the motivation and the encouragement to me to help others do the same.

I would like to do more of this kind of work. Sometimes I dream of starting my own private practice in counseling others about healthy lifestyles. Someday I might. Right now, I am doing it as part of my Health Department role. I am trying to establish such a program as part of the mainstream of what health departments should be doing. This is preventive medicine at its best. It is needed by most of the residents in our community and there is no convenient and inexpensive place for them to go to get such help. Many physicians in private practice are aware that such practices are available and helpful but simply do not have the time with their busy schedules to teach them to their patients. Health Departments are known in our communities as reliable sources of health information and as non-profit organizations we can provide such services at cost.

Obviously, I could go on and on and on, but maybe this is enough for now. I just wanted to give you some impression of how excited I am about my work."

The main task in helping someone to change to a healthier lifestyle is not the imparting of information. Most people already know enough to want to change some aspects of their health affecting behavior. The main task is helping someone to learn certain skills that will enable them to make the changes they have already decided that they want to make. The skills you are learning while practicing waking up, self-observation, and the morning sit are skills you can use to make the changes you want in your life.

Chapter 11
Stress Management

In this chapter I will use stress management as an example of how you can use some of the new skills you are developing. But stress management is only an example, the same skills can be put to use in trying to bring about any changes you wish to make in your life.

First let's review what is known about stress and the body/mind's response to it. Our body/minds are capable of responding to a sudden crisis with remarkable increases in strength and speed. If you are confronted with a sudden danger, say a mugger on the street, your glands will begin secreting more adrenaline, more steroids, and other helpful hormones. Your heart will beat faster, you will breathe more rapidly, and your blood flow will shift away from the internal organs in order to deliver more oxygen loaded blood to your big muscles. You will temporarily become much stronger and faster, enabling you to fight or run much more effectively than usual. I have heard stories of mothers being able to lift a weight several times greater than they normally could, if such a weight should happen to fall on their child. All of these physiological changes are collectively referred to as the "stress response".

This stress response is a healthy, normal response to danger and results in no long-term ills, if it is a brief response and can be immediately followed by the "relaxation response" – the danger passes, we take a deep breath, heave a sigh of relief, the heart rate and breathing slow down, normal blood flow returns to our internal organs, and our glands cease their secretion of extra hormones. Life returns to normal, which hopefully is a peaceful and tranquil existence. All of this is usually going on automatically and unconsciously. And for sudden, big but brief crises, that's wonderful.

But problems with the stress response occur when it is not followed by the relaxation response and things are not peaceful and tranquil. Our body/minds perceive themselves to still be in danger and all of the physiological responses to stress continue. The net effect of having our body/minds continuously in stress response mode is that body parts begin to wear out – cells become damaged and cease to function properly, our arteries get brittle and clog up, our blood pressure goes up. And we wind up with an increased incidence of several chronic diseases like heart attacks, strokes, cancer, and diabetes. The mind, feeling unable to successfully cope with certain stressful situations, represses them, thereby setting us up for a whole host of neurological symptoms, pain, and dysfunctional behavior patterns.

So, for these more common, day-to-day, smaller but longer lasting stressors, leaving things on automatic can be harmful. The solution is obvious. We need to bring a little more awareness into the process. You need to know what is going on. Your self-observation and wake-up routines can help you here. You know that you usually function by alternating among several subpersonalities, so observe which subpersonalities are being stressed by which situations.

Understand that some stressful situations are okay. A certain amount of stress in life is considered helpful. Our responses to stress help us to grow, to mature, enabling us to handle more and bigger responsibilities. Such stressful situations you can accept willingly, but know that your stress response has been put in play, so plan an exit strategy. Plan some relaxation into your schedule, so you can trigger the relaxation response. Some stressors you will not want to accept and the skill to develop here is to be able to stop the stress response with a relaxation response as soon as you observe what is happening. Eventually you can learn to keep the stress response from ever getting started.

Let us say you were in a meeting yesterday at work and gave your opinion on something and someone responded by saying,

"That's really dumb", and then proceeded to give his opinion. You felt attacked, hurt, and embarrassed. You immediately challenged him back and a heated argument issued. For the rest of the day you kept replaying the scene, coming up with several pithy remarks you wish you had thought to say. You found it difficult to be kind, loving, and generous with your family that evening. You had trouble sleeping and this morning during your Morning Sit, you found it impossible to keep from replaying the same scene over and over again. The stress response is in full force now and may get re-enforced some more today if you run into him again.

If that example doesn't exactly fit into your life, I'm sure you can come up with others that are similar. The problem is the automatic nature of the response. We've been doing this for years. It is now an ingrained habit. A certain stimulus invokes the same response. A little self-observation will tell you that this is so. As you get better skilled at waking-up and being a little more self-observant all the time, you will notice what has happened soon thereafter. As your more aware Self, you will note that your stress response has been invoked. You will realize that this is not really a life-threatening situation and that you need to bring on a relaxation response. Sometimes just taking a slow deep breath will do it. Remember that the stress response has you breathing rapidly and shallowly. A slow deep breath will interrupt the automatic process and let you start to relax. You will realize that the stressful event is over now. You no longer need to fight. You can analyze whether the angry exchange was useful or not. But after a few minutes, tell yourself again that the argument is over. There is other work to do and you have other subpersonalities wanting to do other things right after work. So, there is no time to think about this exchange any longer. As soon as you observe that another thought has arisen about the incident, you will be able to note it, name it, and then send it away with a smile on your face. All the experience that you have gained doing this at your Morning Sit will serve you well now.

If you run into situations like this frequently, you will soon learn to "wake-up" as the situation is still unfolding and you may be able to stop the stress response from ever getting started. All you need to learn to do is to insert a little space, a brief moment of time, in between the stimulus and your automatic response. During the little space of time you will be doing a lot consciously. You will be functioning in a higher state of consciousness and you will have time to ponder what the most appropriate response should be. As your more aware Self, you are feeling OK, you are not embarrassed, hurt, or attacked. Only one of your subpersonalities is. As Self, you can take a broader perspective of the meeting. You will want to listen. What is he saying? Can you agree with any of that? What is the goal of the meeting? Will it help accomplish the goal if you assertively defend your opinion? Or would it be better to drop this discussion completely? You may want to suggest that we go on to more appropriate matters. Whatever you decide to do will be okay, because you will have managed to stop the automatic stress response from occurring.

Here is another instance where the experiences you are having during your Morning Sit can help. Hopefully by now you have developed some skill at being able to notice a thought arising and at being able to let it go. You may have noticed that some of these thoughts come prepackaged with anger. Often such thoughts arise with the anger directed at some person. These are "attack thoughts". And hopefully you have learned to let these go as well.

Attack thoughts are especially dangerous ones to entertain from a stress response perspective. They initiate a chain of events that begin with anger, and if not stopped right then and there, may proceed to rage and violence. Just as you have learned to let go of attack thoughts during your Morning Sit, you can now extend your lookout for them throughout the rest of the day. There is almost never a reason any more to entertain an attack thought. Learn to spot one as soon as it arises, label it, and let it go. It is easier to let go of an attack thought than it will be later to let go of the anger that will soon follow.

Some people do not react with anger in stressful situations, but instead react with anxiety, worry, and feelings of inadequacy. These, too, start off as attack thoughts, only this time one of your subpersonalities is directing attack thoughts towards you. Treat them the same, note them, label them, and let them go.

Remember, as Self, you are feeling OK. The feelings of inadequacy belong to one of your subpersonalities.

The above examples work well if the stressor is a well-defined and circumscribed incident, especially if it signals its arrival with the opening line of "That's really dumb!" But most of us are faced daily with a lot of smaller stressors coming from our co-workers, children, spouse, and/or significant others. And we may feel as though our body/minds are constantly reacting with the stress response – that tightness in the neck and shoulders, the low-grade headache, that queasy feeling in your stomach.

Under these conditions it is best to schedule several regular doses of the relaxation response. You can take a slow deep breath every time you "wake-up" enough to do a self-observation. You can tighten a few big muscles for a while, and then let them relax. One common relaxation technique will have you systematically go from your toes to your head, alternately tightening and relaxing as many muscle groups as you can find. A session of yoga or tai chi would work well here also. Your Morning Sit also qualifies as a relaxation session. Sitting quietly, calmly watching your thoughts come and go, will slow your heart rate, lower your blood pressure, and repair some of the damage already done.

Physical exercise is also a very good relaxation technique, especially if most of your day is spent sedentary. Running, tennis, golf, a long walk, are all opportunities to give your mind a rest and your muscles a workout. As the muscles are challenged, the stress response is invoked, but then you stop, and trigger the relaxation response. The point being that the relaxation then corrects not only for the exercise induced stress but also for a lot of the other stresses that have accumulated in your body/mind. But don't overdo on the exercise, too vigorous a workout may induce more of a stress response than the subsequent relaxation can correct. It's the relaxation you are after, not the stress.

Exercise is a good example of a stressor on your system that is healthy, if you don't overdo it. The right amount of a workout will strengthen your muscles and train your heart and blood vessels to deliver more oxygen to your muscles more effectively. Your body will be better able to perform a greater workload in the future without feeling it as a stressor.

I hope that you are not thinking that you do not have time to work in an exercise activity or a relaxation technique. By now you should know that this is simply a matter of "waking-up", and then as Self, deciding on your priorities, and then directing your ego subpersonalities to act accordingly. Remember, you as Self, are in charge. If you have trained your will sufficiently, you can direct how the rest of your life will go.

The above techniques may be all you need, to help you deal with the stresses with which you are being faced every day. But maybe not. Your work situation or your home situation may be such a stressful environment that you may need to consider drastically altering that environment.

The way you respond to stresses in your environment is part of your life script. You have learned that this is what works best for you. Some respond with anger, some with anxiety. Some respond by overeating, some by lighting a cigarette or taking drugs. As you become more aware of what is going on here, you may decide that you would like to make some changes in this life script of yours.

Whether you are wishing to make major changes in how your life is going or whether you only wish to make some minor adjustments, you may be able to benefit from doing a few "life-script reviews".

Chapter 12
The Life-Script Review

As you gain more experience functioning as your more aware Self and as you gain more confidence in being able to direct some of your ego activities, you will naturally come to the point where you will want to re-write some parts of your life script. Remember that your parents, your culture, and your childhood experiences have written for you the life script that you are now living. This is a good thing, whenever your script is handed to you as a way to live until you can wake-up enough to write your own. It becomes undesirable only when it ceases to work for you and your culture insists that you continue to live out that script and not change any parts of it.

As you become more awake, you will begin to think of your life as a work of art that you as the artist are creating. You can think of your life as a three or four act play, the first two of which you may have already lived according to your unconscious script. Now may be the time to consciously re-write the rest of your life script.

It's probably best not to try to make any sudden drastic revisions. Your will may not as yet be strong enough to pull that off. And it may be unkind to all of your significant others. It's probably better to start off with minor changes, and work up slowly to any major changes. However, any re-writing of a life script is a major undertaking. It may help if you begin by noting carefully where the momentum of your life is heading now. This is the purpose of a Life-Script Review.

To do this well, you will need to set aside a time when you can do some work without interruptions for at least an hour or two. You may want to write down some of what develops during this session, so sit at a table or desk with a pen and some paper.

Begin your session by repeating your "Hello, World!" wake-up message, sit quietly for a few minutes, focusing on your breathing if you find that helpful. Gently let go of any worries; you can attend to them later. When your body/mind has relaxed and you are feeling OK, think about your subpersonalities for a while. Review the script that each one of them is playing out. Get a feel for the momentum of each. Is it getting more demanding, taking up more of your time each year or is it on the wane? How does that make you feel? Which subpersonalities do you wish to make the major players in your future script? Which do you wish to phase out?

Next review your steppingstone periods. Get a feel for their momentum. Can you picture where this life script is heading? Can you already imagine what the next steppingstone period will be like and the next? How does this feel? After you have pondered these questions for a while, take out your paper and pen and write down a brief summary of where you think the momentum of your life is taking you. Record how you feel about that. Finally, jot down a few tentative ideas you may have developed as to changes you would like to see in your remaining steppingstone periods. Label this summary, "My First Life-Script Review", date it, and set it aside for now.

If you haven't already done so, this may be a good time for you to start a journal. You have already written up your wake-up message, your subpersonalities, your steppingstones, and your first life-script review. You may as well organize these writings into some sort of a journal. From time to time I will ask you to record some exercise in your journal because I think it helps the transformation process to write something down instead of just thinking it. It also helps if you have someone to whom you can tell it or read it. You can also record into your journal any life events that bear on what you are attempting to modify. Don't think of your journal as some sort of a diary, into which you will need to write something every day. An occasional entry, whenever you feel moved to do so, is all you will need, to document the growth and development that is taking place.

Soon you will begin to notice that during your Morning Sit, among all the usual thoughts that normally arise each morning, you are now getting thoughts that deal with the changes you have decided to make. As always, try not to get hooked on any of these. Just note them, label them, and let them go. But know that on a deeper level, the transformation is already underway. Even though you may not be consciously directing the process, on an unconscious level your intelligence, your imagination, your will, your memory, and your intuition are all adjusting to the creative changes you are initiating.

It may help you to periodically repeat your Life Script Review. Go back and sit at the same desk or table. Read what you had written up about your previous life script review. Read all the journal entries you have made since your last review. Then sit quietly and again review the direction and momentum of your subpersonalities and steppingstone periods. Has anything changed? Have you experienced any successes or disappointment? Do you now wish to modify in any way the new script you are writing? At the end of your session, record in your journal a summary of this review and schedule your next session. How often you will find it helpful to do this depends on the magnitude and timing of the changes you are trying to make. Once a year may be enough for some, for others a weekly review may be optimal.

The reason I am making such a big deal about re-writing your life script is because I do not believe you can make even minor changes in your life without making a big deal out of it. Consider how many resolutions you have made in the past – to lose weight, to quit smoking, or to spend more time with the kids, only to note that six weeks to six months later you were again back to your usual routine behavior patterns. It is just plain hard to change a life script.

Let us say you are overweight and you decide that you do not wish to stay that way for the rest of your life. This is a major undertaking. First you will need to consider why you are overweight. Is overeating a response to stress? Have you been overstuffed by a loving parent or grandparent and now equate food with love? Do you get to avoid certain relationship problems by being overweight? Can you learn to wake-up and self-observe before each intake of food? Ask yourself, "Why am I planning to eat?" Can you substitute doing something else rather than eating? You can learn to actually prefer the feeling of being slightly hungry to feeling overstuffed. As Self, you know that this is healthier. You can use "feeling slightly hungry" as a trigger to wake-up and self-observe. Then as Self, you can decide whether it is time to eat or whether you would rather go on to doing something else.

Observe carefully which subpersonalities are overeating and which would prefer to be thinner. You may be able to find more time for those who want to be thinner and some other rewards besides food for those who are overeating.

Set modest goals. If you can just stop gaining, that's a victory. Most people gain weight as they get older. If you want to lose some weight, how about five pounds in five years as a beginning goal. Don't fall for the latest fad diet. The best way to lose weight and keep it off is to educate yourself as to the basics of a healthy eating pattern, plan to switch to it over a period of time, and then stay with it for the rest of your life.

Stopping smoking or drugs is more difficult, but the same procedures apply. It is the automatic routine of lighting up a cigarette that must be observed and changed. Learn to wake-up and self-observe before lighting a cigarette. Ask yourself how you are feeling, note what it is that you are doing, and note what triggered the wish to light up. Was it the situation you were in, had something just occurred, or was it simply the length of time since your last one? After you have noted all of that, go ahead and light up.

After you have learned to do this much, you can try considering whether or not you can do without the next cigarette or whether you can start doing something else that may let you forget about the need for a smoke. Count how many you are smoking per day and record the number occasionally in your journal. Next time you are buying cigarettes, see if you can switch to another brand. Sometimes such relentless observation and interference in the automatic nature of the process is all it takes. Sometimes you may need some professional help – a program, a group, or a psychotherapist. These you can schedule into your new life script.

Sometimes the change in your lifestyle will involve the need to change something about your home environment or something about one or more of your relationships at home or at work. Whatever the change contemplated, the process is the same. You shine the spotlight of your awareness on the automatic habit pattern you are now bound by. With self-observation, you are better able to understand what is going on. With Life Script Reviews you schedule in changes to some of the automatic behavior patterns. And slowly, oh so slowly, the change occurs.

As always, be on guard that it is really you, as Self, who is directing this process. There is always that danger that one of your ego-subpersonalities will find this an exciting new avenue to express itself, and will take over and run the show from now on. You, as Self, may go back to sleep, only to wake up years later wondering where all the time has gone and how you could have slept through it all. This has happened to me several times before I established the Morning Sit as a regular routine.

I soon found it awkward to keep referring to myself all the time as either being "one of my ego-subpersonalities" or as being "my more awake Self." One day I hit upon the idea of giving myself a new name whenever I identified as Self. You too, may find it helpful to adopt a new name.

Chapter 13
Adopt a New Name

L et me share now with you some of my journal entries that describe my motivation and my experiences with adopting a new name. Since I believe so strongly that telling or reading our journal entries to a friend is helpful in supporting our efforts at change and growth, I have always written my journal entries as though I were writing to a friend. And I have actually been mailing some of my journal entries to some of my friends since 1985. The following entry was written in March of 1987.

My full name is Clarence Charles Anthony Skrovan. Clarence Charles was what my parents named me at birth. Anthony is the name I chose for myself at Confirmation (at age 12). I have never used the name. I have never thought of myself as Anthony. I think that maybe the time has come to introduce Anthony into my life.

Throughout my journal I describe the experience of waking up to a more awake, more aware state of consciousness. I am trying to experience this state as often as I can for as long as I can. I think that I may be able to do that better if I try to think of myself as Anthony whenever I am in this heightened state of awareness. The rest of the time, whenever I am functioning in my usual automatic, mechanical, habit-driven state of consciousness, I will, quite naturally, continue to think of myself as Clarence.

In this way, the name Anthony will serve as a trigger or stimulus for waking me up. Anytime that I see or hear the name, I will be reminded to wake up and to Self-remember. And then, for as long as I am thinking of myself as Anthony, I will know that I am still functioning in my more awake mode. Maybe it will help. It should also help in describing my experiences in shifting back and forth from one mode to the other.

Take yesterday, for example. Yesterday was a warm, clear, sunny Sunday. At about three in the afternoon, Joseph was out mowing the grass, Susan was outside somewhere puttering around in the yard, and I, as one of my Clarence: Doctor subpersonalities, was here in the house, at my computer terminal, trying to solve a problem that I was having with a database program, which I was developing for our immunization records at the Health Department. Suddenly, I, Anthony, awoke and began observing what I was doing and how I was feeling.

I was feeling pretty good. I was enjoying the challenge of the problem. It was not all that difficult and I was feeling confident that I could solve it. But was this really the time and the place to be doing this? It didn't take me long to realize that I really did not want to be here in the house working on an office problem. On a warm and sunny, winter, Sunday afternoon, the place to be is out there in the sun, at least for a little while. I got up to go outside.

I almost didn't make it. For as I was walking through the kitchen, I noticed that there were dirty dishes all over the table and the counter top. Clarence: Family Man almost took over the controls at this point, wanting, at least, to start the dishes. Usually this is what happens; I fall back into this trance I spend most of my life in. When I would have finished with the dishes, the chances were great that I would have gone right back to my computer to work some more on my office problem. This time I was lucky. The momentum of my stride heading for the door, helped me to remember that there was something else that I had been planning to do. I, Anthony, had wanted to go outside.

I walked out the door and into the sunshine, mumbling to myself various exhortations to stay awake, to keep self-observing, and to resist the natural inclination to fall back into my usual state of "waking sleep". I did pretty well. First I stopped to talk to Susan for a while. I asked her what

*she was doing and how she was feeling, and explained what
was happening with me. She gave me all sorts of positive
reinforcement for coming outside. Next I walked over to Joe
and asked how he was doing. He, of course, immediately
offered to let me take over mowing the lawn. I resisted the
immediate urge to respond negatively and thought about it
awhile. I even considered mowing for a while just to
demonstrate once again that I could do something
unpredictable. Eventually I told him, "No thanks", and
headed for the pasture.*

*I had several reasons for heading out for the pasture. I
could check on the condition of the electric fence. I could
go down to the creek and watch the water fall over dead tree
trunks. Maybe I would sit down under a tree and just sit for
a while. Then I noticed the garden. It needed to be
rototilled and prepared for a spring planting. I decided that
I would rototill. One can practice self-observation and Self-
remembering even while doing something practical. I
headed for the garden shed and got out the rototiller. I
noticed that the tines were all wound up in about a cubic
foot of Bermuda grass runners. For me, as Anthony, this
posed no problem; I would simply sit down with my pocket
knife, cut each strand, and slowly unwind all of the grass.
It would be a meditation. I would mindfully cut each strand
and remove it, and all the while I would remember who I
was, and I would observe what I was doing and how I was
feeling.*

*I think I lasted for about 30 seconds before Clarence:
Homesteader took over. Soon I found myself rushing so I
could get in some rototilling before dark. As soon as I
started rushing I started hitting my knuckles against the
tines. As soon as I started hitting my knuckles I started
having attack thoughts. First against Joseph - "Why did he
let these tines get so messed up?" Then against Susan -
"Why hasn't she cleaned them up by now?" I decided that
I would clean exactly half and then get Susan to clean off
the other half. When I had finished cleaning my half, I got
up to get Susan. Couldn't find her. Car was gone. She must
have gotten a call to go to the office or to the emergency
room. I decided to leave those dirty tines for her to do, came*

back into the house, and started working again on my database problem. As I stormed through the kitchen, I decided I would leave all the dirty dishes for Susan to do also.

There must have been something about being back in the same spot at my computer, struggling with exactly the same ambiguous field designations, and seeing the sunshine still streaming into my room, that woke me up again and reminded me that I wanted to be outside. As Anthony, I had a good laugh, thanked whatever powers there may be that help us in times like these, and went outside to finish cleaning the tines. I got them clean and was rototilling away before Susan got back. I never did tell her how narrowly she had avoided an angry run-in with Clarence, her self-righteous homesteader husband.

I have had enough experiences such as the one described above to know that there is a qualitative difference in my functioning depending on whether I am identifying with one of my subpersonalities or whether I am identifying with the self-observing, Self-remembering Anthony. I have gotten enough positive feedback from family, from friends, and from colleagues to know that they prefer to deal with me in my Anthony mode.

What does it mean to wake up from a Clarence subpersonality to feeling as though I were Anthony? And is this a healthy practice to encourage? Isn't there some danger in splitting myself up into a Clarence and an Anthony? There may be. Nothing ventured, nothing gained. But it does not seem dangerous. In fact, it seems downright healthy.

First of all, there doesn't seem to be any Dr. Jekyll vs. Mr. Hyde sort of split operating here. Almost nothing notable happens whenever I wake up from functioning automatically as Clarence to the perceiving of myself as a more awake, more aware Anthony. The change is a subtle, almost imperceptible, shift in attention. I shift away from exclusively attending to whatever it is that I am doing, and I begin to attend to both -- to whatever it is that I am doing

AND to the Clarence subpersonality who is doing it. If I wish, I can simply allow the Clarence subpersonality to continue to do whatever it was that he was doing and no one will notice that I have awakened.

Secondly I perceive no conflict between myself, as Anthony, and myself, as Clarence. Whenever I am functioning as a Clarence subpersonality, I forget that I am Anthony and I function as though that subpersonality, and his particular set of interests, attitudes, and personality traits were all that I am. Whenever I am functioning as Anthony, there is no conflict because I know all about my Clarence subpersonalities; I love them; they are me. I don't know who I would be, if I didn't have my Clarence subpersonalities.

And thirdly, the reason it feels downright healthy has to do with wholeness. As Anthony, I can see the fragmentation and the conflicts in the life of Clarence. His many drives, urges, needs, interests, and character traits have grouped themselves unconsciously into several subpersonalities, with each competing for time to use this one body/mind. The resulting time pressures and stress usually express themselves either as guilt, frustration, irritability, or anger. The more frequently I can wake up and observe this drama going on within, the easier it is to prevent these troublesome emotions or to dissipate their energies once they do arise.

I am convinced that it is healthy to encourage this waking up process and I think that it is helpful to think of myself as Anthony whenever I am awake. I only wish that I could wake up more often and to stay awake for longer periods of time.

But who am I while I am observing or writing about the Clarence subpersonalities? This is taking the Socratic question, "Who am I?" to an entirely new level. While functioning as a Clarence subpersonality, I asked, "Who am I?" and was moved to self-observe. I observed that I was many I's and experienced multiple subpersonalities. I also noticed that it felt as though I had awakened to a higher state of consciousness. While functioning in this more awake state of consciousness, I now think of myself as Anthony. I will need to have more experience at staying awake before I can find out who I really am in this Anthony mode.

However, from the little experience that I have had, I believe that I can make the following preliminary generalizations:

1) The actual moment of waking up to thinking of myself as Anthony is always accompanied by a pleasant feeling, a physically felt relief. It is like the feeling you get whenever you finally remember something you have been trying to remember but couldn't. Or like the feeling you get when you wake up from a dream and remember that you are you in your reality and not the character in the dream in his reality. I immediately feel better, healthier, and happier to have remembered that I am Anthony.

2) My time perspective is drastically different from that of any of my Clarence subpersonalities. As Clarence, I often find myself in time binds of my own setting and then I feel pressured and frustrated as the time slips by. As Anthony, there always seems to be plenty of time. I reschedule things more realistically. I tend to plan things in terms of months, years, and decades instead of minutes, hours, and days. My favorite cartoon on this theme shows two galaxies expanding outward at the speed of light when suddenly one of the galaxies says to the other, "Wait, wait. Before going on, shouldn't we wait to see how much Clarence accomplishes today?"

3) I am more gregarious and sociable as Anthony. Most of my Clarence subpersonalities are rather introverted and private. They hate to be interrupted in their tasks by company dropping in. Most of them hate to go to parties where you have to talk with people. As Anthony, I love to talk with people. I try to get them to tell me their steppingstones; I ask them about their subpersonalities. I really do wish I knew you better. This is why I'm sharing my journal entries with you. I think that for all of us humans to try to get to know one another a little bit better is one of the most meaningful and authentic of human activities.

> *There are a few other glimmerings emerging of how Anthony is different from Clarence, but these are still rather vague and poorly defined. I will just have to experience myself as Anthony a lot more before I really understand who I am as Anthony.*

Pick a name, any name, for any reason, and declare to at least one other person that you are now functioning alternately in two states of consciousness -- one wherein you function as one of your ego-subpersonalities, in your usual culturally created life script, and the other as your more aware, more awake Self.

It may also help if you occasionally use your new name when ordering a magazine or making a contribution to a worthy cause. You will be surprised how quickly your new name will spread as mailing lists are shared and/or sold to others. Then every time a piece of mail arrives at your home addressed to your new name, you can use seeing it as another trigger to "wake-up", do a self-observation, and experience being Self again for a while. Do try it.

Chapter 14
Values and Beliefs

Did you do it? Have you got a new name? Did you tell at least one other person? I do hope that you have adopted a new name and that you are finding it helpful. We still have a ways to go and you will need all the help you can get. The road ahead may get a little scary at times, but I encourage you to trudge on. You can deal with the fear the same way you have learned to deal with anger and anxiety – note it, name it, and let it go. And trudge on. The courage will come, rewards will appear, and joy will manifest. You have experienced this before. This is just normal growth and development. You've done a lot of growing already, from preschooler to elementary school to adolescent to young adult to mature adult. It's just that you thought you were now fully grown and could just continue-on as is, remaining at this stage of development for the rest of your life. And you can. You can stop and rest awhile anytime you wish. Stopping is rather easy. I've done it many times. You simply stop doing your Morning Sit, stop the self-observations, and soon you will be comfortably asleep again in your usual mode of existence. But the urge to grow will come back. You can then restart your Morning Sit, renew your efforts at self-observation and trudge on.

So far we have been working with thoughts and feelings, now we will spend some time working with values and beliefs. Values and beliefs are very important components of any life script. They are usually just accepted as givens – "that's how everyone around here lives." It's the culture; it's what your parents and peers have programmed into you. If you are to make any meaningful and lasting changes in your life script, you will need to observe and understand how your values and beliefs are affecting your life.

You may have already noticed that each of your ego subpersonalities seems to be operating with a slightly different set of values and beliefs. One of your subpersonalities may want to play it safe with money – get out of debt as quickly as possible and save as much as possible for the future. That's only prudent, right? A more entrepreneurial sub may want to get you into debt big time, in order to have more resources working for you in the future. That's courage, boldness, the free market way, right? If you are married, you will run into two similar subpersonalities in your spouse. How you four resolve this is one of the beautiful assignments in married life by which you learn to communicate better and to grow in love with one another.

Another wonderful assignment in married life is deciding whether to have children, when to have children, and how many to have. You may have a parenting subpersonality who wants to have one or more children, but most of your other subs may feel that they don't have the time for that right now. Bring all of these together with similar subs in your spouse and watch the drama unfold. The money question involved only a discussion of which would be preferable for your family. The children questions will bring up even more value and belief issues, such as birth control and abortion, and possibly, feelings of shame, guilt, and sin.

It is very painful to observe this drama play out among the various subpersonalities involved. As an issue unfolds, the subs perform, automatically and mechanically, in the usual human state of "waking sleep" awareness. The drama often gets replayed several times with usually the same outcome. Remember the stimulus-response discussion? Here the same words spoken by one automatically trigger the same response by the other.

I hope that you can see how tough it can be when our various ego-subpersonalities are in control instead of our awakened Selves. It would be preferable if at least one of the partners were able to "wake-up", observe, and understand what is going on. And then, maybe not immediately, but over time, after a few more Morning Sits, and another Life Script Review or two, be able to make some decisions and bring the discussion to a satisfactory resolution.

I'm not saying that it will be any easier, actually it may even take more effort on your part, but a resolution will be reached and, as Self, you will no longer be plagued with feelings of shame, guilt, or sin, whatever your decision. Yes, that's right, no more shame, guilt, or sin. You can eliminate these the same way you got rid of anger and fear, by stopping them at the level of "attack thoughts". That's all that any thoughts of shame, guilt, or sin are, attack thoughts of one of your subpersonalities directed at another. Watch it arise, note it, label it, and let it go.

You, as Self, can do this because you know that you are OK, you are lovable, and you are satisfied that you have considered carefully all the relevant issues and have made the best decision you are capable of at this time. This is your life. This is how you, as Self, are choosing to live it.

You may have observed that some of your subpersonalities are rather selfish, wanting only what is best for you, to hell with anyone else. But some of your other subs may be willing to sacrifice some self-satisfaction if they can see a benefit to others. You may have observed that some of your values and beliefs have changed as you grew-up.

Several researchers who study values and beliefs (e.g. Ken Wilber, Jenny Wade, and Don Beck), have studied these stages of normal human growth and development and have discovered a consistent pattern in the changes we make as we grow up and mature. One such pattern is movement from a basically egocentric orientation (what's best for me), to an ethnocentric or sociocentric one (what's best for my family, my ethnic heritage, my country), and finally to a worldcentric orientation (what's best for humanity, the planet, all life.)

Another pattern is one of movement from pre-conventional to conventional to post-conventional morality, our notion of what is right and wrong. Pre-conventional morality is rather simple – what is right is whatever is best for me, or "might makes right". Conventional morality is defined as following the rules. We conform to the values and beliefs of whichever group we consider ourselves to be a part of – be it the boy scouts, our church, our company, our union, the air force, our nation, etc. In post-conventional morality, we begin to question some of the rules. Do they always apply to everyone? Does this rule apply to me in this situation? Is this a good rule?

These are stages through which all of us grow, we start out as a child at the lower stages and work our way up. Wilber, Wade, and Beck write extensively about these stages and have elaborated seven to eight into which our growth can be sub-divided. We don't need to discuss all of them here, but I think that understanding the following four may help you to understand where some of your subpersonalities are coming from, where they have gotten their values and beliefs. Jenny Wade calls these four stages egocentric, conformist, achievement, and affiliative. Don Beck labels them with colors: red, blue, orange, and green respectively.

Subpersonalities still functioning at the red-egocentric stage see the world as a competitive jungle. There is not enough to go around, so you have to fight all others to be sure you get enough. They believe that only the strong survive and that might makes right. They don't trust others much and want to go it alone. Wilber suggests as examples rebellious youth, frontier mentalities, epic heroes, gang leaders, etc. Many adults are still functioning primarily at this level most of the time.

Subpersonalities at the blue-conformist level have learned it is okay to trust some others as long as they belong to the same group as they do and agree to follow the same rules. If they belong to a church, they believe that their church is the best way to serve God, and that all other religions are inferior, if not downright heretical. If you don't conform to the rules, you will go to hell and burn eternally. Subs at this level exhibit a strong ethnic and national identity. They may say, "My country, right or wrong, my country." They believe there is one right way and only one right way to think about everything. They are strongly conventional and conformist. Wilber's examples include Puritan America, Singapore discipline, religious fundamentalism (e.g. Christian and Islamic), Boy and Girl Scouts, "moral majority", etc. This is probably the most common orientation seen in the world today. Wilber and Beck estimate that approximately 40% of the world's population function at the blue level.

Many subpersonalities prefer to stay at the blue-conformist stage because it is safer and easier to do so. You don't have to think for yourself, actually you are usually encouraged not to think for yourself. Better to just follow the rules and stay with your kind. To grow through this conformist, ethnocentric stage into a worldcentric, post-conventional worldview takes a little courage. Some of your subpersonalities are already there. They are willing to question the rules and to think for themselves. These are primarily of two types – orange-achievement and green-affiliative.

Subpersonalities at the orange-achievement level place a high value on science and reason. If they perceive a conflict between what their church tells them to believe and what science and reason say is so, they feel free to choose science and reason. Rather than feeling satisfaction from being part of a group, they want to achieve individual distinction, to be the best they can be, to accumulate many material goods, and to control their environment. Highly competitive, they will manipulate earth's resources for their strategic gains. Examples are people on Wall Street, emerging middle classes around the world, colonialism, materialism, secular humanism, liberal self-interest, etc. Approximately 30% of the world's population are functioning at this level.

Green-affiliative subpersonalities may also value science and reason, but they are not so individualistic, self-centered, or so achievement oriented. They value being part of a network, wish to work collaboratively with others, believe everyone should have a chance to have their say, all cultures are important, there is strength in diversity. They reach decisions through reconciliation and consensus. Their emphasis is on dialogue and relationships. They highly value intuitive, non-linear thinking. They show a greater degree of affective warmth, sensitivity, and caring, for the earth and all its inhabitants. Wilber's examples include Canadian Health Care, humanistic psychology, liberation theology, Greenpeace, human rights, ecopsychology, etc. Approximately 10% of the population are functioning primarily at this level.

Here are a couple of paragraphs from Wilber's Theory of Everything describing Beck's and Graves' colorful Spiral Dynamics:

In Spiral Dynamics, the preconventional stages are beige (archaic-instinctual), purple (magical-animistic), and red (egocentric). Although red is called "egocentric," the first two stages are even more egocentric (there is a steady decline in narcissism at each and every stage); it is just that red marks the culmination of the highly egocentric and preconventional realms and is now able to act this out forcefully. At the next stage (blue, conformist rule), the narcissism is dispersed into the group -- not me, but my country, can do no wrong! This conventional/conformist stance lasts into orange (egoic-rational), which marks the beginning of the postconventional stages (green, yellow, and turquoise). These postconventional stages (especially orange and green) are marked by an intense scrutiny of the myths, conformist values, and ethnocentric biases that almost always inhabit the preconventional and conventional stages.

In short, as development moves from preconventional to conventional to postconventional (or from egocentric to ethnocentric to worldcentric), the amount of narcissism and egocentrism slowly but surely decreases. Instead of treating the world (and others) as an extension of the self, the mature adult of postconventional awareness meets the world on its own terms, as an individuated self in a community of other individuated selves operating by mutual recognition and respect. The spiral of development is a spiral of compassion, expanding from me, to us, to all of us: there standing open to an integral embrace. [13]

I found this discussion of the various stages of human growth and development very helpful to me in understanding my subpersonalities and my often-conflicting values and beliefs. On reviewing the steppingstone periods of my life, it is easy to see that by the time I entered the Catholic Seminary to train to be a priest, I had been thoroughly enculturated by the Czech-Catholic culture, in which I grew up. My dominant subpersonalities were as conformist, conventional, ethnocentric, (blue), as you can get. I really believed that the Czechs were the best people on Earth and that Roman Catholicism was the best religion. My primary motivation for studying to be a priest was because it was said in my community that the Church needed more Czech priests. And, of course, as a good boy, I only wanted to do what my ethnic-religious community wanted me to do. So, I entered the Seminary.

I realized early that I really did not want to be a priest, but such was the strength of the programming that I was constantly being reminded by my most conformist subs that it really did not matter what I wanted, what mattered was what God wanted. Therefore, I stayed on and lasted for three years.

The seminary routine did allow for many periods of quiet for prayer and meditation. Although at the time I had not yet heard about "Waking-Up", doing a Morning Sit, or a Life-Script Review, there was something about those periods of quiet that allowed me to wake-up, and, as Self, to decide that what I really wanted was to have a wife and family. Therefore, I left the Seminary and after a couple of years of pre-med, entered medical school.

You will recall that I described my next four steppingstone periods (5-8) as an intense enculturation into the academic, scientific, and research community. Compared with the doubts I was beginning to have about some of the blue conformist values and beliefs, I found the scientific worldview a welcome relief and safe refuge. It is so precise, so logical, and so certain of itself. I loved it and so transformed gradually from functioning predominantly at the blue conformist level into the orange achievement stage. Medical school was a competitive environment, and as a good orange achiever, I, too, wanted to be the best.

The clashes of values and beliefs in my transition from blue to orange were obvious in several areas. One was in my motivation for being a physician. It started out as wanting to be a doctor so I could help other Catholic families working in the missions. My motivation then changed to wanting to be the doctor who got the fame and credit for eradicating smallpox in

Africa, malaria in South America, or for preventing the most heart disease in my region of Texas.

Another clash involved my views on artificial birth control. I remember having several very heated debates throughout medical school defending the Catholic Church's ban on the use of the pill and the intrauterine device (IUD). However, by the time Susan and I were married, artificial birth control no longer seemed to us to be wrong at all -- a rather classic example of moving from conventional to postconventional morality.

I didn't know about green-affiliative at the time, but as you read the next entry from my Journal describing the Family Man subpersonality, note the gradual transition from a personal achievement orientation to a family affiliative perspective.

Chapter 15
The Family Man Subpersonality

This is another entry from my Journal dated 2-25-86. The Family Man subpersonality is talking:

The Family Man:

Let me tell you some more about my family. Susan and I are well into our 20th year of marriage and going great. The boys are now 18, 17, and 16. John is a freshman at the University of Texas and enjoying it tremendously. He is currently majoring in Physics and spending a lot of time practicing various forms of the Martial Arts. Randy is a junior at Granger High and is trying to finish up all of his required work this year so he could graduate at the end of his third year of high school. He also plans to attend UT. Joseph is a sophomore at Granger High and is also planning to finish high school in three years. He, too, seems to be leaning towards UT. When we moved to the farm they were 9, 7, and 6. A lot of growing up has taken place in the past nine years, both for them and for Susan and me.

I am enjoying being a parent. I feel like I am participating in an age-old, worldwide drama. How do I get the kids to eat more vegetables? How do I get them to appreciate the value of money? Why don't they put things where they belong? Why don't they go to bed when I think it's bedtime? How do I get them to study more? How do I get them to help more around the house? Why do they waste so much time?

I think that raising children is one of life's most significant experiences. Their needs and demands are so immediate, so definite. They have helped me to grow out of being so involved just with myself. They have helped me to understand what it means to love unconditionally.

All three are showing a big interest in science and math. They all read a lot of science fiction and fantasy and all like to play Dungeons and Dragons. They have learned to program in Basic and when my old TRS-80 (Model I) got too plain for their tastes, they pooled their money and bought themselves an Apple IIc. All three are now running with me each year in the Capital 10 K in Austin. Sometimes we all attend a chess tournament or go hiking in the mountains. Occasionally we take long trips -- to California, to the Rocky Mountains, to the Big Bend, and once to Washington, New York, and Boston. They are not into washing dishes but do help some with the housework and mow the grass whenever their mother or I really insist. For money, of course.

I am also enjoying being a spouse and lover to Susan. She and I are getting along better now than we ever have. I think I love her more now than I did when we were first married. We understand each other better now. We have learned each other's responses to feeling stressed, to being tired, to being scared. It's easier now for us to forgive each other for what we consider inappropriate responses. We have shared enough life experiences to know that our values and goals are compatible and that a future together not only looks possible, but downright desirable and exciting. I still feel unloved and unappreciated at times. But I have come to accept this feeling as a universal human longing and yearning, rather than something I should blame on my family and friends.

I entered my Family Man role back in 1966 pretty much a typical product of our culture. I was a strongly independent, conceited, cocky, ambitious, chauvinistic male. My mother and sister had done all of the cooking and the housework while I was growing up and I assumed that when I married that my wife would accept pretty much the same role in our household. I think that Susan and I both assumed that somehow she would be able to do both -- be a physician and do all the wife and mother chores at home.

Well obviously she couldn't and very early on she would ask for help. Sometimes I helped and sometimes I didn't. After all, that was her job; I had other, more important things to do. There always seemed to be plenty of more important things to do. As I recall the first woman's task that I agreed to do was giving the boys their bath. Susan had argued that it would help develop a good relationship between the boys and myself and that someday I would thank her for having insisted that I do the baths. We had both heard stories about how fathers often became strangers to their kids because they did not interact enough when the children were young, so I agreed to do the baths. Before long I was also cooking meals, washing clothes, and in general helping Susan run the home.

Sometimes I resented it, sometimes I was embarrassed. My colleagues at work soon realized that I did not like to schedule evening meetings or to be out of town for too long because I was needed at home. All of this was rather hard on Susan too, because she still had very mixed role expectations to grapple with in her own mind. All through Medical School she had to fight the bias and prejudice that implied that it was a waste of time to train women because they would stop practicing medicine as soon as they got married and had babies. Susan wanted to practice medicine, but she also wanted to have a home, a husband, and children. But to do all that she needed a husband who understood and was willing to help out at home.

Eventually I understood that and slowly my relationship with housework and parenting grew from resentment and embarrassment to an egalitarian tolerance that it was only fair. Susan and I were equals. We both had our professions. And it was our family. We decided to share the tasks equally. And so, I started to count. How many meals did I prepare and how many did Susan? Who was the last one to mop the kitchen floor? Who's turn was it to get the kids to doing their homework?

What happened next was as unexpected as it was wonderful. Somewhere along the way under the pressure of too many demands, I learned to love, and love made it all easier, love made it a joy. I stopped counting and did as much of the parenting and homemaking as needed to be done. I began to enjoy the role. It was significant, meaningful work.

It was about this time that I really got serious about decreasing my percent employment with the State Health Department from 100% to 50%. At first I ran into a lot of resistance and prejudice. Such a thing just was not done. Some of my colleagues began to question my masculinity, some even my sanity. I was surprised. I had always considered myself to be an outstanding young physician, with good experiences, good credentials, and good references. People at the Health Dept. were generally all happy that I was there and I thought that they would be willing to make this adjustment for my sake. I had what I thought to be a perfectly sound reason, 'Susan is getting busier in her practice now, and I would like to spend more time at home with the kids.'

It wasn't until I found another young physician with training similar to mine who also, for reasons of his own, wanted to work half-time, that we were able to pull it off. We decided to timeshare one job. The position stayed one full time position, but it just happened to have two half-time physicians in it. I stayed as Director; he became Deputy Director. It turned to be a very good deal for all concerned.

Now I have more time to interact with the boys and to help Susan with the housework. I also have more time to put into all my other interests. On a typical day-off from work the Philosopher wants to read, the Homesteader wants to build fences, the Seeker wants to spend more time meditating, and the Kid wants to play more chess. Even the Doctor occasionally has something that just has to be done on that day. So even though I no longer think of housework as woman's work, feel quite comfortable in doing it, and no longer count whose turn it is, it is still hard to motivate myself to do the dishes or to sweep and mop the floors. It's humorous how many different excuses I can entertain for not doing the dishes. My old standby is still, 'I have too many more important things to do.' For a while there I actually convinced myself that Susan would want me to save some of the housework for her to do. My reasoning went something like this: After a hard day at the office doing only Doctor type stuff, she will want to wash the dishes as a change of pace, to give her other subpersonalities a chance to express themselves. My current approach to motivating myself to do the housework is to think of it as a prayer, a meditation, an ascetic discipline, a little dying to self, a mortification, an opportunity for spiritual growth. Of course, now I find myself saving the housework for Susan out of love. After all, she needs opportunities for practicing her spiritual growth also.

When it is about time for the kids to come home, I try to remember to switch into the Family Man role and begin to think kids. First of all, I try to be there when they come home from school, to hear what happened that day and to find out what they are planning for the rest of the day. Secondly, I like to have something baking in the oven when they come in. Homemade bread is best, but it's hard to remember to get started early enough for bread. I usually do something that is quicker, like muffins or Jiffy corn bread. And thirdly, I like to have a home cooked meal every evening with as many of us as possible sitting down together to eat it.

You can read the above as just another example of all of my subpersonalities fighting it out for time sharing my one body/mind. But it also describes a gradual shift in my dominant beliefs and values from an emphasis on what is best for me and my career to an emphasis on what is best for my family and their health and happiness. This affiliative perspective didn't end with just family. At work, I became genuinely interested in hearing opposing viewpoints from my colleagues. And I actually began to value the diversity of perspectives from the various cultures represented on committees.

Wilber and Beck describe normal growth and development as proceeding from blue to orange to green. The orange subpersonalities are the ones more concerned with personal achievement, power, or wealth. The green subpersonalities are more concerned with relationships, connectedness, freeing the oppressed, or safeguarding the environment.

My purpose for going into this discussion of the red, blue, orange, and green color memes is to help you understand that different subpersonalities may be operating with different sets of values and beliefs. Remember that usually all of this is going on rather automatically and unconsciously. What color meme a person is considered to be operating from depends on which subpersonalities he or she happens to be presenting predominantly to the world at that time.

The point of waking-up and self-observation is to help you to understand what is going on and to bring the whole process into the light of awareness. Once you understand about egocentric, conformist, achievement, and affiliative perspectives, you are well on your way to freeing yourself from the automatic habit patterns that characterize those life scripts, eventually transforming yourself up into the next stage of consciousness beyond these four. Jenny Wade calls this next stage, Authentic Consciousness; Wilber calls it Integral: Beck colors it yellow. But before I go on to describe this next stage, I would like to review some of what we have already covered as the differences between <u>Stages</u> of Consciousness and <u>States</u> of Consciousness.

Chapter 16
States vs Stages of Consciousness

You are changing from one state of consciousness to another when you change from identifying completely with one of your subpersonalities, operating automatically, through habit patterns, in a kind of "waking trance", to identifying with Self, as the more awake, more aware state of consciousness. You will recall that deRopp refers to this as moving from the third state of consciousness to the fourth state. Under his scheme, the second state is while we are asleep and dreaming; the first state is being in deep sleep (no dreams). In an effort to emphasize this distinction, while operating in my usual third state of consciousness I think of myself as Clarence, and whenever I awaken to my more aware Self in the fourth state of consciousness, I think of myself as Anthony. Do not confuse these four *states* of consciousness with the four *stages* of consciousness described earlier – the egocentric, conformist, achievement, and affiliative. These four stages pertain to sets of beliefs, values, and behaviors that people have observed their ego-subpersonalities growing through automatically, while operating as usual in their "waking sleep" or third state of consciousness.

To grow through these four <u>stages</u> is normal growth and development, which usually happens without any awareness on our part in the third <u>state</u> of consciousness through the influence of parents, culture, religion, and life experiences. But sometimes, through the pressures of stressful life experiences, this normal growth gets arrested, so that today we are able to observe adult personalities still functioning at some of the lower stages, stages that they should have grown out of, if they were fortunate enough to have been born into a culture that understood and encouraged such growth. Most may stay stuck at blue or orange and may unconsciously and predictably live out their life-scripts for the rest of their lives.

It is easy to observe examples of people stuck at these stages – red, blue, orange, green. The reds are the egocentric ones. They have failed to learn how to love others and are doomed to live lonely lives, not ever trusting anyone. They are stuck at the survival stage. Their goal for the day is to be able to say at the end of it, "Today I ate, and was not eaten." It is easy to understand why someone with this mentality will steal and kill to get food and money. They are operating with pre-conventional morality -- what is right and moral is what best assures their survival.

We all lived through this stage in early childhood. But hopefully, through the enculturation process, grew out of it and learned to love enough to identify with our family, ethnic heritage, our church and local community. This is described by Wade and Beck as the blue-conformist stage and is the stage from which most personalities in the world are operating today. Children born to families who value scientific research and exploration, who encourage the use of logic and reason, and who foster individual development of potential will manage to transcend the blue-conformist stage and move on to the orange-achievement stage and the green-affiliative stages.

Wilber makes a point of stressing that we do not abandon the values and strengths of one stage as we grow into the next. But instead we "transcend and include" each stage as we grow through it. Each stage has its benefits and its weaknesses. At first we master and appreciate the benefits and incorporate the values and skills into our make-up. Then as we get comfortable with this stage we grow dissatisfied with its weaknesses and limitations and feel the urge to move on to the next higher stage. It's like when children learn to crawl, they appreciate the benefits of crawling over not being able to crawl, but soon they become dissatisfied with the limitations of crawling over walking and learn to walk. "Transcend and include" means that even though they have transcended crawling into walking, they still include being able to crawl in their skill set, and are able to crawl should they ever wish to do so again.

In a similar way, we include all of the values and skills we have acquired along the way as we grew through the various stages and we express these through our various subpersonalities. Most of us live in situations where our survival is not at stake, so we do not need to express ourselves through the subpersonality that best incorporates survival skills. But were we ever placed in a survival situation, we could call forth this sub to increase our chance of survival.

Research in this area is complicated by the fact that humans rarely exhibit consistently only one personality, which could easily be categorized as red, blue, orange or green. Since each of us is a composite of several subpersonalities, we exhibit one stage or the other depending on the situation we find ourselves in, either hour by hour as we go through the day or decade by decade as we go through our life.

Beck also describes whole cultures as growing through these stages, meaning that the culture can be categorized by the stage that most of the people living in it are expressing. Some indigenous cultures, in Mexico, Africa, or Australia, are still predominantly living at the survival stage. Most countries are living at the blue-conformist stage, exhibiting a high degree of ethnocentrism with strong national patriotism, sometimes associated with a religious dominance. Bosnia is a good example of where three such cultures are dramatically clashing within one nation. From the northeast, the Bosnian Serbs represent the farthest advance of Eastern Orthodox Christianity. From the northwest, the Bosnian Croats represent the spread from the west of Western Roman Catholic Christianity. Wedging in-between these two cultures from the south are the Bosnian Muslims. So hostile are these three cultures towards each other that NATO forces need to patrol the boundary lines in order to keep peace. It is in the United States and in the countries of Western Europe that the worldcentric values of the orange-achievement and green-affiliative stages are best expressed. The worldcentric value is that all nations should be appreciated for their cultural differences but that all nations should be able to co-exist peacefully.

Beck and Wilber estimate that fully 98% of the world's population can be characterized as functioning predominantly either in the red, blue, orange, or green stages of consciousness development. Beck has developed some bell-shaped curves to describe the color variability mix by country, to point out that no nation has all of its citizens functioning from the same stage of consciousness. Some countries may be predominantly blue with some red and some orange. Another country may be characterized as mostly orange with a lot of green and some blue. Although most countries plot out as a smooth bell shaped curve with only one peak, in some countries like South Africa, Beck found that there were two peaks – one that characterized the black majority, mostly red and blue like a lot of black Africa, and one the white minority, more like the European countries, orange and blue.

Beck at one time served as a consultant to the South African government. He found it very helpful to get everyone familiar with red values, blue values, orange values, and green values. This was so much more accurate and acceptable than to be talking about black values vs. white values. It soon became obvious that Beck wasn't talking about types "of" people but types "in" people. There were white people who demonstrated red and blue values as well as orange and green. And there were black people who demonstrated orange and green values, as well as blue and red. This made it possible, at least for the leaders and negotiators, to understand that a lot of the problems with which they were dealing were better clarified by references to these color stages.

Keep in mind that the purpose of this chapter is to clarify the difference between _states_ of consciousness (we are talking here about only two – deRopp's 3rd: the "consensus trance" or "waking sleep" state, and deRopp's 4th: the more aware, awake state) and _stages_ of consciousness (we are talking now mainly about four – egocentric, conformist, achievement, and affiliative), stages through which we grow normally and automatically, though it may take some time, maybe decades. And remember that it is also possible for you to get stuck at one of these stages and remain there for the rest of your life.

It often takes a major life crisis – a death, a divorce, an accident, a heart attack, to get one unstuck and to allow the personal growth process to continue. But you do not need to wait for a major crisis. It is my hope that if you are stuck in a life script that is not working well for you, that you will be able to use the concepts and exercises in this book to be the stimulus to get you growing again.

However, regardless at which stage you consider yourself to be at present, by "waking-up", at least periodically, to another state of consciousness, you can begin to access the intuitions, the insights, and additional energies that will allow you to grow on until you eventually reach the Authentic Stage – with a healthy functioning ego, free of crippling neurotic symptoms, realizing your full potential; an ego that has its various subpersonalities well integrated, strong enough to assert itself in the world, loving enough to form healthy relationships, competent enough to earn a living; and an ego experiencing an abundance of joy, love, and peace. It is a big step, this next one up to the Authentic Stage. And it will take some more practice in "waking-up", at least periodically, to a higher state of consciousness.

Chapter 17
A Letter to Susan from Anthony

L et me share with you now some more of my experiences in trying to wake-up, at least periodically, to a higher state of consciousness. After I had experimented for a while with associating the name Anthony with me, the more awake, more aware Self, I decided to write a letter to my wife explaining what I thought was going on. I started the letter on May 3, 1988.

Dear Susan,

How do I begin to tell you that sometimes there is someone else sleeping in your bed at night instead of Clarence?

And how do I do it in a way that will simply have you smile and say, "I've noticed," instead of worrying that maybe I have gone off the deep end.

Susan, I want you to help me think through this Clarence vs. Anthony thing? Sometimes I feel as though I am accomplishing a major breakthrough in consciousness evolution. As Anthony, I feel less selfish, less egotistical, more loving, more generous, easier to live with. Other times I worry that I am fooling myself, that I am just pretending that as Anthony I am qualitatively any different from any of the Clarence subpersonalities.

Almost always when I am writing in this journal, I am doing so while at home all alone. It is very easy to feel more loving and more generous when there is no one else around making any demands. The reason I want to bring you into the discussion is to see if there is any observable evidence that my behavior as Anthony is qualitatively different from my behavior as one of the Clarence subpersonalities. What I want to propose are three experiments with you as the principal investigator. The laboratory will be our daily activities and interactions. I would like for us to test three hypotheses:

HYPOTHESIS #1:

Some of my Clarence subpersonalities sometimes do not treat you very well. You and I still at times manage to get into an angry exchange of words. The Clarence subpersonality you are dealing with at that time is acting petty, childish, self-centered, defensive, self-righteous, and scared. He is afraid that you are trying to dominate, manipulate, and control. I know that at times like that I am a pain in the ass to deal with. The first hypothesis which I would like to test is whether you can help free me from that kind of behavior by simply reminding me that I am Anthony. Right now, as I write this, I firmly believe that you can stop abruptly any such unbecoming behavior of mine by simply saying, "Anthony, dear. What's wrong?"

HYPOTHESIS #2:

On the other hand, some of the Clarence subpersonalities are quite lovable and a joy to be around. Sometimes it's nice to be with someone very familiar, very predictable. I know that you know all of my subpersonalities very well and I suspect that at times you try to influence which role you want me to play at any given time. Sometimes you need Clarence: Homesteader to help you out in the yard while Clarence: Philosopher wants to read a book or watch the MacNeil/Lehrer News Hour. As our second hypothesis, I would like to test whether you can wake me up from my automatic role-playing behavior at any time by saying something like, "Wake-up, Anthony, I need you. Can you arrange to put on your Homesteader hat for a while and come help me out?" I think that that is all that it would take. I think that within 30 seconds I can cheerfully switch roles and be on my way out the door to help you outside.

HYPOTHESIS #3:

Or sometimes you might just want to talk to me as Anthony. Will you be able to tell the difference when you are talking to Clarence in one his automatic and very predictable behavior patterns or when you are dealing with me, Anthony? For our third hypothesis, I would like for you to try saying something like, "Wake up, Anthony. I would like to get to know you a little better." And then we'll talk. What will we talk about? What will we do? Will you be able to keep me aware of myself as Anthony? Will you be able to find out anything about me? Will you enjoy talking with me? My prediction for this one is that you will definitely be able to tell the difference, not only in what I say but also in how you feel. And I predict that you will like it. Mainly because, I love you more than Clarence does. And I wish I knew you better.

Love, Anthony

The next Journal entry to refer to this letter was written on July 21, 1990.

Well, I finally showed the letter to Susan. As you can tell from the dates, it took me a long time to get up the courage to give it to her. I started the letter in May of 1988 and had most of it written by August of 1988. Then I kept editing and rewriting it for over a year. But mainly I was stalling. I wasn't sure that I wanted to commit myself to all the implications of those three hypotheses.

And even if I decided that I wanted to so commit, I wasn't sure that I could do it. So, while I was stalling, I was also practicing. Whenever Susan and Clarence would get into a little spat, I would try to remember that I was really Anthony only play-acting a Clarence role. While continuing Clarence's end of the spat, I tried to calm myself, observe what was going on, and then tried to say things which would defuse the issue and allow us to bring about a peaceful resolution.

Same with switching subpersonalities. Whenever Susan would ask Clarence to do something that happened to be outside of the interests of the particular subpersonality he was currently living out, I tried to wake-up fast enough to stop Clarence from responding negatively. And then, during that awkward silent pause which sometimes lasted 30-60 seconds, I tried quickly to switch to the appropriate subpersonality and say, "Sure. I can do that right now."

I also worried about what would happen if she ever actually did come up to Clarence someday and say, "Wake up, Anthony. I would like to get to know you a little better." I had no doubts that I could wake-up but for how long could I keep myself awake and Self-remembering? What would we talk about? I would have to come up with something easy and safe. I wouldn't want to worry her with all the things that are really going through my mind.

When I was confident that I had practiced enough and that I was ready to show the letter to Susan, I developed a new worry. What if the letter freaks her out? What if she gets angry and tells me to quit reading all that transpersonal garbage? I decided that the setting had to be just right. Couldn't just drop it on the table one night when she gets home from a busy day at the office with the Susan: Doctor subpersonality still very much in control. That wouldn't do at all. I had to get her into a romantic mood. Probably would be best to get away from home and into a strange, non-routine setting.

So, then, for several months I tried to schedule a weekend in Austin or San Antonio. We would get a hotel room, have a nice dinner Friday evening, make love during the night, and then late the next morning over breakfast, I would show her the journal entries where I first described Anthony and then the letter. We could talk about it all Saturday and most of Sunday before we came back to Granger. That was the plan.

But, for one reason or another, I simply couldn't decide on a weekend. I kept putting it off. Then out of the clear blue, a doctor friend of ours from New York asked if we would like to get away for a few days. He wanted to visit in Texas for a while, would like to stay out here at our farm, and would take over Susan's practice during our absence. We said "Sure!" and planned a skiing trip to Angel Fire just for the two of us. This was in March of 1990.

Then it hit me. This would be the perfect setting. Angel Fire is in northern New Mexico, just 20 miles east of Taos. We already had romantic memories of Taos. It is an enchanting environment. I quickly put the finishing touches on the letter and carefully and secretly packed it along with several journal entries.

After a couple of days of skiing, I casually asked if she would like to drive over to Taos for dinner. Then on the drive over, I began my pitch. This was no ordinary evening. This was a magical, enchanted evening. Strange powers and spirits were gathering to help us through this night. I reminded her of some of the elder tales in Allan Chinen's wonderful In the Ever After. Things were going to be very different for us ever after this night. Our relationship as we knew it was over, and a new one was about to begin. I promised her that I would ask her again to marry me when this night was over and told her that I wouldn't hold her to her earlier marriage vows if she wanted out.

As we sat in the dining room at the old Taos Inn, I told her that I had written her a letter which I wanted her to read, but that I could not show it to her just yet. First I had to remind her of some of the things she had already read in my journal but may have forgotten -- concepts like waking up, self-observation, and my multiple subpersonalities. Over dessert I showed her the journal entries that introduced Anthony. Finally, as we returned to our lodge at Angel Fire, I gave her the letter.

She took it well. She wasn't worried about the split personality problem at all. She felt that she had already experienced some of the very positive aspects in my behavior changes from a typical Clarence response to an Anthony one. And she liked that. She strongly feels that the proof of any theory or technique lies in its effect on the relationship. And she believes that ever since I have started reading about psychological and spiritual growth and development, that I have been a lot easier to live with.

And she actually got downright excited about the implications for our future. We could plan a future together anew. Our future need not be simply a predictable extrapolation of past routine behavior patterns. We could think new thoughts, make new plans, sing new songs, and accept new challenges.

She even agreed to marry me again!!!

The next entry in my journal that refers to the letter is dated December 10, 1990 and is part of a Christmas letter I was writing to some of our friends.

Dear Friend,

I hope you are enjoying reading my journal entries and that you will be moved to write me and to tell me a little bit more about yourself. Remember that I wish I knew you better.

I am glad that I wrote that letter to Susan about my three hypotheses. We have enjoyed referring to it occasionally over the past eight months. It's just too early yet to try to draw any conclusions. We have not actually ever had an interaction exactly as described in the three hypotheses. The closest that we came to experiencing #1 was one afternoon while my big sister, Loretta, was visiting at our home. I got into a nice, hot, little argument with her and while I was at my hottest, Susan calmly says, "Anthony, remember who you are."

I immediately switched my attention from Loretta to Susan, and began trying to explain to her that I really wasn't angry, that I was just using my angry voice to try to win a point. I felt sheepish, like I had just been caught doing something that I should be ashamed of. Eventually I was able to laugh, and to tell Susan, "Good point, thanks." I don't know what Loretta thought about the exchange. She had no idea who Anthony was, and I did not think that that was the time to try to explain.

On my own, I have been experimenting with switching perspectives from Clarence to Anthony and continue to feel that it is worth doing. I feel better now, physically, psychologically, and spiritually, then I ever have before. My relationships with Susan, with family, with friends, and with coworkers, are better now than ever before. So much so that I again am feeling enthused to share all of this with you and to encourage you to try doing something similar yourself. Give yourself another name, start observing what the old you are doing, and then write me about it all. I'd love to hear it.

If any of you would rather not be on this mailing list of mine, please let me know and I'll let you go. Otherwise stay with me, as we try to find out just who this Anthony character is and becomes.

Love, Anthony

I got several positive responses to this letter encouraging me to keep them informed of my progress as Anthony. I still find adopting a new name to be a very helpful aid in nurturing my psychological growth and development. And I encourage you again to adopt a new name if you haven't already done so. It helps with the feelings. When you first started doing self-observations and waking-up, I encouraged you to do them until you felt the difference, until you experienced that as your more awake, more aware Self, you felt calmer, more at peace, more lovable, more loving. If you have had that experience, these feelings will come back every time you are reminded to wake-up by seeing, hearing, or thinking of your new name.

Don't get discouraged if your family and friends don't share your enthusiasm for your new name. Several years later I asked Susan to re-read the above journal entries. She said that she definitely remembers the letter and the trip to Taos as a wonderful, romantic experience and that she appreciates the effects of all my efforts at personal growth. But she never did take seriously her role as principal investigator of my three hypotheses. She never felt like calling me Anthony and continued to call me Clarence. I am assuming therefore, that by the time of the letter, I had already mastered the task of integrating my various subpersonalities adequately enough that she never felt the need to call on me as Anthony for help in dealing with any of my Clarence subpersonalities.

I do have some friends who knew me first as Clarence and now do occasionally call me Anthony just to remind me that they do remember the various journal entries I have shared with them. And I now have several new friends who only know me as Anthony. These new friends I have made at conferences and retreats of various sorts where I registered myself as Anthony Skrovan and had "Anthony" on my nametag. Since they call me and write to me as Anthony, it is quite a challenge to remain awake and interact with them as Anthony. And that's the benefit; it gives me more practice in functioning for extended periods of time in my more awake, more aware state of consciousness.

Sometimes it can get rather humorous. I will forget and introduce myself to someone as Clarence Skrovan and they ask, "Why does it say Anthony on your nametag?" Sometimes I am asked if friends call me Tony. I tell them no, mainly because I'm not Anthony very often. And then there are the times when I have to sign a check or credit card voucher, which clearly says Clarence Skrovan on it. I use all such opportunities to explain all the advantages of adopting a new name. You, too, can have this much fun, but only if you adopt a new name for yourself. We are not through growing yet and a new name will have some more uses as we go along. So, if you haven't picked out one yet, do so now.

Chapter 18
Meditation

Another help in trying to wake-up, at least periodically, to the next state of consciousness is Meditation. You may have noticed immediately that the Morning Sit is a lot like meditation. I didn't want to call it meditation because a lot of people are put off by the term, either because they worry that it is part of some religion or because they think that it is too hard to do. You may have tried meditation yourself for a while but then dropped it because it didn't seem to you to be worth the time and effort.

There are several different kinds of meditation, but what most have in common is that they ask you to set aside a few minutes each day to sit and try to stop, or at least modify, the usual kind of mental activity that goes on in your head most of the time. It's a kind of constant chatter – we worry, we plan, we whine, we hope, we regret, constantly. We don't know where all of these thoughts are coming from. They just seem to arise, one after another. And we all soon experience that thoughts are very hard, if not impossible, for us to stop. That's why I didn't ask you to try to stop the thoughts from coming during your Morning Sit, only to observe them flowing by and to try not to get hooked – not to identify with the subpersonality entertaining that thought, and then spending most of your sitting time on just that one thought, or worse yet, ending your meditation to attend to some activity one of your subs just decided needed to be done right then.

What causes most efforts at doing meditation to fail is a lack of understanding of the difference between the state of consciousness wherein you identify with one of your ego-subpersonalities and the state wherein you are functioning as Self. Since most people are simply functioning out of the automatic habit patterns of one subpersonality or another, it is usually one of the subs that reads about or hears about meditation and decides to try it. One of the subs decides to try it. I hope that by now you can appreciate how humorous this is about to become. First of all, the subpersonality that wants to meditate may never even get a chance to try. By the time the next morning comes around, some other sub is in charge, doing its automatic behavior patterns, meditation is not one of them, so meditation does not happen. But let's suppose that you have a friend who keeps reminding you and insisting that you try, and eventually does succeed in having you sitting down one morning trying to meditate. Then what happens? As soon as this sub manages to disengage from one of its thoughts, all the other subpersonalities jump in to fill up the empty space. The other subs simply do not have time or any appreciation for this and will always succeed in finding more important things to do. Eventually one stops trying because it doesn't seem to be worth the effort.

To be successful at meditation, you need to understand about self-observation, about subpersonalities, about waking-up, and about the Self. You need to strengthen the Self's will and ability to direct your body/mind's activity for at least 15-20 minutes. You will need to experience the difference in feeling tone and mood while you are functioning as Self vs. functioning as one of your subpersonalities. Only then, when you, as Self, decide you want to meditate, does meditation have any chance of gaining a foothold on your daily "to do" list. If you have that understanding and have managed to work in 15-20 minutes every day for a Morning Sit, then you may as well call it meditation.

What happens during a meditation? For some proportion of the time, your mind will be preoccupied with thoughts, the remainder of the time your mind is sitting there idle — it is in-between thoughts. Both times are important. At first you will experience very little time in-between thoughts. That's okay, don't rush it. It will come. The harder you try, the more impossible it becomes. You sort of have to let go and not give a damn. Just enjoy watching the thoughts and try not to get hooked on any one of them.

Eventually, as you get better at letting thoughts go, you will begin to notice the small gap of space/time that sometimes occurs in-between thoughts. This gap will be experienced as a quiet space or emptiness, a kind of silent hole you can peer into and wonder what is in there. What you have just discovered is an opening into your unconscious and meditation is a method for observing what comes out of your unconscious.

Most of the time while you are meditating, you are bombarded with thoughts and emotions from your most active and demanding subpersonalities, the usual chatter that you entertain all the time – the worries, the plans, the problems, the fears and the joys. We can say that these thoughts and emotions are coming from your conscious mind.

As soon as you start becoming somewhat successful in letting go of these thoughts and emotions, you will occasionally experience a new kind of thought and emotion dealing primarily with a past event. Most of these thoughts and emotions will be coming from your unconscious mind. In your unconscious mind are the stored recordings of all the thoughts and emotions that you ever experienced as you were growing up.

Most of these thoughts and emotions are ones that you simply forgot. They are no longer meaningful to you in your present life situation. As these come tumbling out, you will be able to observe them, label them, and simply let them go. They may be fun to think about again, but you can do that later on ("Hey, Hon, you will never guess what came up during my meditation this morning.") For now, just let them go and return to observing the gap in-between thoughts.

However, what else is over there in your unconscious mind are thoughts and emotions that have been actively repressed by your dominant ego-subpersonalities. One or another of your subpersonalities considered these childhood experiences as threatening and/or not useful in coping with current life situations. Some of these actively repressed experiences from the past may be causing you neurotic symptoms today. As thoughts and emotions associated with these repressed experiences emerge during your meditation, they may be a little harder to let go of. You may also observe old subs emerging from your unconscious and wanting time now to express themselves again.   Some of these old repressed subpersonalities represent your "shadow", a term popular with Jungian psychologists.   Recognizing your shadow subpersonalities, facing them consciously, and understanding that they are part of you will enable you to love them, integrate them into your conscious life, thereby defusing the unconscious inner conflicts they may be causing.

Having to deal now with these repressed thoughts, emotions, and subpersonalities may strike you as a little scary and you may be beginning to wonder why you should continue doing this. The answer is that there are profound benefits to be gained by continuing doing this. Your present life script is being held firmly in place mainly by these unconscious influences. If you wish to transform how the rest of your life will go, these influences will need to be dealt with.

So, I urge you to stick with it, it may turn out not to be as scary as it seems at first.   This repressed material may have been scary to the subpersonality that had repressed it, but to you, as Self, it may not seem so scary now.   After all, most of these materials are childhood experiences. What was scary to a child, may not seem scary to you at all.   Now that you are more mature, now that you have learned to function as Self, you are coming to these experiences from a more secure and loving place.   You can observe them from a higher perspective.   You are more capable now of integrating them into your current life situation.

It is possible that you may have more serious stuff repressed in your unconscious than most of us have and you may want to get some help.   There are psychotherapists out there whose job it is to help you with stuff like this – counselors, ministers, psychologists, physicians.   Sometimes just talking about it with a friend, a parent, or an aunt or uncle may be all the help that is needed. ("Hi, Mom. I'm calling today to discuss something that came up in my meditation this morning.")

There is more help available yet.   Not everything in your unconscious is scary stuff.   There are also helpful and loving influences lurking in there as well. Activating these helpful and loving energies will help you to heal whatever disturbing experiences you may have had in childhood.

Assagioli divides up the unconscious into a higher and a lower. He describes the higher as follows:

> From this region, we receive our higher intuitions and inspirations – artistic, philosophical or scientific, ethical "imperatives" and urges to humanitarian and heroic action. It is the source of the higher feelings, such as altruistic love; of genius and of the states of contemplation, illumination, and ecstasy. In this realm are latent the higher psychic functions and spiritual energies. [14]

You and I can speculate on exactly what this higher unconscious is throughout the rest of this book, but for now, let's just say that working with the repressed thoughts, emotions, and subpersonalities will help you get rid of some of the unconscious blocks that may be restraining your normal growth and development. I encourage you to continue with your self-observations and your daily meditations.

We have dealt with some serious stuff in this chapter. This may be a good time for you to take a break and deal with something lighter and happier, like describing in a little more detail one of your playful subpersonalities. The next chapter describes my Kid Subpersonality.

Chapter 19
The Kid Subpersonality

The Kid subpersonality is one sub that you are sure to have also. The Kid has been with you since childhood. As you grew up you changed the nature of your play, but hopefully you haven't stopped playing. Taking time out to play is also a relaxation response and can help ameliorate any damage stress may be causing in your life. The following is from my Journal written in March of 1986:

The Kid:

With so many of my fellow subpersonalities always wanting to do something serious, responsible, important, or absolutely necessary, it is hard for me to find time for just having fun. But I think that in order to have a healthy well-rounded personality, having fun is just as important as all that studying, shit-shoveling, and meditating. Well-roundedness aside, I may be more effective in whatever impact all these subpersonalities are trying to make on this world if we take a break now and then for some fun.

So what do I like to do for fun? Well, I like to play games. I've played a lot of games over the past few years -- Monopoly, King Oil, Acquire, Bridge, Poker, Chess, Checkers, Dominoes. My Dad liked to play dominoes best, especially Moon. Sometimes my Mom would play with us. Moon is best with three players. With two players, Straight is best; with four, Forty-two is best. I've played some dominoes with my boys, but we seem to enjoy King Oil, Acquire, and Poker more. On one vacation trip to Odessa, while Susan was visiting with her family, the boys and I rented a room in the lodge at Davis Mountains and played King Oil for two days straight. We had planned to hike, but it rained the whole time. We play mostly Poker now whenever we play anything together. Susan and I have played Bridge some, mostly while visiting in Odessa with her family. I like Bridge, but I don't push it because the whole notion of playing Bridge regularly seems to strike everyone around here as such a colossal waste of time. But if someone else wanted to, I would enjoy playing Bridge.

What I really like to play most of all is Chess. I like playing it for fun. I like studying the game. I like to teach it and I like to play seriously at Chess Tournaments. The boys and I have had a lot of fun playing Chess. I've enjoyed teaching them how to play better. At one time, we even started a Chess Club and met regularly once a month. The biggest thrill of all, however, is playing in U.S. Chess Federation (USCF) rated tournaments.

USCF rated means that everyone there has a rating and plays by USCF rules. A rating is so neat. It tells the world exactly how good a chess player you are. Right now, I am at 1587, the boys are all somewhere in the 1200's and rising fast. At 1200 either one of them could probably beat most of the people around the world who are not rated and playing Chess just for fun. 1587 is somewhere around the median of the approximately 30,000 Chess players who are USCF rated. Experts and Masters are rated from 2000 to 2400. Grandmasters go higher than that with the World Champion being around 2700. Every time you play a game, your rating changes plus or minus 16 points for winning or losing and plus or minus 4% of the difference in the ratings. If you beat someone rated 200 points higher, you gain 24 points (16+(.04x200)). If you had lost the game, you would lose only 8 points (-16+(.04x200)). Got it? Almost everyone almost always feels that he is better than his rating. But it is hard to improve your rating. The only way you can do that is to become a better Chess player.

To become a better Chess player you really have to learn to concentrate and it helps to study Chess books. The books are full of advice on how to develop your pieces in the opening, how to work the pieces in combination, and how to safely promote your pawns in the end game. The books are also full of games of other players. By studying these games, you can learn to avoid mistakes faster than if you wait to learn through your own games. I know some Chess players who study the books for five hours each day. I read and study my books as often as I can, which is usually around five hours every year. I also go to as many tournaments as I can, which is usually one or two a year. I hope that that is enough to keep me improving. Someday I want to win the Texas State Amateur Chess Championship -- that's the best under 1999. After that, who knows?

I also like to play around with little bitty electronic things. I like to put together kits of wires, electronic parts, and printed circuit boards with my soldering iron. I have built from kits a couple of short wave radios, a multimeter, an oscilloscope, and a stereo receiver. Lately I've enjoyed interfacing my computer with other electronic gadgets. A few years ago, John and I were studying Morse Code in order to get our Amateur Radio License. First we put together a small oscillating circuit with a telegraph key and speaker to create the dot and dash sounds. Next we connected it to our computer through the input and output ports of a cassette recorder. Now when we use the telegraph key to practice our Morse Code, the computer displays on its screen which letters we are sending to it. We also now have a program, which will generate the appropriate dot and dash sounds, when we press a key on the computer keyboard. Isn't that bad?

I now have a board that has 8 analog input ports and eight output relay switches connected to the computer. At one time, I had it all set up to read temperatures up in our 'solar' attic and to turn on and off our attic-to-house fan depending on the attic and house temperatures. After we got our central heating unit, I set it up to monitor and to give me a printout each day of the times the furnace was on and off and what the temperatures were at the time. The most fun the boys and I have had with this board was to hook it up to a switch at the door and then whenever anyone opened that door, the computer would shout out through its voice synthesizer, 'Intruder Alert. Intruder Alert.' Then it would ask the intruder to come up to the keyboard and identify himself or it would threaten to call the police. We never actually got it set up to automatically dial up anyone yet, but we're working on it.

The computer itself has been a source of fun to me over the past seven years. I must have been the first kid in town to have one, a 1978 TRS-80 Model I with 4K of RAM, Level I Basic, and a cassette recorder. First I upgraded it to 16K of RAM and Level II Basic. It was at this time that I got my Scripsit word processing program and bought a Radio Shack Line Printer IV. Soon the cassette recorder seemed too slow for storing and loading my programs, so I tried Exetron's Stringy Floppy for a while. It took 4 minutes to load Scripsit from cassette and only one minute on the Stringy Floppy. Soon even that seemed too slow, so I got the Expansion Interface with a disk controller board, another 16K of RAM, and a disk drive. Scripsit then loaded in about six seconds. Next I got another disk drive and another 16K of RAM. Then I got a doubler board for the interface, which now stores double the density on my disks. Then I got the RS232 board and the telephone Modem, subscribed to CompuServe, and began reading its bulletin boards and ordering its books on-line. By getting in early and doing all my upgrading just as the prices started falling, I now have a computer system which cost me only about 4 times as much as a comparable system would cost today. But the fun over the years has been worth it. The boys all took to it early. We have all learned to program in Basic and we have all used it as a word processor for writing letters, reports, and my little essays and journal entries.

I really enjoy programming a computer. There's something about the logic and rationality of a program that interests and attracts me. The program will always do exactly what I tell it to do, even though sometimes that is not what I want it to do. That's the fun part, answering the question, 'Why is it doing what it is doing and not what I want it to do?' The challenge is in finding the error. You have to walk through each of your logic sequences step by step in order to find the ambiguous command. Sometimes it takes hours, and the time flies, and it is fun.

So what else do I, as Kid, like to do. I like to read science fiction and go to the movies. Occasionally I camp out or go hiking. I like to take long trips. The essence of being a kid, it seems to me, is to be doing something or going somewhere which takes me away from all the responsibilities of the homestead and the office, and where I can just enjoy being alive, with no worries or cares. Kind of like it used to be when I really was just a kid.

If I have my way around here, the future will be full of long trips around the world, more camping and hiking trips, more Chess tournaments, and more little bitty electronic gadgets and things.

If you haven't yet written up a description of your Kid subpersonality, please do it now. You'll enjoy doing that. Then share your write-up with someone, ask them what they like to do for fun. After you have shared a few laughs, you can tell them about your other subs, your steppingstones, and your morning meditations. Then ask them about their steppingstones. Remember that getting to know one another better is one of the most meaningful of human activities. And getting to know one another better may just be the key to further growth and development. And further growth and development may take you all the way up to the Authentic Stage of Consciousness.

Chapter 20
The Authentic Stage of Consciousness

Obviously, what we are pursuing here is psychological growth and development. Our goal is to develop healthy, strong, well-functioning ego-subpersonalities, which are, at least periodically, under the fully awake direction of Self. If you have adopted a new name for yourself whenever you are functioning as Self, you can ascribe your usual name to your various ego subpersonalities. In my case, Anthony is the more awake one, observing and directing the various Clarence subpersonalities – Clarence: Family Man, Clarence: Philosopher, or Clarence: The Kid, etc.

The task is to get all of your subpersonalities to submit to the priorities and direction of the Self. It is not healthy, nor conducive to happiness, to remain fragmented unconsciously into several subpersonalities, each pulling in a different direction like the horses in Gurdjieff's parable of the stagecoach. The more you can remain awake observing the interaction of all your subs, the easier it will be to bring about some integration or synthesis of their various strengths and weaknesses. You want to be able to draw on the characteristics and personality traits of each of your subs whenever you, as Self, decide the situation calls for them.

This is a kind of self-help psychotherapy. Your self-observations and thought watching give you a lot of information about the day-to-day details of your life. Understanding and working with Subpersonalities, Steppingstones, and Life-Scripts allow you to gradually decrease the amount of dysfunctional behavior of your automatic habit patterns and increase the amount of positive, healthy behaviors that your body/mind truly desires. Doing your Meditation and giving yourself some time in-between thoughts, will allow for the unconscious healing energies to flow, repairing your damaged body organs and giving you the strength to carry on with your task of integration and synthesis.

I mentioned earlier that the end result of all this psychological growth and development will be to have arrived at this stage, the Authentic Stage of Consciousness, with a healthy functioning ego, free of crippling neurotic symptoms, realizing your full potential; an ego that has its various subpersonalities well integrated, strong enough to assert itself in the world, loving enough to form healthy relationships, competent enough to earn a living; and an ego experiencing an abundance of joy, love, and peace.

In the rest of this chapter I will fill out this description of the Authentic Stage with some quotes from Wade, Maslow, and Wilber, as well as some of my experiences with this stage. First, here is a quote from Jenny Wade:

Authentic consciousness resolves both the Achievement and Affiliation dilemmas, using a synergistic blend of both solutions that is greater than the sum of its parts. If love will not conquer all and power does not obtain the more important things in life, the Authentic resolution is, fulfilling one's own personal mission and supporting the personal growth of others along the way. [15]

Quoting from Maslow, Wade further describes this stage by saying:

Authentic consciousness represents the height of most conventional developmental theory. It is familiarly known as Maslow's Self-Actualization (1943, 1982, 1987) ...

His Self-Actualizers have moved past the basic needs for physical and psychological survival supplied by the environment that cause discomfort if they are not satisfied. They are motivated by self-actualization, an intrinsically pleasant state that creates an enjoyable tension defined as personal growth. It is experienced as the ongoing actualization of potentials, capacities and talents, as fulfillment of a mission (or call, fate, destiny, vocation), as a fuller knowledge of; and acceptance of; the person's own intrinsic nature, as an unceasing trend toward unity, integration or synergy within the person. (Maslow 1982, 25) ...

There is a "superior perception of reality," including acceptance of the Self of others, and of the world (Maslow 1982, 26). Life is appreciated in its complex and ever-changing totality replete with existential dilemmas. The "authentic person assumes a new relation to his society and indeed, to society in general. He not only transcends himself in various ways; he transcends his culture" (Maslow 1982, 11). Authentic people identify not with a particular group or society but with the human race. Resistance to enculturation comes from social independence. Unlike Affiliative- and Achievement-oriented people, Self-actualizers do not need the affection or recognition of others for self-validation, since their standards are internal. [16]

One more quote from Wade, and then we will move on.

The Authentic person deeply respects the autonomy of others, including their limitations. Although he considers personal growth for all people to be the highest good, he respects the choice of others who may resist change as their inalienable right. He will help others only if help is desired and mutually worked for by the other party (assuming that party is a competent adult)-not to "rescue" or "straighten out" a person or situation, as would someone at the Affiliative and Conformist levels. [17]

The existential philosophers also write a lot about living your life authentically. You are not living authentically, if you frequently observe yourself giving time to activities not in proportion to what your priorities are.

When we were living in Houston, Susan and I were both very much involved in furthering our careers. Susan was teaching Pediatrics at the Medical School, seeing sick children at a community free clinic, and also serving as the Assistant Dean for Student Affairs. I was an Associate Professor at the School of Public Health teaching and counseling graduate students for master's and doctoral degrees in Public Health, and serving as project director on federal grants creating new roles for community health nurses and health planners. Both of us were making a lot of business trips and frequently brought home work from the office. There was very little time left for parenting our three young sons. Anyone observing our behavior would assume that our careers and making lots of money were our top priorities.

After Susan's mother died, her elderly diabetic father came to live with us. This added a fourth dependent to our household, but one who was quite vocal about how little "care giving" was going on at home. Susan and I were forced to confront "authenticity." We asked ourselves, "What are our priorities?" and "Are we spending our time accordingly?" Once we "woke up" enough to ask these questions, it did not take long to realize that we were not dividing up our time according to our priorities. We did some "Life-Script Reviews" and decided to make some changes. One thing led to another and soon we resigned our positions and moved to Granger, unemployed but happily spending more time with parents and kids.

The challenge to live authentically according to your priorities is a never-ending one. You will need a daily practice like meditation to keep the goal of living authentically constantly in the forefront. You want to actualize in your life the priorities that you, as Self, have. That's why Maslow called people able to do this, Self-Actualizers. He described Self-Actualizing authentic personalities as having an inner feeling of detachment from their culture. In the following quote from *Motivation and Personality*, Maslow describes what others have termed post-conventional and world-centric beliefs and values.

> An inner feeling of detachment from the culture is not necessarily conscious but is displayed by almost all, particularly in discussions of the American culture as a whole, in various comparisons with other cultures, and in the fact that they very frequently seem to be able to stand off from it as if they did not quite belong to it. The mixture of varying proportions of affection or approval and hostility or criticism indicated that they select from American culture what is good in it by their lights and reject what they think bad in it. In a

word, they weigh it, assay it, taste it, and then make their own decisions.

This is certainly very different from the ordinary sort of passive yielding to cultural shaping displayed for instance by the ethnocentric subjects of the many studies of authoritarian personalities. It is also different from the total rejection of what after all is a relatively good culture, that is, when compared with other cultures that actually exist, rather than fantasied heavens of perfection...

Detachment from the culture is probably also reflected in our self-actualizing subjects' detachment from people and their liking for privacy, which has been described above, as also in their less than average need for the familiar and customary.

For these and other reasons they may be called autonomous, i.e., ruled by the laws of their own character rather than by the rules of society. It is in this sense that they are not only or merely Americans, but also to a greater degree than others, members at large of the human species. To say that they are above or beyond the American culture would be misleading if interpreted strictly, for after all they speak American, act American, have American characters, etc.

And yet if we compare them with the over socialized, the robotized, or the ethnocentric, we are irresistibly tempted to hypothesize that this group is not simply another subcultural group, but rather less enculturated, less flattened out, less molded. This implies degree, and placing on a continuum that ranges from relative acceptance of the culture to relative detachment from it. [18]

In his study of healthy individuals, Maslow found that often they reported having experiences for which he coined the term, "Peak-experiences". Here is how he described a peak-experience:

The person in the peak-experiences feels more integrated (unified, whole, all-of-a-piece), than at other times. He also looks (to any observer) more integrated in various ways, e.g., less split or dissociated, less fighting against himself, more at peace with himself, less split between an experiencing-self and an observing-self, more one-pointed, more harmoniously organized, more efficiently organized with all his parts functioning very nicely with each other, more synergic, with less internal friction, etc. ... [19]

The person in the peak-experiences usually feels himself to be at the peak of his powers, using all his capacities at the best and fullest... He feels more intelligent, more perceptive, wittier, stronger, and more graceful than at other times. [20]

With the concepts and exercises in this book – from Self-Observation, Sub-Personalities, Steppingstones, and Waking-Up to Meditation, Life-Script Reviews, and Adopt a New Name, what I am trying to do is to give you a method, a way to help you experience peak-experiences more and more frequently with a more or less permanent sense of being finally on the Authentic Stage of Consciousness.

Finally, here a few more quotes from Maslow describing characteristics of peak experiences and fully functioning on this stage:

A slightly different aspect of fully-functioning is effortlessness and ease of functioning when one is at one's best. What takes effort, straining and struggling at other times is now done without any sense of striving, of working or laboring, but "comes of itself." Allied to this often is the feeling of effortless fully-functioning, when everything "clicks," or "is in the groove," or is "in over-drive."

One sees then the appearance of calm sureness and rightness, as if they knew exactly what they were doing, and were doing it wholeheartedly, without doubts, equivocations, hesitations or partial withdrawal... [21]

The person in peak-experiences feels himself, more than at other times, to be the responsible, active, creating center of his activities and of his perceptions. He feels more like a prime mover, more self-determined (rather than caused, determined, helpless, dependent, passive, weak, bossed) ... [22]

He is therefore more spontaneous, more expressive, more innocently behaving (guileless, naïve, honest, candid, ingenuous, childlike, artless, unguarded, defenseless), more natural (simple, relaxed, unhesitant, plain, sincere, unaffected...), more uncontrolled and freely flowing outward... [23]

Wouldn't it be great to be able to function a little more often like this?

While Maslow says that the benefits of personal transformation into a fully-functioning, integrated, Self on this stage can be "ultimately exhilarating and strengthening," remember also that he says that the process of doing so can be "painful at first." This process forces you to confront your various "sources of external value." You will need to take each value and "weigh it, assay it, taste it, and then make your own decision" about it. You will be living intentionally now instead of simply following your old, automatic habit patterns. You will be taking ownership of your values and beliefs. This takes courage. And it may take some time, so don't be in too much of a hurry. And you don't have to do it alone. Share what you are going through with your family and friends. Their feedback will be of value to you, and what you're sharing may be of some help to them. You may want to share your new name with them as well.

It is really a major accomplishment if you can grow through all the stages of consciousness from Egocentric to Conformist to Achievement to Affiliative, and then up to Authentic. Or as Graves and Beck color them – from red to blue to orange to green and up to yellow. Graves and Beck describe yellow (Authentic) as being on a second tier. Yellow is not just the next stage in the sequence, but qualitatively different from the stages in the first tier, more awake and aware, more integrated, and more under the influence of Self. As Self we realize the shortcomings of our present stage and will wish to move on to the next higher stage. We proceed over time, through each of the stages of the first tier until we are ready to make the jump to the second tier. Sometimes Wilber refers to these stages of consciousness as levels, waves, or memes. He describes the jump to second tier as follows. The italics are Wilber's:

With the completion of the green meme, human consciousness is poised for a quantum jump into "second-tier thinking." Clare Graves referred to this as a "momentous leap," where "a chasm of unbelievable depth of meaning is crossed." In essence, with second-tier consciousness, one can think both vertically and horizontally, using both hierarchies and heterarchies; one can, for the first time, *vividly grasp the entire spectrum of interior development,* and thus see that each level, each meme, each wave is crucially important for the health of the overall spiral.

As I would word it, since each wave is "transcend and include," each wave is a fundamental ingredient of all subsequent waves, and thus each is to be cherished and embraced. Moreover, each wave can itself be activated or reactivated as life circumstances warrant. In emergency situations, we can activate red power drives; in response to chaos, we might need to activate blue order; in looking for a new job, we might need orange achievement drives; in marriage and with friends, close green bonding.

But what none of those memes can do, on their own, is fully appreciate the existence of the other memes. Each of those first-tier memes thinks that its worldview is the correct or best perspective. It reacts negatively if challenged; it lashes out, using its own tools, whenever it is threatened. Blue order is very uncomfortable with both red impulsiveness and orange individualism. Orange achievement thinks blue order is for suckers and green bonding is weak and woo-woo. Green egalitarianism cannot easily abide excellence and value rankings, big pictures, or anything that appears authoritarian, and thus it reacts strongly to blue, orange, and anything post-green.

All of that begins to change with second-tier thinking. Because second-tier consciousness is fully aware of the interior stages of development -- even if it cannot articulate them in a technical fashion -- it steps back and grasps the big picture, and thus second-tier thinking appreciates the necessary role that all of the various memes play. Using what we would recognize as vision-logic, second-tier awareness thinks in terms of the overall spiral of existence, and not merely in the terms of any one level.

Where the green meme uses, early or beginning vision-logic in order to grasp the numerous different systems and contexts that exist in different cultures, second-tier thinking goes one step further and begins to *integrate* those pluralistic systems... [24]

Beck estimates that less than 2% of our population is at this second-tier stage.

Psychological growth up to the Authentic Consciousness Stage requires that you, as Self, focus your attention on helping your subpersonalities achieve their objectives. After all, there is a living to earn, a career to pursue, a family to raise, and/or a work of art to complete. Now that you are more aware and awake, you decide on how much time to give to each subpersonality. You eliminate the fragmentation and integrate the strengths, values, and beliefs of each sub into one, whole, authentic, smoothly-functioning personality.

Under conscious direction as Self, you can literally transform your life. It will be a transformation away from the life script that was written for you by others into a life script of your own choosing. Think of your life as a work of art with you as the artist. You can think of it as a four act play with one or two acts already played out and the rest of the script yet to be written. Or you can think of your body/mind as a sculpture with most of its shape already completed but time enough yet to make a few more improvements. Your life affects not only you but also all of those who know you. You are a role model for several in the next generation. Is the life you are now leading the role model you wish to project or are there yet a few minor (or major) adjustments you would like to make? Just remember that the key to being able to make any changes is to wake up to the higher state of consciousness and to function more and more often under the influence of Self.

Under conscious direction as Self, you can decide on how much you will weigh and what physical shape you will be in. You can eliminate, one by one, stressful emotions like anger, fear, and guilt. You will become less judgmental, more forgiving, more joyful, more loving, more at peace. I'm hoping that this book of mine can contribute to helping more and more people to achieve their goals and to find the joy, love, and peace that we are all capable of experiencing.

You can accomplish all of this from whichever stage of consciousness you are now functioning on. I know that I have been pushing you to keep growing up the stages – from conformist blue, to individual achievement orange, to environment concerned green, and finally to Authentic yellow. But you don't have to; you can 'wake up" to the higher "state" of Self from any of the stages and plan your future life according to the values and beliefs of that stage.

While teaching at the School of Public Health in Houston I had a student (wife of a psychiatrist) come up to me after class one day and say, "I am so tired of being pushed to grow, grow, grow all the time. Can I just stay where I am for a while?" I'm not sure who was pushing her more, me or her husband. I told her, "Sure. You can stay where you are for as long as that stage is working for you."

You, too, can stay on whichever stage you are most comfortable on. The urge to grow on usually comes when you become uncomfortable living with the cultural values and beliefs in which you find yourself enmeshed. Keep in mind that growing up the stages is normal growth and development. It takes time, the urge to grow will come and you can continue growing then. Sometimes the urge is a gentle one and you can smoothly move on up to the next stage. Sometimes the urge comes at a time of a major life crisis. In either case your response should be the same. You wake up, self-observe, and start directing your life as Self.

This sounds like a good place to stop. Quite possibly it may have been wiser to have wished you the best of luck and to have ended this book right here. That I didn't do so is obvious, but you may want to stop here, put into practice the methods and concepts discussed so far, and work to achieve the many goals that your various subpersonalities have chosen to pursue.

But don't lose the book, because at some point in your life, your attention may shift away from a preoccupation with achieving those goals. You may begin to wonder if maybe there aren't yet higher stages of consciousness into which to grow and develop, or if maybe there aren't yet higher states to wake up to.

Although most scientists who study normal human growth and development today perceive Authentic Consciousness (yellow) as the highest stage to which humans can aspire, there are some development researchers, psychologists, and philosophers who do say that there are higher stages and states. There isn't as much known about these higher stages and states. There aren't very many humans at these higher stages available for study. But there are some and there are some first-person accounts available describing what it is like to experience higher states and to function at these higher stages.

The higher stages beyond Authentic are usually referred to as transpersonal, asking what are we a part of beyond our personal ego subpersonalities, and transrational, meaning that our reasoning cannot explain all that we observe happening. To move into the transrational stages you have to be willing to accept that reality may not be exactly as we now believe it to be.

Here is yet another reason that it may have been better to have ended this book right here. The stages up to Authentic have been fairly well documented by several researchers. And more importantly, I feel like I have grown through each of them; I have experienced the different feel and perspective of each of the stages. And I feel very confident that I can help you grow through each of the stages up to Authentic.

I cannot say the same about the stages beyond Authentic. I have not been there yet, but I have been exploring what it means to be transrational and transpersonal. I want to share with you now what I am learning about being transrational and transpersonal, just in case you are already wondering if there are yet any more stages beyond Authentic. Let me share with you first what I am learning about being transrational.

Chapter 21
Transrational?

Transrational is a rather worrisome term to those of us who are very proud of our ability to reason. Most of us were pleased with ourselves when we reached the age of reason and were able to grow out of the pre-rational stages, stages Wilber refers to as magic and mythic, and which Beck and Graves color red and blue. Blue, you will recall, is conformist and conventional, the entire culture held entranced by dogma. Everyone is encouraged to be a true believer; individual thought and reasoning are discouraged and to be a "free thinker" is a very derogatory label. Therefore, we are justified in being pleased with ourselves for breaking free of those limiting worldviews. The next three stages – achievement (orange), affiliative (green), and authentic (yellow) – are the rational stages. Science and logical reasoning are held in high regard. What does it mean to be willing to go transrational? Are we being asked to give up being rational?

Not at all, remember that higher stages "transcend and include" the lower stages. We go into the transrational stages fully armed with all the scientific and reasoning skills we have acquired thus far. All that transrational asks of us at the start is that we accept that our reasoning capacity alone may be inadequate to fully comprehend all that really is going on and that we accept that some things are happening for which science and reason have no explanation.

We can start by first considering some examples of strange anomalous phenomena, which do not fit in well with the dominant scientific paradigm. We have all heard reports of experiences, by seemingly honest people that are hard to believe. These reports are usually dismissed either as fraud, mental illness, or at best, we label them to be strange anomalous experiences, maybe true, but hard to fit into our present understanding of how reality works. Some of these strange anomalous phenomena have been studied scientifically.

The way these studies are usually conducted, one person may be looking at the Golden Gate Bridge and another person, miles away, sitting in a relaxed, receptive state, who has no idea where the first one is, draws what the first person is seeing. What will you say if the second person draws a reasonably accurate image of the Golden Gate Bridge?

Or what if a mother tells you she woke up in the middle of the night convinced that something had just happened to her daughter, who lives several states away. The next morning, she gets a phone call confirming that her daughter was in a car accident right about that time.

Or what would think if, at a conference, miles away from your home, you handed your house key to the woman sitting next to you, and she could describe your house to you in surprisingly accurate detail. She should not be able to do this, right? What's easier for you to believe, that she is somehow getting vibes from the key, or that she is simply reading your mind and getting the description directly from you?

What's going on here? Okay, sometimes it is fraud. Con artists are known to exist who delight in taking money from the gullible in an amazing variety of ways. But I think that enough credible reports of this kind have now been documented that we need to consider these as truly strange anomalous experiences, hard to fit into our present understanding of how reality works, and we must then try to alter our worldview so as to make room for them. Now that we have some experience of functioning both in the ego-subpersonality state and in a higher, more aware state as Self, it may be a little easier to speculate on just what is going on here.

Let's take the mother-daughter event first. As ego-subpersonalities mother and daughter can't communicate in any other way than the usual phone calls, texts, or e-mails. But when something as drastic as a car accident happened to the daughter, the energy of that event registers upward into her Self state of consciousness. Somehow the Self of the daughter is able to communicate immediately with the Self of the mother. The mother wakes up and in her "mother-subpersonality" screams at her husband that something has just happened to their daughter. The father, who isn't as "sensitive" to these Self to Self communications, hasn't gotten the message, so he, in his practical spouse subpersonality, says to his wife, "It was just a dream, dear, go back to sleep. We can call her in the morning." When the phone call comes in the morning telling them that their daughter was in a car accident, he is totally surprised and stumped as to how this could have happened.

As for the remote viewing of the Golden Gate Bridge, I don't think it would work if either stayed in their ego-subpersonality states. In our usual state, I can't see what you are looking at. Both of these people have put themselves into a prolonged meditative state, with the sender having the strong intention of transmitting to the receiver whatever it is that he is looking at. The receiver meanwhile has placed herself into a receptive state, intending to receive the image. And again, in a Self to Self state of consciousness, the communication comes through and she is able to draw the bridge.

The house key experience is a little harder for me. I don't understand how "vibes" could exist in the key. So, for me, it is easier to think of this as another form of extra sensory perception (ESP), another Self to Self communication taking place inside a higher state of consciousness. Information from my mind is somehow getting into your mind. Or is it that maybe my mind and your mind are both part of a greater mind and that this greater mind is handling the transfer of information?

Something wonderfully strange is going on here. How would you explain the above phenomena? It is easier to deny that they are happening, but as you become more open to accepting the possibility that these paranormal events are occurring, you will soon be hearing about more and more of them, and quite naturally, you will try to come up with a worldview to believe, that allows for such events to occur.

Philosophers and researchers have developed the concept of "non-local mind" to help in talking about such phenomena. I first read about non-local mind in the works of Russell Targ and Larry Dossey. Targ writes about the remote viewing stuff [25] and Dossey writes about scientific studies that show that praying for someone's health does work, even if the praying is done from thousands of miles away [26]. They describe what we usually think of as being my mind as "my local mind", a mind that works with and handles all the functions of our body. Targ explains remote viewing and Dossey explains how prayer can heal at a distance as an intent transmitted through the distance via a "non-local mind".

It may be that our ego-subpersonalities are functioning within our local mind and that the Self somehow has access to, or is a part of, this greater non-local mind or consciousness. What is the nature of a Self that can transmit and receive information and intent so quickly over such great distances? There is a mystery here which boggles the rational mind.

Assagioli has often struggled with how to present to his patients the nature of this higher Self. In *Psychosynthesis,* he wrote:

> To many, who are confronted for the first time with psychosynthesis, the concept of two selves (a "personal self" and a "higher Self") seems to constitute an obstacle, but the higher Self, for instance, can -- in the beginning of therapy -- simply be presented as a hypothesis which will be verified or disproved later. With some we advise them not to concern themselves about it, particularly where we are dealing with only a personal psychosynthesis (as distinct from a spiritual psychosynthesis) and the Self, therefore, remains more or less in the background.

> In cases where a patient is proceeding towards a subsequent spiritual psychosynthesis, we first point out that there is a sense of self-identity: "I am myself," but that this self-consciousness is generally hazy, because of its many identifications. Therefore, a process of dis-identification is useful in order to become aware of the self-identity. The discussion of the subject with the patient can well be halted at this point, postponing until a much later stage of the treatment

the question of the higher unconscious or superconscious and the spiritual Self...

To be more specific about the presentation of the higher Self: naturally, the same explanation is not suitable for all patients, but with only a little knowledge of a patient's background and mentality we can easily vary our description appropriately. To all who are religious we can say that it is the neutral psychological term used for the soul; for those who are agnostic we use their language: presenting the hypothesis that there is a higher center in man, and explaining that there is a mass of evidence of direct experience of many people -- some in the West and more in the East -- of becoming aware of superconscious contents and of the Self. For instance, we can quote from Bucke's Cosmic Consciousness, from Ouspensky's Tertium Organum, as well as general Eastern and Western (Platonic) philosophy. As a specific example, the patient can be told: "There is evidence of direct awareness, either through spontaneous illumination, or through exercises of concentration, that such realities exist. Later on, if you are interested and when the treatment requires it, we will explore the situation more deeply."

In such ways, we adapt our presentation to the patient's mentality and terminology. We translate our neutral terminology -- e.g., "Self" or "superconscious" -- into his terminology. [27]

Assagioli is saying that "there is evidence of direct awareness...through exercises...that such realities exist." I hope that by now you can say that through your exercises of self-observation, waking-up, and meditation you have some direct awareness that you are a higher Self. It's important to have had this awareness, because it is only as a fully awake and aware Self, that any growth into the transpersonal and transrational stages beyond Authentic can occur.

But how about his equating Self with Soul? He regards Self to be a neutral psychological term, whereas Soul usually carries a lot of religious baggage that may confuse some believers and turn-off agnostics. Up until now Self has been preoccupied with its subpersonalities and concerned with functioning smoothly in society. Now we must ask again, "What is the nature of this Self? Is it a spiritual entity, as Assagioli claims, which exists as part of a yet higher consciousness, but is also attached somehow to this one particular body/mind that we refer to as "I" or "me"?

From the experiences you have had already, you know that the Self is a point source of intelligence and will. You, as Self, can observe and understand how you are functioning in the world and you can willfully direct, to a major degree, how you are functioning in the world. And you seem to be attached in some fundamental way to this one particular (local) body/mind.

But are you completely attached? Is it possible that you, as Self, could exist and function independently of your physical body? Is there any evidence accumulating that would lead us to conclude that, yes indeed, it does seem that the Self can exist independently of the body? It is one thing to *believe* that such is true because your early religious acculturation told you to so believe. But what I keep asking is whether the preponderance of the evidence is such now that it is more rational to hold a worldview that accepts this as so than to hold a worldview that says it is not so. The way the question is usually debated at some of the conferences I attend, is whether or not this Higher Self, which we can and do experience, is somehow just an epiphenomenon of our material brain and destined to die with it, or is it something completely immaterial, which can and does exist apart from, and does survive the death of, our physical body. If we conclude that the Self can function without a physical body, then the Self must be a spiritual entity and we may as well call it Soul, because that is the common usage of Soul. Maybe we are Souls, having incarnated as a physical body, in order to experience what life is like on Planet Earth.

And just what is this evidence that is accumulating to support the premise that the Self can exist apart from our bodies? There are now several reports from credible, rational people that they have had either an out-of-body experience (OOBE), a near-death experience (NDE), or a past life recall. What all of these experiences have in common is that in each instance the person retains a memory of having existed and of being able to function apart from his or her current physical body. First let's consider OOBEs and NDEs.

Chapter 22
Out-of-Body Experiences

I first read about OOBEs in 1977 in Robert Monroe's book, *Journeys Out of the Body.* Monroe was a normal ordinary business man with a family to support. In the late 1950s he began occasionally to experience vibrations all over his body before falling asleep. This worried him and he discussed it with his doctor. After a thorough exam, his doctor assured him that he didn't think that he was going crazy and that he didn't think he had a tumor on his brain. He was told to relax and to see what would happen. Here is how he describes what happened some four weeks later:

It was late at night and I was lying in bed before sleep. My wife had fallen asleep beside me. There was a surge that seemed to be in my head, and quickly the condition spread through my body. It all seemed the same. As I lay there trying to decide how to analyze the thing in another way, I just happened to think how nice it would be to take a glider up and fly the next afternoon (my hobby at that time). Without considering any consequences -- not knowing there would be any -- I thought of the pleasure it would bring.

After a moment, I became aware of something pressing against my shoulder. Half-curious, I reached back and up to feel what it was. My hand encountered a smooth wall. I moved my hand along the wall the length of my arm and it continued smooth and unbroken.

My senses fully alert, I tried to see in the dim light. It was a wall, and I was lying against it with my shoulder. I immediately reasoned that I had gone to sleep and fallen out of bed. (I had never done so before, but all sorts of strange things were happening, and falling out of bed was quite possible.)

Then I looked again. Something was wrong. This wall had no windows, no furniture against it, no doors. It was not a wall in my bedroom. Yet somehow it was familiar. Identification came instantly. It wasn't a wall; it was the ceiling. I was floating against the ceiling, bouncing gently with any movement I made. I rolled in the air, startled, and looked down. There, in the dim light below me, was the bed. There were two figures lying in the bed. To the right was my wife. Beside her was someone else. Both seemed asleep.

This was a strange dream, I thought. I was curious. Who would I dream to be in bed with my wife? I looked more closely, and the shock was intense. I was the someone on the bed!

My reaction was almost instantaneous. Here I was, there was my body. I was dying, this was death, and I wasn't ready to die. Somehow, the vibrations were killing me. Desperately, like a diver, I swooped down to my body and dove in. I then felt the bed and the covers, and when I opened my eyes, I was looking at the room from the perspective of my bed.

What had happened? Had I truly almost died? My heart was beating rapidly, but not unusually so. I moved my arms and legs. Everything seemed normal. The vibrations had faded away. I got up and walked around the room, looked out the window, smoked a cigarette.

It was a long time before I had the courage to return to lie down, and try to sleep. [28]

Monroe then paid another visit to his psychologist friend, Dr. Bradshaw and told him what had happened. He also told him he was worried that he would die. Here is the dialogue that followed:

I met with Dr. Bradshaw, my psychologist friend. He was even less helpful and far from sympathetic when I told him the story. He thought I should try to repeat the experience if I could. I told him I wasn't ready to die.

"Oh, I don't think you'll do that," Dr. Bradshaw stated calmly. "Some of the fellows who practice yoga and those Eastern religions claim they can do it whenever they want to."

I asked him "do" what.

"Why, get out of the physical body for a while," he replied. "They claim they can go all over the place. You ought to try it."

I told him that was ridiculous. Nobody can travel around without their physical body.

"Well, I wouldn't be too sure," Dr. Bradshaw replied calmly. "You ought to read something about the Hindus. Did you study any philosophy in college?"

I said I had, but there was nothing I could recall about this traveling-without-the-body business.

"Maybe you didn't have the right philosophy professor, that's what it seems to me." Dr. Bradshaw lit a cigar, then looked at me. "Well, don't be so closed-minded. Try it and find out..." [29]

Monroe did try it and he found out a lot. Soon he lost his fear of leaving his body behind and learned to leave the room he was in to visit friends and places. At first he always traveled with the intent of seeing something during his OOBE that he had not seen before, which he could later describe and thereby prove to himself that he was really there. Here is a quote from his notes of 9/10/58:

Again, I floated upward, with the intent of visiting Dr. Bradshaw and his wife. Realizing that Dr. Bradshaw was ill in bed with a cold, I thought I would visit him in the bedroom, which was a room I had not seen in his house and if I could describe it later, could thus document my visit. Again, came the turning in air, the dive into the tunnel, and this time the sensation of going uphill (Dr. and Mrs. Bradshaw live in a house some five miles from my office, up a hill). I was over trees and there was a light sky above.

Then I came upon Dr. and Mrs. Bradshaw. They were outside the house, and for a moment I was confused, as I had reached them before I got to the house. I didn't understand this because Dr. Bradshaw was supposed to be in bed. Dr. Bradshaw was dressed in light overcoat and hat, his wife in a dark coat and all dark clothes. They were coming toward me, so I stopped. They seemed in good spirits, and walked past me unseeing, in the direction of a smaller building, like a garage, Brad trailing behind as they walked.

I floated around in front of them, waving, trying to get their attention without result. Then without turning his head, I thought I heard Dr. Bradshaw say to me, "Well, I see you don't need help anymore." Thinking I had made contact, I dove back into the ground (?), and returned to the office, rotated into the body and opened my eyes. Everything was just as I had left it. The vibration was still present, but I felt I had enough for one day.

Important aftermath: We phoned Dr. and Mrs. Bradshaw that evening. I made no statement other than to ask where they were between four and five that afternoon. (My wife, upon hearing of the visit, said flatly it was not possible, could not be so because Dr. Bradshaw was home in bed sick.) With Mrs. Bradshaw on the phone, I asked the simple question. She stated that roughly at four twenty-five they were walking out of the house toward the garage. She was going to the post office, and Dr. Bradshaw had decided that perhaps some fresh air might help him, and had dressed and gone along. She knew the time by back-checking from the time they arrived at the post office, which was twenty minutes to five. It takes roughly fifteen minutes to drive to the post office from their house. I had come back from my trip to them at approximately four twenty-seven. I asked what they were wearing. Mrs. Bradshaw stated she was wearing black slacks, and a red sweater which was covered with a black car coat. Dr. Bradshaw was wearing a light hat and a light-colored topcoat. However, neither saw me in any way or were aware of my presence. Dr. Bradshaw had no memory of saying anything to me. The great point is that I had expected to find him in bed, and didn't.

The coincidences involved were too much. It was not important to prove this to anyone else. Only to me. It proves to me – truly for the first time – that there might well be more to this than normal science and psychology and psychiatry allow – more than an aberration, trauma, or hallucination – and I need some form of proof more than anyone else, I am sure. It is a simple incident, but unforgettable. [30]

Monroe made many more out-of-body trips and founded the Monroe Institute to help others learn to have OOBEs. You can read about them all in his three published books. For now, all I am asking you to do is to be open to this possibility, just in case you find yourself someday outside of your body.

Michael Murphy, in his book, *The Future of the Body*, describes several OOBEs reported in the literature. One story concerns an S.R. Wilmot, who while on a ship at sea, dreamed that he was visited by his wife:

> Toward morning I dreamed that I saw my wife, whom I had left in the United States, come to the door of my state-room, clad in her night-dress. At the door, she seemed to discover that I was not the only occupant of the room, hesitated a little, then advanced to my side, stooped down and kissed me, and after gently caressing me for a few moments, quietly withdrew.

> Upon waking I was surprised to see my fellow-passenger, whose berth was above mine, but not directly over it, leaning upon his elbow, and looking fixedly at me. "You're a pretty fellow," said he at length, "to have a lady come and visit you in this way." I pressed him for an explanation, which he at first declined to give, but at length related what he had seen while wide awake, lying in his berth. It exactly corresponded with my dream. [31]

When he returned home, his wife asked him if he had noticed her visit. She then said:

"Tell me, do they ever have state-rooms like the one I saw, where the upper berth extends further back than the under one? A man was in the upper berth, looking right at me, and for a moment I was afraid to go in, but soon I went up to the side of your berth, bent down and kissed you, and embraced you, and then went away." [32]

Wilmot then states, "The description given by my wife of the steamship was correct in all particulars, though she had never seen it." [32]

Another OOBE that Murphy describes is one where a Mr. S.H.B. made an out-of-body visit to Misses L.S. and E.C. Verity and both of the Veritys confirmed having seen him in their room at 1 am. Murphy then states:

Experiences such as the Wilmots' and the Veritys' resemble a phenomenon long reported in the contemplative traditions, namely bilocation, the simultaneous appearance by a yogi or saint in more than one location. In the New Catholic Encyclopedia, bilocation is listed among the principal charisms of Christian devotion. It is also a result of the akasha and moksha siddhis of Indian yoga and is described in the lore of Taoism, Tibetan Buddhism, and Sufism. Rejecting the superstitious belief that such experience involves the physical body's existence in two places at once, we find witness to traveling clairvoyance among both modern and ancient peoples. But as we have seen, such events are not limited to religious adepts. They frequently occur spontaneously, during illness, near-death experience, vivid dreams, or intense adventure. A rock climber, for example, claimed that "about 15 or 20 feet above the ground, I slipped and fell. As I fell, I seemed to be about 5 or 10 feet out from the face, looking at my body falling. I vaguely recollect moving around to the other side of my body to look at it. Once I hit the ground, I was immediately preoccupied with my pain. "[33]

Besides reporting on OOBEs, Murphy's whole book is a compendium of strange anomalous phenomena that the rational mind finds hard to understand.

One night, soon after I began reading Monroe's "Journeys Out of the Body", I found myself floating near our bedroom ceiling. I remember having the thought, "Hey, I did it. I'm having an OOBE, just like Monroe." Next morning, I dismissed the whole experience as being simply a dream. Told myself that before I would say to anyone that I had had and OOBE, I would have to be able to move out of our bedroom and go, at least, to the next room to visit where our boys were sleeping or three rooms over to where Susan's dad was sleeping.

I did experience being out of my body, floating near our ceiling, three more times over the next two weeks. But I was never able to leave our room. I just remember floating there near the ceiling for a while.

In January 1978, our son John and I were involved in a major car accident. Our legs were crushed and both of us had broken bones in our legs. My head hit the steering wheel and I drifted in and out of consciousness for thirty minutes. The accident occurred about one mile from home while we were driving the three miles between my sister's home and our house. It was around 7 pm.

I don't remember much of what happened immediately before or after the accident but one memory I distinctly do have is of floating out of my body about 50 feet above the mangled cars. I remember looking across the field towards our farmhouse and thinking, "Wow! Look how far I am now from my bedroom ceiling." That's it, that's all I remember. I know it would make a better story if I could say that I zoomed down to look over our injuries and then zoomed over to our house and tried to get Susan's attention. Maybe I did, but I don't remember.

Brief and unsatisfying as this experience was, the memory of it has stuck with me. I now know what it feels like to exist outside of my body. And I continue occasionally to try willing myself out of my body and zooming over to a friend's house, then calling her the next day to verify what I saw. But with no success, so far. I mentioned this to a friend one day and he surprised me with several stories of his own of having had OOBEs. And he had two friends who also have had OOBEs. Perhaps it is not as rare as we now think, since people usually do not talk readily about such experiences.

Further evidence that our Self can exist independently from our physical brain is accumulating in reports of people having Near Death Experiences (NDES). Let me share with you now what I am learning about NDEs.

Chapter 23
Near Death Experiences (NDEs)

NDEs have been studied extensively since 1975 by many research scientists, most notably by Raymond Moody, M.D. and by Kenneth Ring, PhD. NDEs happen to people who almost die but are then resuscitated and live to tell the story of what happened. The near death can be from any cause – a drowning, a car accident, a heart attack, etc. One Gallup survey estimated that approximately "15% of all adult Americans or about 23,000,000 people, said they had a close brush with death involving an unusual experience and of that number about 8,000,000 have experienced some sort of mystical encounter along with the death event." [34]

Before 1975 most physicians were reluctant to give any credence to reports by their patients of the fantastic experiences they had during the time they were almost dead. In 1975 Dr. Moody published *Life after Life*, a groundbreaking book wherein he described accounts of fifty NDE stories that he had heard. Such was the impact of this book that others soon began listening for NDE stories from their patients. Some scientists undertook research studies to document the commonalities. NDEs happen to children as well as to adults and although no two stories are exactly alike, all have one or more of the following characteristics: 1) an out-of-body experience (OOBE), 2) passage through a dark tunnel, 3) meeting the Bright Being of Light, 4) encounters with dead loved ones, 5) a life review, and 6) a decision to return to their injured bodies.

During the OOBE, the Near-Death Experiencers (NDErs) sense themselves floating above their injured bodies and witnessing all the efforts by others trying to revive them. They can remember enough of what they witness that they can later tell the others what they were doing, much to their amazement. Several of the NDEs occurred in hospital settings, after a patient's heart stopped beating. During the resuscitation efforts of doctors and nurses, the patients experienced themselves as Selves floating above the body, witnessing all of the efforts below. After the successful resuscitation, the patients were able to describe in surprising detail to the doctors and nurses what they observed while floating out of their bodies - things like what was said, who was in the room, who did what. Some were even able to report on seeing things that could not have been seen from room level. One reported seeing a shoe on a ledge outside a window several floors higher. A nurse on hearing this claim went up to the window, leaned out and verified that the accurately described shoe was indeed there.

Dr. Ring reports that even blind people have such OOBEs and can also describe what they "saw" while floating above their bodies. This usually really amazes people but it really isn't any more amazing than OOBEs described by people with normal vision because during this particular time the physical eyes are closed. The observations are taking place through means other than the usual retina via optic nerve to the visual cortex. Some NDErs remember nothing more than their OOBEs before they return to their bodies and to life.

Others may next feel themselves to be in a dark tunnel, whooshing rapidly towards a light at the end of the tunnel. When they reach the light, they describe it as a very bright light that completely envelops them. They feel the presence of a loving Being in the light. Some call it a Being of Light. They feel loved by this Being of Light like they have never been loved before. Depending on their religious beliefs and stages of consciousness, they think of the Being of Light as Jesus, or Buddha, or Krishna, or by some as God. There are even some reports by atheists and agnostics saying something like, "I don't know who it was, but I really did feel loved by that light."

Thoughts are exchanged. No words as such are spoken, but communication does take place between the Being of Light and the NDEr. For some a life review takes place wherein they experience again all the encounters they ever had throughout their life. This review is described as taking place in a loving environment. There is no sense of judgment or threat of punishment. They simply feel the effects their actions had had on others. The life review goes by very quickly, some saying that it is almost like you get it all at once.

One man described an incident that took place when he was eight. He was told by his father to go mow his Aunt Gay's yard. Previously Aunt Gay had told him not to ever cut down some weeds in a corner of her yard that had some wildflowers growing on them. She wanted to make tiaras for some girls from them. But in a fit of rebellion, he decided to cut them down. Nothing was even said at the time, but thirty years later during his life review he experienced the feelings Aunt Gay had on finding the flowers cut down. On a much more serious note, another man reported that he had been an assassin for the CIA and had actually killed several people. During his life review, he experienced the feelings of the dead man's wife and children and was shown how the death had affected the rest of their lives.

Before, during, or after the life review, some were visited by some of their dead loved ones. These dead loved ones don't usually "say" much, but hover around to greet and support the NDEr. In 1984 I was sitting by my mother's bedside as she lay dying at our local hospital. At one point, she started telling me that her mother, father, brothers, sister, and some friends were there to greet her. She faded in and out of consciousness all that afternoon. Later that evening my wife came by to visit and started to talk with her. My mother opened her eyes and exclaimed, "Susan, what are you doing here?" Susan explained that she had been in the hospital making rounds on her patients and that she dropped in to see her. At this point my mother said, "I mean, what are you doing HERE?" It was obvious to us that my mother didn't consider herself to be in a hospital anymore. She closed her eyes and never again regained consciousness.

The NDErs report that at one point they were told that it is not yet time for them to stay and that they must return to living. Some pleaded to be allowed to stay but were told that there was still something they needed to accomplish on earth. Some NDErs report that they were given a choice in this matter and that they chose to come back because someone here needed them.

So, what are we to make of these NDE stories? Throughout this book I have encouraged you to develop the skill of switching your sense of "I" from a complete identification with your body and ego subpersonalities to identifying with the Self, a Witness observing what the ego subpersonalities are doing. This is difficult to do under normal circumstances, so we have to develop specific practices like self-observation, waking up, life review, and meditation, all of which try to give you the experience of functioning as the Witness or Observer. But usually it is only a partial experience because it is hard to shed the identity of our ego subpersonalities. What is going on here with the NDErs is that they are experiencing what it is like to completely function as Self or Soul, because they have left their bodies and ego subpersonalities behind.

The near-death experience has had a tremendous impact on all who have had one. Their subsequent lives have been transformed. They no longer fear death. They are now convinced that there is more life after this life. Those who have encountered the bright, loving, Being of Light now know that life after death takes place in a loving environment. Remember from the stats given earlier, there are now millions of NDErs throughout the world, all telling their children and grandchildren about the loving Being of Light and what happens to you right after you die.

Is it proof of life after death and proof of God's existence? I think not, certainly not by what most scientists and philosophers regard as proof. But it is something; it is more evidence that will need to be considered by us as we formulate our own worldview or story of what this life on earth is all about, a story by which we will live the rest of our lives.

If you have been swayed by the theory that the NDE is merely the result of oxygen deprivation to the dying brain, there is now some evidence that you do not have to nearly die to have an experience of the Being of Light. In the Afterword to the 2001 edition of *Life after Life,* Dr. Moody describes a startling phenomenon that he calls "the empathic death experience." He says:

> It is very common for someone at the bedside of a person who is dying to participate empathetically in the dying experience of that other person. Hundreds of wonderful people from all walks of life have related to me that, as a loved one died, they themselves lifted out of their own bodies and accompanied their dying loved ones toward a beautiful and loving light. They also describe seeing deceased relatives coming to greet the one who was passing away. In fact, all of the elements commonly thought of as defining the near-death experience also are mentioned by those who report empathic death experiences. [35]

More evidence that we may not need to wait until we die to encounter the Being of Light is to read about the experiences of the mystics and saints. Judith Cressy has studied the writings of mystics and saints, describing experiences they have had while doing contemplative prayer or meditation. Cressy found similarities in their stories to those reported by the NDErs. One of her examples is the following quote from St. Theresa of Avila:

> I thought I was being carried up to Heaven: the first persons I saw there were my mother and father, and such great things happened in so short a time. I wish I could give a description of at least the smallest part of what I learned, but when I try to discover a way of doing so, I find it impossible, for while the light we see here and that other light are both light, there is no comparison between the two and the brightness of the sun seems quite dull if compared with the other. (Afterwards) I was...left with very little fear of death of which previously I had been very much afraid. (Theresa 1960, 361-63) [36]

Cressy goes on to say:

> ...NDErs and mystics differ, however, in intention, preparation, understanding, techniques, and communities for reintegration. On the spiritual path, growth is slow. Each experience is accompanied by an integration of the emotional,

intellectual, and physical components of the individual. Unlike the mystic, the NDEr is suddenly jettisoned unprepared into another world and the higher reaches of spiritual consciousness. Often the NDEr must make up emotional and intellectual deficiencies by entering school, counseling, a new career, or a spiritual path. Unlike the mystic, NDErs return to an alien community rather than to a monastery. They return to a culture dominated by secular materialism, with little understanding of and less interest in mysticism. They may misunderstand their own experience. The difficult task of reentering life and recovery from death is compounded by the often-negative feed-back provided the NDEr by his/her own community. [36]

And finally, there is Kenneth Ring to tell us that you do not need to have an NDE to benefit from its life transforming effects. Although most of Ring's research has been on the transforming effects the NDE had had on the NDEr, he also explored the effects that simply reading about NDEs has had on people. He is now convinced that by becoming familiar with NDE stories, you, too, can experience many of the same beneficial changes in your life. Here is how he describes this research in *Lessons from the Light*:

In general, then, the overall pattern of our data here gives us a strong suggestion that merely acquiring knowledge about NDEs can act rather like a "benign virus"; that is, by exposing yourself to NDE-related information, you can "catch it," because the NDE appears to be contagious. Therefore, it seems quite plausible to argue that in this way you can reap some of the benefits of an NDE -- possibly for life -- without having to go to the extremity of throwing yourself under the wheels of the nearest oncoming train, like a modern-day Anna Karenina, in order to induce the experience. Clearly, this book is based on that very premise, and if it is correct, you should already be showing some signs of having contracted the condition from which NDErs "suffer" and thus seeing the world with eyes not unlike theirs. [37]

Dr. Ring has taught classes on the NDE at the U. of Conn. for over 15 years. During the classes the students read many books written by NDErs and many books by researchers on

NDErs. They were shown video interviews and had guest lecturers come in to describe their own NDEs and to answer questions. After the Course was over, Ring would query the students about the effect that exposure to the NDE has had on them. The following are some of the responses he has received:

I feel I have become more spiritual, and it also has reinforced my beliefs about the unimportance of wealth and material objects.

I feel that the most important thing I gained from my study of the NDE is a higher spiritual sense and a greater belief in God.

I have less fear of death ... [and] am more spiritual.

[What] I have gained most from studying NDEs is that love is the driving force of all humanity. I have reevaluated my beliefs about God, reincarnation, and spirituality in that my belief in them is stronger. I felt that, with this course, I have grown as a person.

What I have gained from studying the NDE this semester: (1) more compassion for all people; (2) less fear of the ending of this life; (3) more open-mindedness to learn as much as I can, while I still can.

I have found a spirituality that has been hiding within myself. I see how I affect others more, and I want to let this new spirituality grow over time.

I have felt a feeling of being set free from much of the negative aspects of life. I have gained some profound self-knowledge and an increased sense of self-worth. I have become more appreciative of life and love. I feel less negative -- and I have less animosity toward others. I feel this course has been extremely helpful in my life.

A more spiritual view of myself and the world. The understanding of what is REALLY [her capitalization] important in life, and a break from some of the materialistic values that I had.

The very exposure to NDEs was interesting and enlightening. I feel this course has made me more open-minded and caring...The NDE has given me a positive outlook on death and life. [37]

Ring then goes on to elaborate on the study design and points out some conclusions he has reached:

This little survey of mine has since been repeated in two more NDE courses -- one that I taught the following semester, the other, a similarly structured course at another university -- with virtually identical results. This makes it clear that these findings do not depend in any way on the instructor involved, and makes it more likely they can be attributed solely to the content of the material presented in NDE courses.

Now that we have a general picture of the outcome of these studies, what is it reasonable to conclude in regard to the benign virus hypothesis?

Despite the small, self-selected nature of the samples and the ad hoc character of these surveys, one general finding shines forth from these studies that is undeniable: These students expressed sentiments, feelings, values, and beliefs that are indistinguishable from those commonly uttered by NDErs themselves. The same effects that NDErs tend to attribute to their experience, these students indicated derived from their exposure to their course on NDEs. What this suggests is certainly in accord with the benign virus hypothesis: It appears as if some of the benefits of the NDE can be transmitted vicariously, simply by presenting relevant information on the subject to individuals who are or become interested in NDEs. The implications are obviously profound. And specifically, for readers of this book, there is now additional evidence not only to support the idea that what happened to my students can also happen to you, but, in all probability, it already has. [37]

He's right. I think that I have caught that virus, for I, too, no longer fear death, think of it as merely a transition, and I look forward to meeting that Being of Light and having my life review.

Actually, I may be having my life review already. I am finding similarities between what is happening in my morning meditation sessions and some of the life review as described by the NDErs. Frequently while sitting quietly in meditation, thoughts from my past come up dealing with unkind things I have done to others. Even though I try not to get hooked on them, during the few moments that I do dwell on them, I feel some of the remorse and sadness for not having been more kind and loving at the time. Maybe some of these experiences during meditation are having the same effect on me as the NDErs report their life review had on them. We both are becoming more kind and loving now in our relationships with others.

So, go read Ring's book, *Lessons from the Light*, you'll enjoy it and you, too, may catch the benign NDE virus. This will be a very transrational thing for you to do, and you may earn yourself some "unpredictability" points.

What are we to make of these reports on OOBEs and NDEs? On hearing such a story from only one person, it would be easy to dismiss it as dream imagery, but on noting the consistency in the reports from several people, who had not compared stories beforehand, I have to conclude that, yes, it does seem like, as Selves, we are able to function independently of our physical brain. But what about you, dear reader? Are you ready to conclude that what you have experienced as a Self may indeed be able to function independently of your physical body? Need more evidence? Okay, let me now share with you what I am learning from reports on past lives.

Chapter 24
Past Lives

Another set of evidence that, as Self, you can exist and function outside of the body are the scientific studies on past life experiences. Ian Stephenson, a physician and head of the Dept. of Psychiatry at the U. of Virginia Medical School, has documented hundreds of reports in children who remember having lived a past life. He has conducted numerous field trips in Lebanon and India to verify these children's stories by interviewing them as well as interviewing the rest of the family of which the child claims to have been a member.

The usual report goes something like the following. A child starts telling his parents that he has another family in another town and describes that family's composition in great detail complete with names. The child states that he would like to visit his previous family. The parents contact someone they know in the other town and find out that indeed such a family exists and that that family had lost a child. Often they would then pay a visit to the previous family. The child then demonstrates that he is able to identify each of the members of the previous family and tells stories from memory that no one else could have known except their child who had died.

Dr. Stephenson would interview both families to ascertain their credibility and to detect if there was anything for anybody to gain by fabricating such a story. Sometimes he got to the previous family before the current family had a chance to visit them and then he could witness the identifications and disclosures first hand. As a result of his field investigations, Stephenson has become convinced that reincarnation is happening and that there are now enough of such reports that any open-minded person will be led to allow for reincarnation in his or her worldview. Probably the easiest way to acquaint yourself with Stephenson's work is to read Tom Shroder's *Old Souls*. Shroder is a reporter who accompanied Stephenson on some of his field investigations. He started out as a skeptic, but slowly as his encounters with these children and their families continued, he, too, became convinced.

Another series of books that influenced my view of reincarnation were those by Brian L. Weiss, MD, another psychiatrist, who practices in Miami and gives workshops around the country. In his first book, *Many Lives, Many Masters*, he describes himself as one who did not believe in reincarnation until he worked with Catherine, a Catholic, who also did not believe in reincarnation. Catherine had been suffering from panic attacks and anxiety. She was referred to Dr. Weiss. After 18 months of regular psychotherapy, which had not reduced the symptoms, Weiss suggested they try hypnosis. Here is how he describes hypnosis:

"Hypnosis is an excellent tool to help a patient remember long-forgotten incidents. There is nothing mysterious about it. It is just a state of focused concentration. Under the instruction of a trained hypnotist, the patient's body relaxes, causing the memory to sharpen. I had hypnotized hundreds of patients and had found it helpful in reducing anxiety, eliminating phobias, changing bad habits, and aiding in the recall of repressed material. On occasion, I had been successful in regressing patients back to their early childhoods, even to when they were two or three years old, thus eliciting the memories of long-forgotten traumas that were disrupting their lives. I felt confident that hypnosis would help Catherine." [38]

While working with her in this way, Catherine remembered traumatic incidents in her life from the time she was six years old back to when she was three years old, but none of these memories helped in relieving her symptoms. Then one day, frustrated that none of the memories elicited so far were able to relieve her symptoms, Weiss instructed Catherine to, "Go back to the time from which your symptoms arise." He says he was "totally unprepared for what came next." What Catherine recalled was a memory of a past life in which she had a child, who she was able to recognize as Rachel, who is presently her niece. Weiss continues:

I was startled. My stomach knotted, and the room felt cold. Her visualizations and recall seemed so definite. She was not at all tentative. Names, dates, clothes, trees-all seen vividly! What was going on here? How could the child she had then be her niece now? I was even more confused. I had examined thousands of psychiatric patients, many under hypnosis, and I had never come across fantasies like this before-not even in dreams. I instructed her to go forward to the time of her death. I wasn't sure how to interview someone in the middle of such an explicit fantasy (or memory?), but I was on the lookout for traumatic events that might underlie current fears or symptoms. The events around the time of death could be particularly traumatic. Apparently, a flood or tidal wave was devastating the village. [39]

Catherine describes what she sees happening:

"There are big waves knocking down trees. There's no place to run. It's cold; the water is cold. I have to save my baby, but I cannot . . . just have to hold her tight. I drown; the water chokes me. I can't breathe, can't swallow . . . salty water. My baby is torn out of my arms." [Catherine was gasping and having difficulty breathing. Suddenly her body relaxed completely, and her breathing became deep and even.] "I see clouds. . .. My baby is with me. And others from my village. I see my brother." [39]

Weiss continues;

She was resting; this lifetime had ended. She was still in a deep trance. I was stunned! Previous lifetimes? Reincarnation? My clinical mind told me that she was not fantasizing this material, that she was not making this up. Her thoughts, her expressions, the attention to particular details, all were different from her conscious state. The whole gamut of possible psychiatric diagnoses flashed through my mind, but her psychiatric state and her character structure did not explain these revelations. Schizophrenia? No, she had never had any evidence of a cognitive or thinking disorder. She had never experienced any auditory hallucinations of hearing voices, visual hallucinations or visions while awake, or any other type of psychotic episodes. She was not delusional, nor was she out of touch with reality. She did not have multiple or split personalities. There was only one Catherine, and her conscious mind was totally aware of this. She had no sociopathic or antisocial tendencies. She was not an actress. She did not use drugs, nor did she ingest hallucinogenic substances. Her use of alcohol was minimal. She had no neurological or psychological illnesses that could explain this vivid, immediate experience while hypnotized.

These were memories of some sort, but from where? My gut reaction was that I had stumbled upon something I knew very little about -- reincarnation and past-life memories. It couldn't be, I told myself; my scientifically trained mind resisted it. Yet here it was, happening right before my eyes. I couldn't explain it, but I couldn't deny the reality of it either. [40]

There were several other past lives explored during this session. Afterwards Weiss worried that Catherine, prone to anxieties and fears to begin with, might be too frightened to undergo hypnosis again. Weiss continues:

One week later, Catherine bounced into my office for her next hypnosis session. Beautiful to begin with, she was more radiant than ever. She happily announced that her lifelong fear of drowning had disappeared. Her fears of choking were somewhat diminished. Her sleep was no longer interrupted by the nightmare of a collapsing bridge. Although she had re-membered the details of her past-life recall, she had not yet truly integrated the material.

The concepts of past lives and reincarnation were alien to her cosmology, and yet her memories were so vivid, the sights and sounds and smells so clear, the knowledge that she was there so powerful and immediate, that she felt she must have actually been there. She did not doubt this; the experience was so overwhelming. Yet she was concerned about how this fit in with her upbringing and her beliefs. [41]

Weiss, too, was having problems with how this fit in with his upbringing, beliefs, and training:

> With a new insatiable hunger for any scientific papers that had been published on reincarnation, I hunted through the medical libraries. I studied the works of Ian Stevenson, M.D., a well-respected Professor of Psychiatry at the University of Virginia, who has published extensively in the psychiatric literature. Dr. Stevenson has collected over two thousand examples of children with reincarnation-type memories and experiences. Many exhibited xenoglossy, the ability to speak a foreign language to which they were never exposed. His case reports are carefully complete, well-researched, and truly remarkable.
>
> I read an excellent scientific overview by Edgar Mitchell. With great interest, I examined the ESP data from Duke University, and the writings of Professor C. J. Ducasse of Brown University, and I intently analyzed the studies of Dr. Martin Ebon, Dr. Helen Wambach, Dr. Gertrude Schmeidler, Dr. Frederick Lenz, and Dr. Edith Fiore. The more I read, the more I wanted to read. I began to realize that even though I had considered myself well educated about every dimension of the mind, my education had been very limited. There are libraries filled with this research and literature, and few people know about it. Much of this research was conducted, verified, and replicated by reputable clinicians and scientists. Could they all be mistaken or deceived? The evidence seemed to be overwhelmingly supportive, yet I still doubted. Overwhelming or not, I found it difficult to believe.
>
> Both Catherine and I, in our own ways, had already been profoundly affected by the experience. Catherine was improving emotionally, and I was expanding the horizons of my mind. Catherine had been tormented by her fears for many years and was finally feeling some relief. Whether through actual memories or vivid fantasies, I had found a way to help her, and I was not going to stop now. [42]

Weiss continued to work with Catherine and over the next several sessions, as Catherine continued to improve, both came to accept that this was indeed past life recall and that it was helping her with her symptoms.

Weiss has now worked with many more patients and has written several more books. In his book, *Only Love is Real*, he tells the story of Pedro, whom he had regressed several times and had in his records several past lives that Pedro had recalled. In one life, he is dragged to death behind some soldiers' horses. He remembers dying with his head cradled in his daughter's lap. He also recalls one life in Mongolia in which he returns home from an excursion and finds his village plundered and all his family killed. His young wife was missing and he never saw her again. He assumed she was dead.

Weiss also tells the story of Elizabeth, another of his patients, and he has in his records several of her past life recalls. In one life, she remembered cradling her father's head in her lap as he lay dying after being dragged behind some soldiers' horses. And she also recalled one life in which her...

> ... husband was away with most of the other men, hunting and raiding. The enemy struck, flying in on waves of horses against the depleted defenders. Her husband's parents were killed first, hacked down by broad, razor sharp swords. Her baby was killed next, gutted by a spear. A shudder convulsed her spirit. She wanted to die, too, but such was not her destiny. Captured by the young warriors because of her beauty, she became the property of the strongest of the invading horde. [43]

She lived with her abductors for several years before committing suicide.

Elizabeth and Pedro did not know each other. One evening as Weiss was reviewing his patients' records, he became convinced that Pedro and Elizabeth had been in each other's past lives several times. He writes:

> But they did not know. Only I knew. Father and daughter. Childhood lovers. Husband and wife. How many more times throughout history had they shared their lives and their love?

They were together again, but they didn't know it. Both were lonely, both suffering in their way. Both were starving, and yet a feast had been set before them, a feast they could not yet smell or taste.

I was severely constrained by the "laws" of psychiatry, if not the subtler rules of karma. The strictest of the laws is that of privacy or confidentiality. If psychiatry were a religion, breaching a patient's confidentiality would be one of its cardinal sins. At the least the breach could constitute malpractice. I could not tell Pedro about Elizabeth, nor Elizabeth about Pedro. Whatever the karma or spiritual consequences of intervening in another's free will, the consequences of violating psychiatry's main law were quite clear.

The spiritual consequences would not have deterred me. I could introduce them and let destiny take its course. The psychiatric consequences stopped me cold.

What if I were wrong? What if a relationship between them began, soured, and ended badly? There could be anger and bitterness. How would this reflect back on their feelings about me as their trusted therapist? Would their clinical improvement unravel? Would all their good therapeutic work be undone? There were definite risks.

I also had to examine my own subconscious motives. Was my need to see my patients become happier and healthier, to find peace and love in their lives, affecting my judgment now? Were my own needs urging me to cross the boundary of psychiatric ethics?

The easy choice would be to leave well enough alone, to say nothing. No harm done, no consequences. When in doubt, do no harm. [44]

But Weiss soon found that he couldn't leave at that. He continues:

I was wrestling with time, and it had me in a bear hug. Pedro was about to finish his therapy and move permanently to

Mexico. If Pedro and Elizabeth did not meet soon, they would be in different countries, and the likelihood of their meeting in this lifetime would be dramatically diminished. Both of their grief reactions were resolving. Physical symptoms, such as quality of sleep, energy levels, and appetite, were better in both patients.

Their loneliness and their despair of finding a good and loving relationship remained intact.

Anticipating Pedro's termination of therapy, I had reduced the frequency of his appointments to every other week. I did not have much time left.

I arranged for their next visits to be sequential, for Pedro to follow Elizabeth in the hourly schedule that day. Everybody entering or leaving my office has to pass through the waiting room.

During Elizabeth's session, I worried that Pedro might not come in for his appointment. Things happen-cars break down, emergencies arise, illnesses develop-and appointments are changed.

He appeared. I walked into the waiting room with Elizabeth. They looked at each other, and their eyes lingered for longer than a moment. I could sense the sudden interest, the hint at worlds of possibilities lying under the surface. Or was this just wishful thinking on my part?

Elizabeth's mind quickly reasserted its customary mastery, telling her she needed to leave, cautioning her about appropriate behavior. She turned to the outside door and left the offices.

I nodded to Pedro, and we walked into my office. "A very attractive woman," he commented, as he sat down heavily in the large leather chair.

"Yes," I answered eagerly. "She's a very interesting person, too."

"That's nice," he said wistfully. His attention had already begun to wander. He turned to the task of terminating our sessions and moving on to the next phase of his life. He had pushed the brief meeting with Elizabeth out of his mind.

Neither Pedro nor Elizabeth followed up on this encounter in the waiting room. Neither asked for more information about the other. My manipulation had been too subtle, too fleeting.

I decided to try the back-to-back appointments again, two weeks later. Unless I chose to become more direct and to breach confidentiality by speaking directly to one or both of them, this would be my last chance. It was Pedro's final appointment prior to his move.

They gazed at each other again as I escorted her to the waiting room. Their eyes met and lingered even longer this time. Pedro nodded and smiled. Elizabeth smiled in return. She hesitated for a moment then turned to the door and left.

Trust yourself! I thought, trying to mentally remind Elizabeth of an important lesson. She did not respond.
Again, Pedro did not follow up. He did not ask me about Elizabeth. He was absorbed by the details of his relocation to Mexico, and he ended his therapy on that day.

Perhaps this is not to be, I thought. They were both improved, although not happy. Perhaps this was enough. [45]

That was all Weiss could do, but other forces at play in the universe would not let this life end without Elizabeth and Pedro getting back together again. Their love story is not germane to our discussion here. If you want to know the rest of the story, you'll have to go read *Only Love is Real*. I just wanted to give you yet another example of some strange anomalous experiences that lend support to the premise that as Self, you may have functioned here on earth before with another set of ego-subpersonalities.

Then I ran across the story of Jenny Cockell. Jenny is married and has two children. She lives and works as a chiropodist in Northamptonshire, England. Since early childhood she has had dreams that she had lived before, that in that life she had eight children, and that she died while the children were all very young. During the day, she would also recall episodes from that life concerning her children. It wasn't until after she had her children that she decided that she must try to find out what actually did happen to her previous children.

Through regression therapy she was able to recall many more particulars of that life including that she had lived in Ireland, just north of Dublin. She drew pictures of the houses and roads she remembered. Finally, one day she took a trip to Ireland to look for the place where she lived her previous life. Although much had changed in the old neighborhood, she saw enough to know that this was the place where she had lived. She estimated that it had been about 50 years since she had died in her previous life.

Eventually she found people who remembered her previous family. The children had been split up with some going to orphanages. She announced through newspaper articles and mail outs that she was looking for the children of the family who had lived at that home. Finally, one day she got a call from the daughter of one of her sons. Jenny told the daughter her story and the daughter told her what she knew about her aunts and uncles. Eventually Jenny was able to meet most of her children. All of them were very skeptical at first, but after she was able to tell each of her children, stories of their early childhood, which they felt only their mother could have known, most of them slowly accepted that this woman somehow had their mother's memories and they made her a part of their family. You can read her whole story in *Across Time and Death: A Mother's Search for her Past Life Children*, by Jenny Cockell.

What do we do with stories such as these? Most Christians will probably say that they do not believe in reincarnation. But what about Purgatory. Most Catholics will probably say they do believe in Purgatory. Purgatory is said to be a place where Souls wait until they are able to enter Heaven. What are the Souls doing while they are waiting? Maybe they are reincarnating again and again until they learn what it is that we are here to learn before we can enter Heaven.

Regardless of what you decide to believe about reincarnation, remember that these past lives stories, along with all the reports of out-of-body experiences and the near-death experiences, are being presented here to lend support to the notion that the Self/Soul may indeed be able to function without a physical body.

This brings us back to the question of what is the nature of a Self/Soul that can exist without a physical body. Depending on whether you consider yourself to be an atheist or a theist, an agnostic or a gnostic, you are reacting very differently to this discussion of the Self/Soul being able to function without a physical body and to continue to exist after death. It may help to clarify at this time how I am using the terms, theist and gnostic.

Chapter 25
Doubting Theists and Hopeful Agnostics

Atheist and agnostic are fairly common terms and most people understand what these two words mean, but fewer people are as comfortable in using the companion words, theist and gnostic. A theist is someone who believes that there is a God; an atheist is someone who believes that there is no God. The agnostics will say they don't know if God exists or not, while the gnostics know that God exists. The agnostics reason that since that there is no scientific proof that God exists and since they have not had any direct experience of God, then the only rational stance they can take is to say that they don't know if there is a God. A gnostic is one who has had a direct experience of God and therefore knows that God exists. To "wake up" to the higher states of consciousness is to move towards becoming gnostics, those who know that God exists because they have experienced God as that greater consciousness of which we are all a part.

Most people start out as theists, enculturated by their family and church to believe that God exists. Depending on the culture they are in and the experiences they have had, some theists can fervently and happily remain believers for the rest of their lives. Some, however, at some point will start to have doubts about whether or not God exists, at least the kind of God presented to them by their church. Once the doubts begin, some will progress to becoming agnostics, some will become atheists, but many remain as doubting theists. Being an atheist is an irrational stance, because atheists cannot prove that God does not exist. If they wish to be rational about it, atheists should switch to being agnostics.

Being a theist is not irrational. The rationale for being a theist is that while you may not have had an experience of God, others have had, and you can choose to believe in God based on their witness. Most of the saints and sages are gnostics; they have had an experience of God. However, one need not be a saint or a sage in order to have an experience of God. This experience can occur to anyone. The experience will be interpreted quite differently however, based primarily on the stage of consciousness to which he or she has already grown.

Using Beck's color scheme for stages of consciousness, most of the people still at the blue (conformist, conventional) stage are theists. Some of the people who grow out of blue and into the orange, green, and yellow stages will reject the image of God as preached by the blues. Some of these will become agnostics or atheists but a lot will remain theists primarily because they have had a set of experiences, great or small, that have allowed them to grow up the stages of consciousness, modifying their image of God as they went along, to fit in with their changing view of reality.

There are many different kinds of theists. All theists do not hold exactly the same image of God in their minds and hearts. Some theists imagine God to be someone entirely separate from themselves. It is easy to see why this is so. As long as you identify with one of your subpersonalities, you will naturally see yourself as separate from all others, and therefore separate from God. It is easy to imagine such a subpersonality saying, "God is God, and I am I. God is watching how I am living. He will judge me when I die and will either reward me or punish me." This is the image of God that most agnostics and atheists are rejecting. A more believable image of God is that of the mystics, saints, and sages – God as a Greater Consciousness of which we are an integral part, a God who loves us all and is waiting patiently for all of us to "wake up".

Fundamentalists are theists who are stuck at the blue conformist stage. These can be Christian fundamentalists, as well as Islamic or Jewish fundamentalists. Fundamentalists are theists who when confronted with the science, the philosophy, and the values of the modern world, rather than embracing them as the leading evolutionary edge of human development, are frightened by them, and choose to retreat to the science, the philosophy, and the values of pre-rational medieval times. Now there may be a lot with which to disagree in the science, the philosophy, and the values of the modern world, but the challenge is to grow through this phase of human development into whatever lies ahead. Transcend and include. Our task is to make whatever lies ahead better than the science, the philosophy, and the values of the modern world.

In my own journey, I started out as a very blue theist, a True Believer for most of Act I, up until the time I entered medical school. The influences of medical school and the existential philosophers I was reading, plus my life experiences over the next several years (Act II) turned me first into a doubting theist, and then into a hopeful agnostic.

Doubting theists are persons who still believe that God exists. They go to church and mingle and pray with the fervent theists, but secretly, down deep inside, they are beginning to have doubts about some of the dogma that their church preaches and about some of the activities that the church either insists on or forbids. Doubting theists would love to talk about their doubts about God and their disagreements with the official dogma, but in most churches they are not allowed to and instead are exhorted to "have faith". Doubting theists are crying out to their churches for methods to help them grow out of their childhood images of God, to help them reconcile their faith with experiences they are having in their life, and to help them to continue to grow as theists up the stages of consciousness. If they are lucky enough to be members of a church that does help them in these ways, doubting theists can remain theists for the rest of their lives.

But many are not that lucky and as they approach Authentic Consciousness in their growth and development, they will have to admit to themselves and to the world that they are really agnostic. By now you know enough about subpersonalities to know that such decisions are usually not all or none. Some subpersonalities will want to remain as doubting theists in their behaviors, some will become hopeful agnostics, and some will want to completely reject any further association with religion and churches. The struggle within one person of these competing values and beliefs can be very intense and stressful. But eventually a compromise of some sort is reached, and one's behavior becomes increasingly consistent.

Some agnostics, e.g. the scientific materialists, are content to think no more about God and religion. These can live for many years not knowing nor caring. Some agnostics, however, are on the lookout for books, workshops, experiences, relationships, or churches that will somehow provide them with the evidence that will lead them to conclude that God does indeed exist. I call these latter ones, the hopeful agnostics.

Hopeful because the writings of the mystics and sages suggest that it is possible also for you and me to "wake up" to a state wherein we experience ourselves as part of a greater consciousness, at first maybe only fleetingly, but eventually maybe also more or less permanently.

Regardless of whether you consider yourself a fervent theist, a doubting theist, or a hopeful agnostic, our challenge now becomes, "What can we do to increase our chances of having a direct experience of God so that we can become gnostics, those who know that God exists?" It's probably easiest for fervent theists to become gnostics. Since they already believe that God exists, it may not take as dramatic an experience for them to be able to recognize that "that there" was indeed an experience of God. Most of the known saints in the middle ages were probably very fervent theists, who occasionally had experiences that they recognized as a direct experience of God, thereby reinforcing their decisions to live their lives in ways that eventually led to there being recognized as saints. For the doubting theists and the hopeful agnostics, the experience will have to be very profound, dramatic, and clear, before we will be able to recognize it and accept it as having been "truly" an experience of God.

So how do we go about having such an experience? Wilber has already warned us that we don't get there by just thinking or reading about it. The only way to get there is by following the injunctions, by doing the experiment. These injunctions usually involve asking us to try "waking up" more frequently and to increase the time we spend in meditation. But in between our silent sits, I don't think that it will hurt us to try thinking about it rationally.

While waiting to become gnostics, it is also possible for doubting theists and hopeful agnostics to become fervent theists again, but this time with a very different image of God. That is what happened to me. Three pages ago I told you that early in my life I lived as a fervent theist, later on I evolved into a doubting theist, and then to being a hopeful agnostic. I did not stay an agnostic for too long. The authors I was reading, the presenters at conferences I attended, the discussions I have had, the pondering I have done, the meditations I have sat through all soon convinced me that the preponderance of the evidence now points to the conclusion that God does exist. I would like to review this evidence with you in the next chapter.

Chapter 26
Does God Exist?

K en Wilber starts off his major tome, *Sex, Ecology, Spirituality: The Spirit of Evolution (SES)* with these words:

IT IS FLAT-OUT strange that something -- that anything -- is happening at all. There was nothing, then a Big Bang, then here we all are. This is extremely weird.

To Schelling's burning question, "Why is there something rather than nothing?" there have always been two general answers. The first might be called the philosophy of "oops." The universe just occurs, there is nothing behind it, it's all ultimately accidental or random, it just is, it just happens -- oops! The philosophy of oops, no matter how sophisticated and adult it may on occasion appear -- its modern names and numbers are legion, from positivism to scientific materialism, from linguistic analysis to historical materialism, from naturalism to empiricism -- always comes down to the same basic answer, namely, "Don't ask."

The question itself (Why is anything at all happening? Why am I here?) -- the question itself is said to be confused, pathological, nonsensical, or infantile. To stop asking such silly or confused questions is, they all maintain, the mark of maturity, the sign of growing up in this cosmos.

I don't think so. I think the "answer" these "modern and mature" disciplines give -- namely, oops! (and therefore, "Don't ask!") -- is about as infantile a response as the human condition could possibly offer.

The other broad answer that has been tendered is that something else is going on: behind the happenstance drama is a deeper or higher or wider pattern, or order, or intelligence. There are, of course, many varieties of this "Deeper Order": the Tao, God, Geist, Maat, Archetypal Forms, Reason, Li, Mahamaya, Brahman, Rigpa. And although these different varieties of the Deeper Order certainly disagree with each other at many points, they all agree on this: the universe is not what it appears. Something else is going on, something quite other than oops... [46]

Another conference I like to attend as often as I can is one called "Towards a Science of Consciousness" held every two years in Tucson, Arizona. I've done three so far. This conference is attended by physicists, philosophers, psychologists, neuroscientists, and neurosurgeons all trying their best to communicate with one another their understanding of human consciousness. One of the key features of the conference format is that, in addition to concurrent sessions of interest, every day there are general assemblies which everyone is encouraged to attend. But even though communication is taking place, the differences in paradigms remain and the dominant paradigm is that of scientific materialism, the philosophy of "oops."

The philosophers of "oops" claim that matter is primary and obviously existed long before there was any consciousness. They believe that matter appeared on the scene in the big bang approximately 13.7 billion years ago, but that consciousness didn't appear on the scene until some 13 billion years later, only when the size of the animals' brains became large enough and complex enough, did consciousness somehow emerge. They usually refer to our consciousness as an epiphenomenon of our brain. How this could have happened is the big question and no scientist has a clue. The philosophers of "oops" just don't know how something as immaterial as consciousness could have emerged from something as material as matter, and they cannot explain phenomena like OOBEs, NDEs, past lives, non-local activity, and mystical experiences. It is best, they claim, to just ignore that these phenomena are happening.

The philosophers of "something else is going on" hypothesize that consciousness is primary and existed before there was any matter. They believe that consciousness existed even before the big bang, that consciousness caused the big bang, and that to this day, consciousness is creating and supporting the "form" that matter takes, be it the form for an atom, an amoeba, a tree, a cat, a human, a planet, or a star. These philosophers have no "proof" this is so, their big point is that consciousness coming first seems to explain better all the human experiences we have observed throughout the ages. And this is what good philosophy is. It takes into account all that has been proven scientifically, combines that with all the observable human experiences, and comes up with a story, a worldview that seems best to account for it all.

Does your worldview take into account the testimonies of those who have experienced near death experiences? They have left their unconscious bodies behind and yet experience conscious interactions with people they have known who have already died. Some of them experience meeting with a conscious bright loving light. I think that such experiences can only take place within a consciousness that is somehow bigger than our own. And there are more such experiences still being reported every day. These reports should not be ignored.

What about the testimonies of people who recall having lived other lives? They are now conscious of living this life. Yet they also remember having lived consciously in other bodies. Some even remember being conscious in-between two lives. Doesn't that argue that there must be an intelligent, conscious field of some sort in place in which all of that is occurring?

Finally recall what I said earlier about the testimonies of the mystics, saints, and sages from various traditions. I have attended several conferences where representatives of these traditions have met to dialogue about their similarities and differences. Usually their traditions were started by someone who had awakened to these higher states of consciousness. These traditions have practices or paths, which they encourage their members to follow in order to experience these higher states for themselves. And all traditions have testimonials about what was experienced while in these higher states. What they often report on are "intense experiences where they perceive all of us, not as separate individuals but as parts of a single whole. Our consciousness is experienced to be but a part of a greater consciousness." What to call this greater consciousness stirred up the most debate. Some wanted to call it "Emptiness", and claimed that all forms come from Emptiness. Some called it Brahmin, some Allah, some God. They finally agreed that the best term would be "Ultimate Reality". But whatever you wish to call this ultimate reality, I think that so many traditions claiming that they have men and women who have experienced contact with a greater consciousness is also something we need to take into account in our search for evidence for the existence of God.

There you have it, my arguments for believing that God exists. And why I am now a fervent theist again. It's not quite proof for the existence of God, but it comes pretty close. It's a philosophical argument that says that there is enough evidence available now for a reasonable man or woman to agree that the preponderance of the evidence points to one conclusion: "the universe is not what it appears. Something else is going on, something quite other than oops. . ." Which makes more sense to you, the philosophy of "oops" or the philosophy of "something else is going on"? Think about that.

The God, who I now believe does exist, is not a God that is wholly other. It is a God that we are a part of. Such a God is usually referred to as panentheistic, which makes me a fervent panentheist. In Greek, pan means "all", en is "in", and Theos is "God", which makes panentheism a belief that "all is in God". The "all" means our entire universe – all the galaxies, solar systems, planets, plants, animals, humans, you and me. God is the consciousness who created this universe and continues to this day to ensoul the universe. The universe is the material body of God. God is the soul manifesting as our entire physical universe, just as we are parts of God's soul, manifesting as our physical bodies. Please keep this panentheistic definition of God in mind for the rest of this book.

So, dear reader, do you believe that this God exists? This is, obviously, a very important question. How you answer it, will determine how you will live the rest of your life. If you are an agnostic, you can continue your search for an experience of emptiness, of enlightenment. Then you, too, will become a Gnostic, for you will "know" what "Ultimate Reality" feels like. If you are a theist, we can continue on, searching for an experience described by others as "Union with God", an experience that will also turn us into Gnostics. But to have such an experience, we will have to awaken to more states of consciousness.

Chapter 27
More <u>States</u> of Consciousness

At one point along the way I learned about the Institute of Noetic Sciences (IONS) and attended several of their conferences. It continues to this day to be an excellent source of information, nourishment, and inspiration. IONS was started by the astronaut, Edgar Mitchell. Mitchell is one of the few astronauts that made it to the moon and back. In 1971 while viewing the Earth from outer space, he had a mystical experience, which he describes in his book, *The Way of The Explorer.*

> What I experienced during that three-day trip home was nothing short of an overwhelming sense of universal connectedness. I actually felt what has been described as an ecstasy of unity. It occurred to me that the molecules of my body and the molecules of the spacecraft itself were manufactured long ago in the furnace of one of the ancient stars that burned in the heavens about me. And there was the sense that our presence as space travelers, and the existence of the universe itself, was not accidental but that there was an intelligent process at work. I perceived the universe as in some way conscious. The thought was so large it seemed at the time inexpressible, and to a large degree it still is. Perhaps all I have gained is a greater sense of understanding and perhaps a more articulate means of expressing it. But even in the midst of epiphany I did not attach mystical or otherworldly origin to the phenomenon. Rather, I thought it curious and exciting that the brain could spontaneously reorganize information to produce such a fantastically strange experience. [47]

Mitchell is an engineer, had never heard of such experiences, and wondered what had just happened. On returning to Earth he talked about this experience with others and was told that what he had, sounded like a peak experience into a higher state of consciousness. Therefore, Mitchell started studying psychic phenomena and the inner experiences of mystics from all cultures. Here is another quote from Mitchell:

Perhaps the most thorough and detailed mapping of inner experience comes from the Buddhist and Hindu mystics. The Tibetan Buddhist monks in particular have approached the subject with scholarly intent and precision for centuries. The most exalted state of awareness is described in the mystical literature as the nirvikalpa samadhi, a name derived from the Sanskrit. This is a state of awareness in which there is only Self; there are no thoughts or objects in the mind. Indeed, Self is expanded and merged into the entire field of mind so that pure awareness is all that appears to exist. The state is accompanied by an ecstasy that seems to permeate every cell of one's body and results in a feeling of certainty about the eternal nature of Self. Beyond this simple description, the state is ineffable, which is to say the description falls short and doesn't assist others in attaining it (although it does help one recognize the experience when and if it occurs.) The state must be experienced to capture its complete essence, however.

In Christian literature, the phrase "the peace that passes all understanding" is often used to imply the ineffable character of the inner experience. The theological meaning often given to this samadhi state is that of "union with the godhead," or, to use Paul Tillich's phrase, "union with the ground of our being." I would suggest, however, that the meaning assigned is not inherent in the experience, but rather is the result of attempting to describe the experience in accordance with one's theological beliefs. We do not "see" God in such an experience. Nor do we experience union with God – unless we are already predisposed to expect that this is what the experience means. [48]

Mitchell decided to start an Institute that would study scientifically what was the nature of a consciousness that could have such an experience and what such experiences tell us about the nature of reality. He named it the Institute of Noetic Sciences (IONS).

Noetic means mind or consciousness and for over 30 years now, the Institute has been funding studies of strange anomalous phenomena that do not fit into our current scientific paradigm. Every two years IONS puts on a conference to report on the latest developments in the Noetic Sciences. That's where I learned about some of the research that is being done on the strange anomalous phenomena like Remote Viewing, OOBEs, NDEs, and Past Lives. Also at these conferences there is a lot of philosophical speculation about the possibility of anyone of us experiencing still higher states of consciousness.

The theory or map goes something like this: to experience higher states one needs to undertake an inner journey, an inner journey exploring our inner psyche, venturing deeper into our subconscious mind. You have already started on this exploration into your subconscious mind if you are doing your daily meditations. If you are doing your "Waking Up" and "self-observation" exercises, you have already experienced what it feels like to wake up to one higher state of consciousness. You undertake the inner journey in order to wake up to still more, higher states of consciousness. How many more are there? Various traditions have described at least two more, maybe three or four.

Wilber describes three such states (the psychic, the subtle, and the causal) as the worldviews of the Yogi, the Saint, and the Sage. He claims that hints of these higher states can be experienced by any of us, regardless on which stage of consciousness we are currently operating. At first these experiences will be brief and fleeting. You catch a glimpse, but then it's gone. But if we keep at it, over time we, too, may begin to sound like yogis, saints, and sages.

Why would we want to experience these higher states? For at least two reasons: knowledge and bliss. Persons experiencing these higher states are said to have access to knowledge about the nature of reality obtainable in no other way. And the experience is usually accompanied by intense feelings of extreme joy, love, bliss, and ecstasy.

A third reason might be "because they are there." These states might represent human potentials. Waking up to these higher states may be the main purpose of our being incarnated here on planet Earth. Maybe we keep reincarnating until we manage to wake up to these states.

Some traditions refer to reaching these states as becoming "Enlightened." Others refer to reaching them as having achieved "Union with God." But all traditions seem to agree that in order to start our journey towards these higher states, we must be willing to go Transpersonal. Let me next share with you what I am learning about being Transpersonal.

Chapter 28
Transpersonal?

Transpersonal, like Transrational, is another rather worrisome term to most of us. Transpersonal means "beyond the personal". And what is personal? Well, almost everything about us. Each of us is a unique set of ego-subpersonalities, each having a particular set of assets, attachments, and personality traits. We have a name and a personal history with several steppingstones. We have come to know and love our person. We wish to stay this person. So, what does it mean to go beyond this person?

We go "beyond the personal" whenever we are willing to dis-identify with some of the many preoccupations of our various subpersonalities and to identify more and more frequently with our life as Soul. It is only as Soul, that we can "wake up" to the higher states of consciousness, so we need to leave behind as much of our personal baggage as we can.

This process of leaving behind a host of time consuming activities precious to the various subpersonalities has been a lot easier to do ever since I have adopted my new name, Anthony, because now it is not "me" that is about to go out of existence, it is only the personal Clarence part that I am being asked to drop. As Anthony, I will live on. Now the question becomes, "What would life be like if we identified more often as Soul?"

We can get some glimpses of what that life is like and why we would want to go there by reading about the lives and experiences of mystics, saints and sages, for it is they who have experienced most intensely what it is like to live as Souls. Reports on the lives of mystics, saints, and sages throughout history and continuing to our time vary somewhat depending on the cultures in which they are embedded. But they also show a remarkable consistency across cultures, be they Buddhist,

Hindu, Jewish, Christian, or Sufi. Mystical experiences are said to be ineffable, meaning that they are difficult if not impossible to describe in words. Sometimes we are given injunctions, which if carefully followed, will lead us to having the same ineffable experiences. But some have tried to express in words their ineffable experiences, and what they often report on are intense experiences where they perceive all of us, not as separate individuals but as parts of a single whole. Our consciousness is experienced to be but a part of a greater consciousness. What some experience emotionally are profound feelings of joy, love, and peace. They leave the experience motivated to love one another and to help others to achieve the joy, love, and peace that they have experienced. They encourage us to look inward, to question the story by which we are living our lives, and to go, boldly, up a path less traveled.

For those of us who haven't had any of these profound experiences, it is hard to imagine what it means to perceive ourselves as not being separate. Growth through all the stages up to Authentic requires that we perceive ourselves to be separate distinct individuals, at some stages (red, orange) being very competitive with other individuals and at other stages (blue, green) emphasizing cooperation and communion with one another. But always with the sense that we are separate entities, separate wholes if you will.

Assagioli also had something to say about how we can feel very separate but also feel part of a greater whole:

> Very often patients ask for specific clarification on the quality of the Self and of so-called higher experiences. In such cases, we explain some of the main characteristics. The chief quality is the experience of synthesis or the realization of individuality and universality. The real distinguishing factor between the little self and the higher Self is that the little self is acutely aware of itself as a distinct separate individual, and a sense of solitude or of separation sometimes comes in the existential experience; In contrast, the experience of the spiritual Self is a sense of freedom, of expansion, of communication with other Selves and

with reality, and there is the sense of Universality. It feels itself at the same time individual and universal. [49]

The concept, transpersonal, suggests the possibility of the Self having an identity as part of something greater than the lone separate person it has experienced itself to be up to now. What does it mean to live as though I were part of a greater consciousness? And what would be the nature of such a greater consciousness?

Even though it may be hard for us to understand the nature of this next greater consciousness, it should not be hard at all for it to understand us. This greater consciousness may have been trying to communicate with us ever since we developed a consciousness of our own. The wisdom sayings of the mystics, saints, and sages may be attempts to put into human concepts, insights that this greater consciousness is trying to pass on to us. Insights like that maybe we should love one another just like this greater consciousness seems to love us. Some who have felt this love have likened it to that of a parent for a child. Some have called Him, "Father". Some have called Her, "Mother Earth". This experienced greater consciousness is now sometimes referred to as Ultimate Reality, but most people still prefer to refer to Him/Her/It as God.

You may be beginning to worry now that all of this talk of a greater consciousness and God may be an attempt to bring you back to accepting the religious dogmas we have rejected in transforming out of the blue conformist stage of consciousness to the rational, post-conventional stages. Some very rational and very personal minds find very worrisome any references to religious terms. Wilber quickly assures us that the higher unfolding into these other states is not at all like what is usually meant by religious terms.

> Wilber: First and foremost, if this higher unfolding is to be called "religious" or "spiritual," it is a very far cry from what is ordinarily meant by those terms. We have spent several chapters painstakingly reviewing the earlier developments of the archaic, magic, and mythic structures (which are usually associated with the world's great religions), precisely because

those structures are what transpersonal and contemplative development is not. And here we can definitely agree with Campbell: if 99.9 percent of people want to call magic and mythic "real religion," then so be it for them (that is a legitimate use); but that is absolutely not what the world's greatest yogis, saints, and sages mean by mystical or "really religious" development, and in any event, is not what I have in mind.

Campbell, however, is quite right that a very, very few individuals, during the magic and mythic and rational eras, were indeed able to go beyond magic, beyond mythic, and beyond rational-into the transrational and transpersonal domains. And even if their teachings (such as those of Buddha and Christ and Patanjali and Padmasambhava and Rumi and Chihi) were snapped up by the masses and translated downward into magic and mythic and egoic terms -- "the salvation of the individual soul" – that is not what their teachings clearly and even blatantly stated, nor did they intentionally lend any support to such endeavors at all... [50]

To take the Christian example, biblical scholars are still trying to figure out which of the reported sayings of Jesus are truly his sagely wisdom and which sayings were simply fabricated and inserted later to "clarify" or "elaborate" on a point that the writer, usually operating at the mythic (blue) stage, had decided were important. And even among the accepted truly sagely wisdom sayings of Jesus, we are still trying to understand what exactly Jesus was trying to communicate.

Given what we now know about higher states of consciousness, we can assume that somehow Jesus did manage to "awaken" to these higher states and did experience a consciousness that seemed to love him as a parent would a child. So he called this consciousness, "Father". Later on, he had experiences that made him realize that his own consciousness seemed to be but a part of this loving consciousness so he says, "The Father and I are one." This experience is now referred to as having achieved "Union with God."

Jesus then spends the rest of his short life trying to teach all who would listen that they, too, should try to awaken to these higher states of consciousness. Most of his truly sagely wisdom sayings are transpersonal. One saying that I often ponder is his realization that the "Kingdom of Heaven" is already within us. What does that mean? And what kind of a heaven would that be? This may be as good a time as any to share with you a longer description of my Seeker Subpersonality who's been doing most of this pondering.

Chapter 29
The Seeker Subpersonality

One of my subpersonalities, the one I am calling Clarence: the Seeker, has long had an interest in reading about saints and mystics and in trying to understand what they are trying to communicate. Here is what I sounded like in 1986:

The Seeker: (3-10-86)

It may be that I tend to rely too much on logical, rational thinking and don't spend enough time getting in touch intuitively with my inner strengths and sources of wisdom. There may be a way of arriving at understanding which has nothing to do with rational and logical thinking. This way is the way of the inner search, a search for the inner or spiritual resources to which we have access. But the way to gain access to these inner resources seems to be by stepping aside, by not trying, by letting go. It all sounds rather paradoxical.

The main thing that I may need to let go of seems to be my intellect's insistence on always thinking or worrying about something. I'm trying to develop some skill at being able to stop thoughts, to allow for some experience of what life is like between thoughts. This I find hard to do.

I practice thought stopping in several ways. Sometimes I just sit and meditate, concentrating either on some sound or on my breathing, or simply just observing the thoughts come up and go away. Usually the thoughts represent one of my other subpersonalities breaking in. Either the Doctor is worrying about something that needs to be done at the office, or the Philosopher wants to think about what is the nature of the space between thoughts. I try to recognize that, to understand that, and to postpone all such thoughts until later.

Sometimes I practice thought stopping while doing something else. Some of the Family Man's and Homesteader's chores provide excellent opportunities for this practice. While washing the dishes, I try to focus my attention exclusively on the dishes -- four scrubs clockwise, four scrubs counterclockwise, check the plate, four scrubs clockwise, four scrubs counterclockwise, check the plate; no other thoughts allowed; all thoughts to be postponed until after the dishes are done.

I also try my thought stopping while practicing my yoga or tai chi or while running. During yoga or tai chi, I try to concentrate on my body. I try to feel which muscle groups are being stretched and which are relaxed. Where's the weight? Which leg is yin and which leg is yang? No other thoughts, just feeling the body. Trying to experience the energy flows. Three times a week I go out for a run and for 30 minutes I try not to think of anything. I try just to be there, to notice the sky, the plants, the animals, the sounds, the smells. Most of the time the thoughts are too insistent, too hard to get rid of. But sometimes, all too rarely, something else happens. I begin to feel really good. I feel as though I were becoming a part of some greater life and life force.

I have experienced this feeling of being a part of a greater life at other times in many different situations -- while hiking in the mountains, while looking at the stars, while delivering a baby, while watching someone die, while participating in a group celebration. These have come not while trying to stop thoughts, but as spontaneous breakthroughs into my thoughts. I experienced a sense of wonder, of awe, of peace so profound that all thoughts simply disappeared, until I recovered, and then all the thoughts came rushing back in.

What's happening at these times? Could it be that between thoughts, I am no longer me, but that I become part of some other life, a greater whole, and that then it lives me? Do I then get to participate, to share in its life and its life-giving, life-promoting energies? Is that why it feels so good? Is that what grace is?

How can I experience this feeling more often? Maybe thought stopping is the key. Maybe that is why it is so difficult to learn. This difficulty may be the gatekeeper, the guard who protects the riches, the treasure within. And what is this treasure within? It may be nothing less than the Kingdom of Heaven, the pearl of great price for which one would give all that one has.

It may be, I don't know. But that's my motivation for continuing my practice of thought stopping, to explore what lies beyond that gate within. If I find anything valuable, I'll let you know. Better yet, why don't you come and explore with me. If I am not me between thoughts, then you are not you between thoughts, and all of us together may then make up this other life who then lives us. If we combine our experiences, we will have a better insight into the nature of this greater whole which we are simply parts thereof.

If we are all part of some greater whole, then we are not really all that different from one another. It may be only the logical and rational side of our brain that likes to analyze and to make distinctions, to separate us, isolate us in a skin enclosed bag of bones, and to make us think that each of us is a different unique individual. While we are thinking we may all appear to be different, but when we are between thoughts, we may not be all that different from one another at all.

This may be the explanation for a whole host of poorly understood phenomena. It could form the basis for postulating a common unconscious through which we occasionally make connections across space and time and which we describe as mental telepathy, precognition, clairvoyance, or telekinesis. This greater whole could be the source of the healing energies, which occasionally bring about what to us seem to be medical miracles. It could be the source of the energies, which a practitioner of the martial arts calls on, channels, and feels a part of. And it may be the source of the energies we feel whenever a group of us get together in a common effort, be it a protest, a network, or a sunrise celebration.

Here's another paradox. I was born into a warm and loving family, community, and culture. I enjoyed it for a while but all too soon I began to feel entrapped. I wanted to break free. I no longer wanted to do what others thought I should do. The values, beliefs, and mores of my culture did not encourage my enthusiasms, aspirations, and drives. So I separated. I individuated. I became my own man. I developed a strong ego and an independent personality. But soon I began to feel isolated. As an isolated individual, life had no meaning. I felt the urge to become a part of something again. But how does a strong independent ego become a part of something again? Only by dying a little to self.

So I have this tension. I fought so hard to become independent and strong, and now I'm feeling the urge to give up some of it. An urge which says that true meaning, peace and happiness lie not in more independence and more isolation but in the opposite direction, in more interdependence, more community, more willingness to do the will of others.

So I practice dying to self a little by sometimes cheerfully doing what Susan wants me to do instead of doing something else that I would rather be doing. Or by cheerfully doing what my sons want me to do, or what my sister, or my friends, or my employees want me to do. I practice dying a little to self by letting go of some of my attachment to the things and to the habit patterns which have defined me in the past.

Dying to self is hard to do. It's a little like trying to stop thoughts. Could this be another gatekeeper to the Kingdom of Heaven within? Is dying to self what Jesus had in mind when he asked the rich man to sell all that he had, to give it to the poor, and to follow him? Is this what Jesus meant when he said, "Only he that is willing to lose his life for my sake, will gain it"? Is this why we have been encouraged to pray, "Not my will, but Thine be done, O Lord"?

So I practice my thought stopping and dying to self every time I think about it and for as long as I can hold to doing that. Which right now is not very often nor for very long, but I want you to know that I am being drawn in this direction. Who knows where such practice will lead. Maybe I'll become an impeccable warrior like Don Juan or a saint like Francis of Assisi. Or maybe at the very least I can become a happy old man who radiates warmth and love to all who come near me.

While my mother was alive I would often go over to her house for a visit. She would serve me a cup of coffee and a kolache, usually poppy seed and then we would talk about some of the topics I have discussed here. I think she enjoyed very much these conversations, but she usually adopted a worried, conspiratorial tone as she talked. It was almost as if these were topics one should not be discussing out loud and she was worried that we may be found out by the authorities or by the neighbors. Once she asked me, 'Surely, you don't go around talking like this in front of others?' And then she pleaded with me not to do so. I guess she figured it was bad enough to have a son who did housework. People would really think I had lost it if they knew I was going around looking for the Kingdom of Heaven within me.

For a long time, I did keep "talking about such topics," safely locked up in one of my many closets. Just another subpersonality, I would tell myself, and a rather impractical one at that. After all, I had a family to support, and public health responsibilities to honor.

This description of my Seeker Sub was written in March of 1986. I was in my Steppingstone period #10 which I am calling "A New Beginning". I already gave you a brief description of this period way back in the chapter on Steppingstones. At the time, I left the closing date open, as one should when writing up the present period. I think that period came to a close in the Fall of 1986 when I went back to work full time for the health department. Let me share with you now what happened since then.

Chapter 30
Steppingstones Updated

From 1980 to 1986 I worked half-time for the Health Department and spent the rest of my time helping with the parenting and householder chores at home. It was also a period when I had more time to read, attend Transpersonal conferences, and to write up what I was learning in the various journal entries I am quoting in this book Here is what I wrote about this period on 9-10-1986:

Period #10: A New Beginning (1977-1986)

One of the advantages of doing the Steppingstone exercise is that it helps you to plan and to prepare for some of life's major transitions. By looking back over all the steppingstone periods, you can spot the major trends and the minor variations. You can see more clearly where the energy is going. At each transition point, there are some activities, which now need to decrease, and others, which now need increased attention. I feel as though I am entering such a transition right now, as Steppingstone Period #10 is coming to a close.

One of the characteristics of this present period was the heavy involvement with my own and extended family. However, the need for this involvement is now waning rapidly. I am having two opposing reactions to this continuing decrease in family responsibilities. One reaction is to intensify my parenting activities -- cook more meals, bake more bread, spend more time with the kids. The Family Man does not want to go out of existence. He is already making plans with the Homesteader to turn this place into a really neat farm for the grandchildren to visit. Occasionally he even dreams of turning this really neat farm into a daycare center. One could even teach the kids about computers and how to play chess.

The opposite reaction is to ease off, to begin letting go, to practice dis-identifying with the parenting role. Maybe now is the time to give more attention to some of my other interests or to cultivate new ones. Already the Doctor is negotiating with the TX Dept. of Health to work himself back up to a full-time position. My sons have made it quite clear that they now need more money a lot worse than they need more parenting time.

I can predict that Period #11 will be quite different from Period #10 in some respects. However, there is also a longer-term trend in force now, and in that respect Period #11 will most likely be still a part of the movement that had its beginning with Period #9 with the move to Granger. Sometimes it looks to me as though I were in the middle of the third act of a four-act play.

From this perspective, Act I of my life strings together the first four steppingstone periods and the action there centered around my struggle between accepting the blissful cultural belongingness or breaking free and initiating growth towards individuation and separation. I was born into a cultural matrix. I wanted to fit in. I did what others wanted me to do. All of which resulted in my being in a Catholic Seminary studying for the priesthood. But I was not content to stay a part of that matrix. I had an enthusiasm and a drive for something more or other. Emotional turmoil resulted. This emotional energy together with the fact that I prayed and meditated a lot in those days, somehow helped me to tap into an intuitive, inner source of guidance and support which gave me the courage and the strength to counter the cultural pressure to stay where I was. So I broke free. The day I walked out of that seminary, I felt like a newborn, ready to start my growth as an independent individual.

Act II chronicles this growth and development through Periods #5 through #8. The two years in Austin were a kind of re-experiencing of childhood and adolescence and this time I decided to go to Medical School. Immediately the academic and scientific establishments took over my conditioning and under their guidance and nurturance I grew up strong and independent. I enjoyed it. I liked being me. Life was fun. I tried on the roles of a budding young scientist, a research assistant, a physician, and finally an Associate Professor at the University. But I also became an existentialist of sorts. I had become free and independent, but soon began to feel too alone, too isolated, too separated. I began to experience nothingness and meaninglessness. Why was I doing what I was doing? Was I being authentic, did my activities and behaviors accurately reflect who I was, my values and beliefs? What were my values and beliefs? Act II ends with a certain amount of disillusionment and confusion.

Act III begins with the move to Granger and the action now centers on my efforts to live more authentically and to be able to do so with at least a modicum of grace, serenity, and joy. And it is in this sense that Period #11 will be a continuation of some trends which got their start in Periods #9 and #10. One of these trends is the re-emergence and continuing growth of the Seeker subpersonality. It is the Seeker's contention that the reason I got into trouble there toward the end of Act II is because I had ignored for too long the spiritual aspect of human nature. I had over-nurtured the body and the mind at the expense of the spirit. The Seeker's admonition was that maybe if I went to church more, I'd get to feeling better. I tried that, but for some reason my spirit was not getting any nurturance, enthusiasm, or inspiration by going to church.

Where I finally did find inspiration and enthusiasm was at meetings and workshops of the Association for Transpersonal Psychology. These meetings were fun. They were balanced. There were Yoga, Tai Chi, Aikido, and Fun Runs for the body. There were lectures and discussions for the intellect. And most importantly these meetings provided rituals for the experiencing of Spirit. We did Sufi dances and chants. We did group meditations. We practiced visualizations accompanied by the sounds of a Shaman's drumbeats. The Seeker was soaking it all up. At these workshops, I found out about Zen Buddhists, Sufis, Taoists, and Indian Shamen. Religion and spiritual growth took on a new meaning. I was surprised to find out how culturally narrow my experience had been. It was interesting to note how many Catholic rituals and beliefs had their counterparts in these other spiritual traditions. But most interesting of all was to notice that at some of these exercises I was experiencing the same kind of spiritual high that I used to feel at church receiving the sacraments. Susan would often comment about my need to periodically go off to a meeting to get my fix of spiritual infusion. These meetings became my Sacraments; they were where I went to get Grace. I seriously began to consider that maybe I should switch to one of these other traditions.

It was at these meetings that I found out about Sufi teaching stories. There is one story, which always struck me as particularly funny. This was the one where the Mulla Nasrudin is looking under the street lamp at the corner for something that he had lost. He is asked where specifically was it, that he had lost this something. He replies that he lost it back at home. He is then asked why he was looking for it at the street corner. To which he replies that it was easier to look for it there as the light was better. I was in Boston at a meeting of the International Transpersonal Association when I was asked why I was there. Suddenly I realized that, I too, was looking for something I had lost back home and that I was looking for it in Boston because it was easier to look for it there. What I had lost was my sense of connectedness to the earth, to the universe, to God. And I could look for that right here on the farm, in my own home, and in my own Christian tradition. The direction I needed to head was not outward to explore superficially other traditions, but inward and deeper to explore more fully my own Catholic heritage. Just because I don't agree with all of the views and values of the current hierarchy of the Roman Catholic Church doesn't mean that I have to leave the church. I can stay and work with others to reform and improve the church. I'm reading some more church history, getting reacquainted with some of our saints and mystics, and trying to understand what the Christian experience throughout the centuries can teach me about human consciousness, about spiritual growth, and about our relationship with God.

What's going on here? Did I find the real world threatening and scary? Am I simply retreating back to the warmth and cultural security of Act I? I may be, but I think not. I think that during Act II I had become enough of a scientist and enough of an existentialist that there is no going back to the simple belief structure of the Czech-Catholic kid from Granger. Somehow during Act III I will need to reconcile the various approaches of the scientist, the philosopher, and the mystic to come up with a belief system and a set of spiritual practices with which I can live and grow.

So, another reason that I enjoyed so much the meetings of the Association for Transpersonal Psychology is that they addressed this issue. There was food for thought at these meetings for the scientist and the philosopher as well. People were talking about new scientific paradigms, the study of consciousness, and the farther reaches of human nature. I enjoy exploring these new paradigms. I want to study the nature of human consciousness. I want to understand how psychological growth relates to spiritual growth. I want to learn the disciplines and techniques for doing this through my own experiences, which is why I have been experimenting with steppingstones, subpersonalities, self-observation, meditation, visualization, journal writing, and a host of other related techniques. And I am sure that this experimentation will continue well into the next Steppingstone Period.

And what about Act IV? Act IV will start after I have learned to stay awake for longer periods of time, after I have integrated a little bit better all of my various subpersonalities, and after I have come up with that acceptable worldview or story, that believable set of beliefs, or at least after I have become a little more content to live with a modicum of uncertainty and doubt. By then I will have accomplished some transformation towards a life filled with more joy, love, and peace. I picture Act IV as an exciting, highly creative and productive time, one that is in some major way of service to our planet and its people. I'll let you know as soon as I think it has started.

In the meanwhile, back in Act III, I intend to chronicle the growth, the searching, the transformation with dated essays, letters, and journal entries.

With that hopeful and optimistic note, I ended Steppingstone Period #10 and started Period #11, which I will call "Back to Full-Time Work" (1986-1997). From 1986 to 1992 I worked full time as the Director of the Williamson County and Cities Health District and from 1992 to 1997 I worked full time as the Director of a 30 county Region of the Texas Department of Health. In 1997, at age 60, I decided to retire, mainly to give my Seeker Subpersonality a lot more time to do his seeking. Here now is what I wrote in my journal about this period on my last day at work, September 30, 1997:

Period #11: Back to Full-Time Work (1986-1997)

Today is my last day as a Regional Director for the Texas Department of Health. I have now worked for the State of Texas for 25 years. That seems like enough for one lifetime. It feels right to move on now. "There is a time and place for everything and everything has its season." Now I can say that I've been there, done that. What's next?

But before we explore what's next, it seems fitting that I try to bring you up to date on what has happened since 1986. I had intended to chronicle this period with frequent journal entries, but actually very few got written. Okay, only seven got written.

Normally one might feel a little guilty about having written so little over such a great stretch of time. But Ira Progoff specifically addressed this issue in one of his Journal Workshops. As I recall, he completely freed us from any compulsion to write in our journals at any set frequency. He also assured us that growth and change in our consciousness continue to occur even though we are not writing. I found that thought very reassuring then and I doubly appreciate it now. Without any apologies, I will continue on as though seven entries in ten years were normal for this kind of work at this stage in my life.

But I do think it will be useful if I try to understand and explain why so little was written. The biggest reason is simply that I spent most of this time in what deRopp called "waking sleep" and rarely "woke up" to the more aware and awake state of consciousness. I underestimated how much going back to work full time would rob me of creative free time with which to explore further the nature of human consciousness and the meaning of the various psychological and spiritual stages and states of growth and development. You may recall that most of the journal entries I have shared with you were written while I was working half-time at my Health Department job. In the fall of 1986 I went back to work full time, thus doubling my time commitment there while the parenting and homesteading chores at home continued. Then in 1992 I agreed to become the Regional Director of the Texas Department of Health for the 30-county area in Central Texas surrounding Granger. Now with a staff of 250 employees and several new programs, the time commitment increased even more.

I also got hooked on the stock market. With Susan and I now working full time, we were finally beginning to have some money left over in the bank at the end of the month, which could be invested somewhere. We still had debts and Susan wanted to pay all of them off first. But I would rather have $20,000 in debts and $20,000 in stocks than $0 in debt and $0 in stocks. Susan and I struck a deal, half of what we saved would go towards debt reduction and half would go into the stock market. My bet with Susan was that I could grow the savings at a faster rate than the interest on our debt. I learned to make some very pretty graphs showing the rate of growth of our stocks compared with the interest on our debts.

If any of you really would like to know more about what I learned about the stock market and want to see some of my graphs, just ask Clarence: Master Trader. He will be very happy to give you all of the details. All I want to say now is that I did occasionally wake up enough to be embarrassed about how much time I was spending just counting my money and watching it grow. It was a classic case of playing what deRopp called the "Hog-in-a-Trough Game." You can imagine what that game is like even if you have not read deRopp's, The Master Game.

Occasionally my cattle herd would break out and I would have to go bring them back in and fix the fences. With all three boys at the University of Texas, it seemed like there was always something there that needed to be done or to go see. Once I even drove them to Wisconsin to attend a national Dungeons and Dragons Convention. That was fun. Then when two of them scattered off to Idaho and California, there were trips to visit them there. I even managed to attend a couple of chess tournaments. I am sure that you will recall that in 1986, my chess rating was 1587. It has slipped over the years to 1585, and of course, I still feel that I am better than that. And then Ken Wilber kept writing, so, of course, Clarence: Philosopher had to read all of that. Finally, I have had to keep upgrading those computers. I have gone from the Tandy 1000, to an AMD 386, then to an AMD 486, and finally to an Athlon. And of course, a hard drive failed occasionally. Pain. Does anyone really ever keep backing up often enough?

That's why I did not get around to writing much during that time. But I do believe that all along growth and change were taking place. I did spend some time practicing waking up and self-observing, as well as thought watching and meditation. And I think that helped. I spent some time observing how my various fragmented subpersonalities compete for use of my one body/mind. By understanding better who is wanting to be active and when, I have learned to better timeshare among them. And with the better timesharing, I have noted a definite decrease in troubling emotions like anger, frustration, or irritability. Also with better synthesis and integration, I have noted a definite increase of positive emotions like joy, peace, and love. All of the various subpersonalities seem to be much better integrated now. I am able to move more gracefully from one to the other. Susan tells me that now, whenever she asks the wrong subpersonality to do something, I have learned the trick of very quickly and silently switching to the appropriate subpersonality and saying, almost immediately, "Sure, I can do that right now."

As Anthony, I feel whole, and I experience frequently, what can only be called, extreme states of joy and psychological well-being. I have never felt this good in all of my life. Maybe it is just a coincidence, but I think the well-being is a direct result of the work I have been doing with this waking up phenomenon and the experiencing occasionally of a higher state of consciousness.

And I have started the process of dis-identifying from some of these subpersonality roles. Clarence: Family Man has very little parenting which needs to be done any more. Several weeks ago, the time came to buy some more cows. Clarence: Homesteader did some shopping around, found four beautiful young Brangus heifers, and agreed to buy them. Then something woke me up. I wondered why we would want to continue putting time and energy into cattle raising. I talked it over with Susan and we decided to cancel the order. Our neighbor, who raises horses, needed more pasture, so she agreed to rent our pastureland and to buy our bull and cows. So now we get to enjoy watching colts and calves outside of our windows without any of the work and responsibility.

I am also wondering if going to Chess tournaments is something I really like doing or was it just something The Kid insisted on doing every once in a while, to get away from home chores and to take my mind off of the problems and stresses of work. Will any of you actually find it easier to love me if I can get that rating up into the 1900s where it really should be? I also hope that I can put the Master Trader to rest. I think we have enough money now. Is it really worth the time investment to try to make our savings grow any faster than simply putting them all into a well-diversified mutual fund? If the money runs out before we die, we can practice Poverty. And now that I am quitting my day job, I can drop the biggest time consuming role of all – Clarence, the Doctor/Administrator.

So, what am I going to do with all of this time I am freeing up? That's a very good question. Clarence: Philosopher is already planning on reading and re-reading all of Ken Wilber's books. Also, a lot has been published on the science of consciousness which I will want to catch up with. Actually, both the Philosopher and the Seeker have our dining room table full of books waiting to be read. The Seeker would like to visit a Monastery and/or a Retreat Center. The thought of just sitting and meditating for a week sounds delicious. The Seeker and the Kid are wanting to team up and do a lot more hiking and camping out. I think there is a Writer subpersonality wanting to be born. I could write self-help books or maybe novels, which would present in fiction form some of these really neat self-help techniques. Susan, of course, is an infinite resource for ideas on how I could spend my time.

It will be interesting to see what I will choose to do. I am trying not to rush into making any new plans any time soon. I want to give myself some time for quiet and rest. I will call my next Steppingstone Period: #12 – Retirement (1997 -).

Retirement has turned out to be a very wonderful time. I love it and have never regretted retiring as soon as I did. But there never seems to be much time for quiet and rest. It's amazing how quickly the mind can come up with a "to do" list too long to finish in one day. I had expected that each day would have long periods of down time when I would find myself wondering what to do with it. Doesn't happen, even with the Doctor/Administrator Sub's time now vacant. The other subpersonalities simply moved in and took over. So once again, I had to "wake up" and as Anthony, step in and set some priorities.

I decided that one of my priorities will be to intend, undertake, and commit to, the spiritual journey towards awakening to higher states of consciousness, to experience "Union with God", thereby becoming a Gnostic, one who knows that God exists. And I decided that I would finish this book, so I could share with you what I am learning about Waking Up, Transforming Consciousness, and Undertaking the Spiritual Journey.

Chapter 31
Undertaking a Spiritual Journey

The Spiritual Journey is a psychological inner journey. We do not need to go anywhere physically. We can stay right where we are. We are going to go inside, exploring our subconscious minds, and looking for those inner narrow gates that will allow us to enter the higher states of consciousness. We will be seeking access to knowledge about the nature of reality obtainable in no other way and seeking to experience those intense feelings of extreme joy, love, bliss, and ecstasy.

To undertake this inner journey, we will need to commit ourselves to trying to wake-up more frequently, spending more time as our more aware Self and decreasing the amount of time spent on what our ego-subpersonalities are doing. It will be a conscious purposeful dying to our old selves and giving birth to our new Self. It is only as our new Self that we can make it through that narrow gate.

I undertook my Spiritual Journey in order to experience Gnosis, and to become a Gnostic, one who knows that God exists. But I soon learned that it might be better to stop using the term, Gnostic, because it has a bad historical press. It turns out that in the first and second century there was a movement or a cult within Christianity called Gnosticism. We don't know much about these gnostics but we do know that the other Christians criticized their beliefs and called them heretics. From what little I have learned about these early gnostics, I do not think that I would want to be associated with them either.

In the Christian tradition, the mystical state of consciousness wherein one experiences God's being is called Contemplation. So, I now say that I am striving to become a Contemplative instead of a Gnostic. I want to live a Contemplative life. My Spiritual path is Contemplation.

This is an old tradition, going all the way back to Jesus. Jesus is often said to have withdrawn to go pray. One time it is reported that he went away to pray for as long as 40 days. He went off to pray to experience his oneness with God. He taught others to try to awaken to this state of contemplation. Many of the early Christians did awaken to this state which gave them the courage to withstand the many persecutions they had to suffer. Monks and nuns in monasteries and cloisters have kept this tradition going throughout the centuries to this present day. But one need not be a monk in a monastery or a cloistered nun to be a contemplative; it is possible for you and me to also strive to experience this state called contemplation.

In the fall of 1997 I decided that I would like to attend a 10-day retreat put on by the Cistercian Monks at their monastery in Snowmass, Colorado, thinking where better to learn how to strive to be a contemplative than from the monks themselves. I had read a magazine article about a monk, Abbot Thomas Keating, who in the 1960s had decided to hold a workshop to share with the general public the method the monks have been using in their monasteries on a day to day basis for centuries in their efforts to become contemplatives. He was pleasantly surprised at how much interest there was for such workshops. Soon, so many were clamoring for more, that he quit as Abbot, moved to the monastery in Snowmass, and now devotes full time going around the country, holding conferences and retreats, encouraging everyone to begin a daily practice of what he calls Centering Prayer (CP). He has formed an organization called Contemplative Outreach that is now organizing the workshops around the country.

The magazine article said that 10-day retreats were being held at Fr. Keating's monastery at Snowmass 10 times a year and that the next one was in January of 1998. I called up the monastery, got the registrar and told her I would like to come to the one next month. She told me that they were all filled up for that one, also filled up for over a year and that I would have to wait until January of 1999 for one that had an opening. Next she asked if I had ever attended a shorter retreat closer to home. I said that I had not and then she rather gently suggested that before I attempted a 10-day retreat, that maybe I might want to try a weekend one and then a 5-day one. She said that there were several being held in Central Texas and asked me to contact Tim and Barbara Cook at the Church of Conscious Harmony in Austin. So I did.

During 1998, I attended a weekend one at Bishop Reicher's Ranch near Austin and then a 5-day one at the Cedarbrake Retreat Center near Belton. At each of these retreats, I would introduce myself simply as "I'm Anthony." People would then usually ask where I was from and I would answer "from Granger." Some people started calling me "Anthony from Granger." I liked the sound of that, so since then I have been introducing myself as Anthony from Granger. You, too, can call me Anthony from Granger. That way I'll know you have read my book. I learned and experienced a lot at these retreats and received a lot of encouragement to continue on with Centering Prayer.

I did finally make it up to Fr. Keating's monastery for the 10-day retreat in January 1999 and had a wonderful 10 days of trudging through the snow from my small hermitage where I slept, to the monastery chapel for services, and then to the retreat center where we ate and had our CP sessions. The center has a library; the monastery has a book store. Our days were spent in silence except we could talk at suppertime. I read a lot and enjoyed many walks.

The basic unit of CP is a 20-minute sit. You sit quietly in a chair, with your feet flat on the floor, your back straight, your hands in your lap, and your eyes closed. You begin by "centering" yourself, which using our terminology means you "wake-up" from your usual state of "waking sleep" into your more awake, more aware mode as Self or Soul, you quiet down the usual chatter of your ego-subpersonalities, and try to sit there without getting hooked on any thoughts that may arise. If you have been doing your morning sits and meditations, you will be well prepared for this.

Once you feel centered you tell God that you "intend" to sit quietly, aware of His presence, for the next several minutes, in silent communion, open to any insights or intuitions He may want to send your way. The key defining characteristic of CP is that you are asked to adopt a sacred word to use whenever you notice that you had been hooked by a thought, to bring you back to center. No matter what thought, image, feeling, or itch disturbs your quiet communion, you are to note that that has happened, think of your sacred word, and gently, so very gently, return to your silent communion. Fr. Keating's suggestion for a sacred word is to pick any short word of one or two syllables that means something holy to you, like maybe, Spirit, Love, Grace, Peace, Jesus, Mary, Father, etc. The idea here is not to keep repeating your sacred word throughout your 20-minute sit, but to say it to yourself quietly only when you have noticed that you had been hooked by a thought.

Fr. Keating says to imagine yourself sitting in a small boat on a big river. What you want is just to sit there doing nothing but watching the water flowing by. But instead what you have is a lot of boats floating by. The boats symbolize your thoughts. Some are big; some are small. Some come by with a lot of emotion on board. Therefore, you watch the boats. The skill he is trying to teach you is to be able to sit there and watch all the boats float by. But some boats are so attractive that you attach yourself to that boat and go down the river with it. Once you realize what has happened, you need to say your sacred word, dis-attach from the boat, paddle back to your place, and wait quietly for the next boat to come along.

When the gong goes off announcing that the twenty minutes are up, you are asked to remain sitting quietly for a few more seconds with your eyes closed and slowly become aware that you will soon have to open your eyes and go about your next task. The way we practiced CP during the retreat was to have three such 20-minute sessions back to back with a 5-minute slow meditative walk in between each session. There were about 30 of us there and we would do our CP sitting around in a circle. When the gong sounded to end a 20-minute session, we would wait about a minute or so and then get up and walk slowly in a circle following one another. When we got back to our seat we would sit down for the next session. We did a set of three sessions in the morning before breakfast, then another set of three mid-morning, and a third set mid-afternoon. We also watched videos of Fr. Keating talking about CP a couple of times a day. The rest of the time we were free to read, take walks, and join the monks for services in their chapel.

It was a great environment. The meals were good. Everyone was acting very lovingly. I recommend it highly. The 10 days there will be a healthy break from your usual routine and it will help you tremendously with your meditations. You will find out a lot about yourself in 10 days of meditative sits. And you will get all the physiological benefits of meditation as the relaxation response kicks in –blood pressure comes down, the heart rate slows, stress hormone levels decrease.

Imagining yourself in God's presence also has some psychological benefits. Fr. Keating refers to God as the Divine Therapist. A lot of old, deeply buried stuff will come out as you sit there hour after hour, day after day. You may recall childhood experiences where you felt embarrassed, humiliated, and shamed. Or situations that got you angry with parents, siblings, or peers. These experiences had happened to a lone young subpersonality doing the best it could, given the situation. But now, centered, fully aware as Soul or True Self, sitting in God's presence, you can accept the situation as a learning experience. You can let it go, forgive the perpetrators, and become more loving towards those involved. Fr. Keating often refers to our having developed several "programs for happiness" as we were growing up. These he refers to as childhood programs or childish programs. We have a lot invested in these and continue to try to get happiness by using them. But most of these don't work anymore if they ever did. These, too, we can recognize and learn to let go, substituting more mature behaviors in their place.

I encourage you to give CP a try. The psychological insights will help you move up the stages of consciousness. You will become a healthier and happier person. Your life will go better, with more joy and peace. But Centering Prayer also promises growth into higher states of consciousness. It is presented as a time-tested method for achieving moments of contemplation or Union with God. CP is a kind of intermediate practice between meditation and contemplation. We can learn to meditate, but we do not know how to get to contemplation. CP is a practice we can learn to do, which may carry us from a meditative state to a contemplative one.

Very soon into the 10 days I decided that CP was the practice for me. It builds so nicely on all I was already doing with my self-observations, my meditations, and my efforts at staying aware of myself as Soul. CP adapts easily to viewing God as a consciousness of which we are integral parts. CP does not require any particular belief or allegiance. It doesn't matter if you are a fervent theist, a doubting theist, or a hopeful agnostic. All it asks is that you sit for a while, try to stop all the internal chatter, and be still. We have the monks', the mystics', and the sages' word for it, "Do this and spiritual awakening will follow!"

On the last evening of the retreat we were given an opportunity to share what we had experienced. It soon became obvious that most of the people there were fervent theists and several gave glowing reports of feeling helped by God. But no one described anything that sounded like they had experienced a contemplative state. When it came my turn to talk, I asked about that. I asked if they were keeping any statistics on outcomes. You know stats like, "What per cent of the retreat participants ever reach the contemplative state?" and "On average, how long does it take?" They are not keeping any statistics on outcomes. The impression I got was that they consider what happens in CP to be a private matter between each individual and God. Given what we now know about stages of consciousness and multiple subpersonalities, we can understand how differently the contemplative experience would be perceived by someone at the blue conformist stage as opposed to people at the orange, green, or already at the Authentic stage and on the "brink of the transpersonal." The end points would be really hard to measure.

The monks, however, are convinced that CP works because they have experienced the positive benefits among their community in the monastery. A couple of years later I asked another monk from another monastery how many monks living in monasteries did he think ever achieved the state of contemplation. He replied that he thinks only about 10%, maybe less. Whether or not CP will work in the general public, remains to be seen. For the present, all that we know is that more and more people are accepting it as their spiritual practice and sticking with it.

I decided that I, too, would give it a try. And almost every morning since then, going on eighteen years now, I have started my day with a CP sit, at first for 20 minutes; now I am up to 25 minutes. Even though I have not as yet had my contemplative experience, I am getting enough positive feedback from how the rest of my day goes to keep me at it every morning. While I am waiting for that contemplative moment when all will become clear, I continue going, once or twice a year, to a retreat or a conference to hear from people and to meet with people who are also on the Spiritual Journey. And I am reading a lot of books.

I won't bore you with a list of all the conferences I am attending or a list of all the books I am reading but I do want to mention a few that have helped me and which I think may help you to better understand the meaning of, and the value of, contemplation.

For a while Susan and I attended almost every visit that Fr. Keating made to Texas. He was usually invited by church congregations to describe what Centering Prayer is and to help them through a few CP sessions. I liked hearing him talk. I always felt good in his presence. Unfortunately for you, Fr. Keating has stopped doing these because of his age. He now rarely leaves the monastery. But there are videos, DVDs, and books, which can be had if you want to experience Fr. Keating. Check with Contemplative Outreach to see what is available at contemplativeoutreach.org.

Fr. Keating also occasionally presented at major conferences. Susan and I attended one in Albuquerque, which he co-hosted together with Father Richard Rohr. I was very impressed with Richard Rohr, a Franciscan monk, who had started the Center for Action and Contemplation in Albuquerque several years ago. Richard also traveled all over the world talking to all who would listen about contemplation. He has produced many CDs, DVDs, and books that are a joy to listen to and read. And although he has now cut down on many of his travels, he still does hold conferences in Albuquerque and Santa Fe. He has also started a school with a two-year program for students who wish to become contemplatives and then to go out and act in the world.

If you would like to know more about Richard, you could start by reading his book, *Everything Belongs: The Gift of Contemplative Prayer*, which has much to teach us about our Spiritual Journey. Richard sends out a daily meditation by email every morning, which I have found to be very helpful. I read it every day just before my morning meditation session. Doing so improves the quality of the thoughts that I have to contend with during the 25 minutes of my morning sit. You can find out more about Richard and his center at <cac.org>. The website will invite you to join his mailing list for his daily meditations. Here are a few samples from his daily emails:

From Jan.25, 2017: The most unfortunate thing about the concept of mysticism is that the word itself has become mystified and relegated to a "misty" and distant realm that implies it is only available to a very few. For me, the word simply means experiential knowledge of spiritual things, as opposed to book knowledge, secondhand knowledge, seminary or church knowledge. Most of organized religion has actually discouraged us from taking the mystical path by telling us almost exclusively to trust outer authority (Scripture, Tradition, or various kinds of experts) instead of telling us the value and importance of inner experience itself. In fact, most of us were strongly warned against ever trusting ourselves.

From Jan. 26, 2017: As I shared yesterday, mysticism is experiential knowledge of spiritual things. Franciscan mysticism is a trustworthy and simple—though not necessarily easy—path precisely because it refuses to be mystified by doctrinal abstractions, moralism, or false asceticism (although some Franciscans have gone this route). Franciscanism is truly a sidewalk spirituality for the streets of the world, a path highly possible and attractive for all would-be seekers. You don't need to be celibate, isolated from others, highly educated, or in any way "superior" to your neighbor. In fact, it is much better if you are none of these.

From Jan. 30, 2017: The nondual, contemplative mind is a whole new mind for most people! With it, you can stand back and compassionately observe the self or any event from an appropriately detached viewing platform. This is the most immediate and practical meaning of "dying to self" I can think of. As a general rule, if you cannot detach from something, you are far too attached to it! Eventually, you can laugh or weep over your little self-created dramas without being overly identified with them or needing to hate them. Frankly, few people fully enjoy this emotional freedom.

From Feb. 8, 2017: Most of us have lived our whole lives with a steady stream of consciousness, with a continual flow of ideas, images, and feelings. And at every moment of our lives we cling to these thoughts and sensations, so much so that I don't have the idea; the idea has me. I don't have the feeling; the feeling has me. We have to discover who this "I" really is, the one who has these always passing feelings and thoughts. Who am I behind my thoughts and feelings? The fixed point that watches things pass through me—is the real ME! Learn how to abide there in peace.

I'm sure that most people in the Western world have never really met the person they really are. We have to find a way to get beyond our self-image and our ideas about who we are. We have to discover the face that we already had before we were born, who we were in God all along, before we did anything right or wrong. This is the first goal of contemplation. This "I" is capable of union with God.

From Feb. 9, 2017: In our regular contemplative "sit" (time of silent prayer) we are actually practicing being awake. Religious teachers, including Jesus, the Buddha, as well as many Hindu sages, are always telling us to wake up—to be alert, alive, awake, attentive, or aware. You might call it the AAAAA recovery program! But how can you do that? What does being awake actually mean?

Being conscious or aware means:

- I drop to a level deeper than the passing show.
- I become the calm seer of my dramas.

- I watch myself compassionately from a little distance, almost as if "myself" is someone else.
- I dis-identify with my own emotional noise and no longer let it pull me here and there, up and down.
- I stop thinking about this or that and collapse into pure or "objectless awareness" of nothing in particular. I don't get there; I fall there.

At first, it does not feel like "me." It is unfamiliar territory because up to now I thought that my thinking was "me," yet now my thinking has ceased. I believe this is the meaning of Jesus' teaching on "losing oneself to find oneself" (see Luke 9:24).

This new and broader sense of "me" gradually, over time, begins to feel like my deepest and truest self; it seems solid and unchanging. At this point, God, consciousness, I, silent emptiness, and fullness all start to feel like the same wonderful thing! This is what spiritual teachers mean by growth in holiness. This deeper self is what most traditions refer to as "the soul" or the True Self...

You could start reading Richard's daily meditations every morning and then you could go attend his next conference in New Mexico. While attending Richard's conferences I got introduced to several other spiritual guides offering to help fellow travelers on their journeys. Let me introduce you to three -- James Finley, Cynthia Bourgeault, and Mirabai Starr.

James Finley's Spiritual Journey started in a monastery where he had Thomas Merton as his novice master. After 5½ years there he decided that the life in the monastery was not for him and left. His website states that he "later earned degrees from the University of Akron, Saint John College, and the Fuller Theological Seminary. Today James Finley is a husband, father, writer, and psychotherapist in private practice, but all the while he has continued his contemplative path in the world. He shares his journey with us in his books, workshops, and newsletters. His books include Merton's *Palace of Nowhere* and *The Contemplative Heart.*" You can find out more about Jim at: http://contemplativeway.org/.

Cynthia Bourgeault is described on her website (http://www.contemplative.org/cynthia-bourgeault/) as "a modern-day mystic, Episcopal priest, writer, and internationally known retreat leader. She divides her time between solitude at her seaside hermitage in Maine, and a demanding schedule traveling globally to teach and spread the recovery of the Christian contemplative and Wisdom path."

She has been a long-time advocate of the meditative practice of Centering Prayer and has worked closely with fellow teachers and colleagues including Thomas Keating, James Finley, and Richard Rohr. Cynthia's latest book is *The Heart of Centering Prayer: Nondual Christianity in Theory and Practice*. Cynthia and James are currently two of the core faculty members at Richard's Living School for Action and Contemplation. Here are two more quotes from Fr. Rohr's daily meditations introducing Cynthia and James:

> From Feb. 1, 2017: Over the next few days I'd like to share insights from my fellow CAC faculty members, Cynthia Bourgeault and James Finley. I trust Cynthia and Jim because they are truly grounded in the Christian and wider wisdom Tradition, Scripture, and their own authentic experience. They are part of the vibrant movement that is rebuilding Christianity from the bottom up, reclaiming long-forgotten or misunderstood teachings and practices. Today Cynthia clarifies the various meanings of nondual consciousness:

> The third major approach is to see nondual as basically the same as what Christian tradition has classically known as "the unitive state," the highest level of spiritual attainment according to the traditional map of purgative, illuminative, and unitive. Both Eastern and Western traditions hint at a permanent, irreversible shift in the seat of selfhood and in the perception, that flows out from this new identity. The former sense of self dissolves, and in its place, there arises a capacity to live a flowing, unboundaried life in which the person becomes "oned" with God (as Julian of Norwich famously expressed it) and oned with one's neighbor. However, in the East, the experience tends to be monistic: one discovers one's own deepest essence and nature as identical with that Oneness— "I am that." In the West, the unitive state is looked

upon as relational: a mystical marriage, in which one is fully joined to God in love, subsumed in God through that love— but one does not become God. In the Western Christian tradition, nondual realization is always one of union ("two become one"), not identity. (Adapted from Cynthia Bourgeault, The Heart of Centering Prayer: Nondual Christianity in Theory and Practice (Shambhala: 2016, pgs. 43-47)

From Feb. 3, 2017: Today's guest writer, CAC faculty member James Finley, shares what it is like to be within nondual consciousness.

We approach nondual consciousness by means of our contemplative experience...In my most childlike hour, I have tasted the presence of God that is perpetually manifesting and giving itself to me as my very life. While the value of my life is not dependent upon the degree to which I realize this unitive mystery that is always there, the experiential quality of my life is profoundly related to the degree to which I am learning to live in habitual awareness of and fidelity to the God-given, godly nature of the life that I'm living.

I cannot make moments of nondual consciousness happen. I can only assume the inner stance that offers the least resistance to be overtaken by the grace of nondual consciousness. Two lovers cannot make moments of oceanic oneness happen, but together they can assume the inner stance that allows them to be overtaken by the oceanic oneness that blesses their life.

My spiritual practice is to sit each day in childlike sincerity with an inner stance that offers the least resistance to being overtaken by the God-given, godly nature of myself just the way I am.

This is my sense of what nondual consciousness is and the contemplative way of life in which we, with God's grace, become ever more habitually grounded in it. (Adapted from James Finley, exclusive CAC Living School curriculum, Unit 1.)

Mirabai Starr describes herself "as a fellow traveler immersed in the ongoing adventure." I met her at Richard's 2016 conference in Albuquerque. Her website (http://mirabaistarr.com/) describes her as one who "writes, speaks and leads retreats on the inter-spiritual teachings of the mystics. Known for her revolutionary translations of John of the Cross, Teresa of Avila, and Julian of Norwich, Mirabai renders mystical masterpieces accessible, beautiful, and relevant to a contemporary circle of seekers. Her commentaries on the interconnected wisdom of all traditions are lyrical and evocative.

"Mirabai builds bridges not only between religious traditions, but also between contemplative life and compassionate service, between cultivating an inner relationship with the Beloved and expressing that intimacy in community, between the transformational power of loss and longing for the sacred."

If you have started on your spiritual journey, you will enjoy reading Mirabai. I suggest you start with *God of Love: A Guide to the Heart of Judaism, Christianity and Islam* and then go on to the rest of her books. To give you a feel for the way she writes, here are a few quotes from *God of Love*:

> The third section [of each chapter] is memoir. This is the riskiest part for me. All my previous books have been translations of or reflections on the wisdom teachings of others, and I have avoided sharing episodes from my own life or exposing my personal beliefs. Yet what I crave when I read about the spiritual path is stories about real people who, like me, have wrestled with the Divine in the effort to break through to the ultimate. This time I offer glimpses from my own journey, not as someone who has arrived somewhere, but as a fellow traveler immersed in the ongoing adventure. I also include stories of people I know and love, who represent a particular aspect of the question at hand. [51]

Here is a section where she is addressing someone who is beginning to have doubts about all she had been taught about God. The italics are Mirabai's:

While once you were fed on the Word, now you find the Holy One in the center of a luminous silence. In the face of that radiance, all concepts vanish. You rest in the emptiness of unknowing. The hymns and prayers that used to fill your heart with the presence of God have become dry husks. Where did the juice go? you muse, more curious than distressed. The doctrines that had sustained you are beginning to sound ridiculous. Even as you recite the familiar liturgy, you find yourself perplexed: What in the world does that mean?

You dare not speak these questions aloud. Not to your parents. Not to your priest or minister, not to your sheikh or your rabbi. It took these people decades to establish a solid foundation of belief amid the ever-shifting tectonic plates of this life. To them, this dropping down into emptiness is not good news. It looks like a crisis of faith. They will rush in to fix you. But you are intrigued by your own unraveling. You would like to see what comes next. It is a relief to know nothing, to want nothing. *If this is an ailment, you think, may I never recover.* [52]

Another paragraph in Mirabai's book that I found helpful is where she writes that at some point your heart will become...

...so drenched in love for the Beloved that it overflows into everything you do. You are incapable of making distinctions between the sacred and the profane: each act has become an act of prayer...Now you wash dishes for God. Now when you dance the tango you are dancing with the Holy One, when you check email you are corresponding with the Holy One, and when you grade papers you are giving encouragement to the Holy One. Undressing your lover is unwrapping a divine gift; eating chocolate is partaking of a sacrament. [53]

I can do all of that for God's sake. I think that writing my book, also "showing glimpses from my journey, not as someone who has arrived somewhere, but as a fellow seeker immersed in the ongoing adventure," can be considered an action for God's sake as well.

Okay, so here you have quotes from four contemplatives. Pick the quote with which you resonated the most and buy his or her book. Or better yet buy at least one book from each. Then see with which writer you resonated the most and buy the rest of his or her books. You can never have too many books lying around.

After several years of reading and listening to these and others and after many years of sitting daily in Centering Prayer, here is a summary of what I think is going on. Contemplation is an awakening, however briefly, to a higher state of Consciousness. Sometimes it happens suddenly and unexpectedly; sometimes it happens while one is immersed in meditation or centering prayer.

While in a meditative state, for a prolonged period of time, one has ceased thinking; all reference points to any thoughts or worries of any subpersonalities have disappeared; one loses all sense of being a separate ego personality; and one enters a stillness, an emptiness, which for a theist is experienced as a very joyful, blissful Union with God.

Experiencing this emptiness, this very joyful, blissful Union with God, is also said to be getting a glimpse of the Kingdom of Heaven. For Heaven is now no longer viewed as a physical place somewhere up there or far away. You don't have to wait until after death to get there. You can go there now while still alive in this life, because the Kingdom of Heaven is within you. Heaven is a state of consciousness, a waking-up and remembering, a knowing of how things really are, a felt sense of oneness with all that is, accompanied by the intense feelings of bliss.

Your consciousness has just merged with God's Consciousness. You are now one with God. God can show you whatever He thinks you want to know. He will answer immediately whatever questions you may have. But unfortunately, this moment of our merging with God will be brief and immediately we will return to our usual state of consciousness, wondering, "Wow, what in God's Heaven was that?"

From then on we will try to awaken to that state again. Maybe we will, maybe we won't. Some do manage to do so, and depending on the frequency of the awakenings, may enter into a more or less permanent higher stage of consciousness beyond Authentic or Integral. These then become our mystics, saints, and sages, who, for the rest of their lives, live and love as though they were connected with God most of the time. For these nothing much happens at death. They simply, consciously, decide to leave their physical bodies behind and join God in the consciousness state that we call the Kingdom of Heaven. There they go on to do whatever God has in store for them next.

For the rest of us the dying experience will be our last chance to awaken to God's Consciousness and go join the mystics, saints, and sages. If we don't manage to awaken to Union with God while still alive here on Planet Earth, we will simply reincarnate as another human being, with another unique set of givens – DNA, personality, parents, nationality, culture, and go have another planet side lifetime experience.

The consciousness state where souls, who did not wake up to heaven, go immediately after death, is called the Bardo. There they have their life review and based on lessons learned and not learned, they will decide into which situation they would like to be born next. Then they are born and try again to make it to heaven in that lifetime before they die. These birth and rebirth cycles may go on for centuries, allowing our consciousness to evolve gradually up the stages and states of consciousness. Eventually we will all make it to Heaven. The contemplatives are trying to get there in this lifetime. Deciding to undertake the Spiritual Journey to reach the state of contemplation, is to get started on your journey to Heaven.

It is not a journey for us to undertake lightly for our friends and relatives will surely notice that we are acting rather transrationally and transpersonally, and not understanding these terms, they will worry about us. Part of my motivation for writing this book is to explain to them what we are up to. We are not losing it; we are simply listening to a different drummer, a drummer to whom we also encourage them to listen. Are you interested in joining me on this journey to Heaven? If not now, then maybe later? Or maybe you could start slowly now, and speed up later. Or at least, make a vow now that you will re-read this book every five years. But in any case, for now, just read on. I want to share with you what I think is the essence of a contemplative journey and share with you what I am doing along the way.

Chapter 32
The Contemplative Journey

The essence of the Contemplative Journey is to attempt to wake-up more often each day to our more awake, more aware state of consciousness, our true Self. Then try to remain in that state for longer and longer periods of time throughout that day, remembering all the time that you are negotiating with God to have Him merge your consciousness with His. And, while in that state, try to love all those you live with and all others you encounter during that day. The next day we will try to do all of that again. That, pretty much, is all there is to it. But as the saying goes, "Easier said than done." We can measure our progress by noting each day what percent of the time we were functioning as our small self – automatically, mechanically, habitually as in a cultural trance, and what percent of the day we had managed to wake-up from that trance and began to function as our more aware, conscious, eternal Self, remembering that we were on our journey to Heaven.

This is very much like it was when I first started doing Centering Prayer. I was asked to wake-up to my true Self, to imagine myself to be in the presence of God, and to stay so identified for the whole 25 minutes. Then I was encouraged to try to maintain that identification as long as I could throughout the rest of the day. But all too soon, I again fell back into my usual automatic habit patterns as Clarence – watching the TV, reading the paper, answering emails, paying bills, cooking meals, helping Susan. Most of these things do need to get done, but I could be doing them more lovingly in my more conscious mode as Anthony, with awareness of God all around me. I soon decided that what I needed were some more rituals throughout the day that would remind me to get back into that Anthony mode of being, like the CP session did every morning.

The first new ritual I added was to have a cup of green tea around midmorning every day and while sipping my tea I do some spiritual reading. This is working pretty well. I almost always remember to take that midmorning break. I enjoy drinking the green tea. That in itself may be a benefit. The green tea may have some nutrients that are good for my body and it does put some more liquids into my bloodstream, with which the kidneys can do their work.

But the main benefit is a spiritual one. I remember to wake-up, get into my awareness of God mode, and even after my spiritual reading is over, I do manage to stay in my Anthony mode for a while longer. The spiritual reading is also helpful in keeping me on my contemplative journey. Right now, I am alternating between two books for my spiritual reading.

One book is *The Mystic Hours: A Daybook of Interspiritual Wisdom and Devotion* by Wayne Teasdale. The book is divided up into 365 pages, so you can read one a day for a year and then start over again. It is subtitled as an Interspiritual Daybook to emphasize the growing realization among contemplatives that other spiritual traditions are also encouraging their members to undertake a spiritual journey to reach higher states of consciousness. And that we can learn something from them to help us on our contemplative journey. Here, for example, is a quote from the Sufi tradition:

Fakhruddin 'Iraqi (1213-89), Persian mystic and poet, explores the Sufi notions of fana and baqa. Fana is annihilation of the self, the letting go of ourselves into the Divine, while baqa is about union with Allah or God. Like many Christian mystics, Fakhruddin expresses the relationship in the language of love mysticism. This wise Sufi tells us to cut ourselves off from our senses to attain union. The senses and reason are usually concerned with external matters, but this mystic stresses the necessity of abandoning them in the pursuit of the Divine and intimacy with it. [54]

Here is a quote from another Middle Eastern tradition:

"It is not for him to pride himself who loves his own
country, but rather for him who loves the whole world.
The earth is but one country and mankind its citizens."

Baha'u'llah

Baha'u'llah, the founder of the Baha'i tradition in Iran,
saw the terrible toll the nation state and blind nationalism
took and would continue to take in world history. Love
of one's own country, although admirable, could not
hold as a virtue for the whole world. Our own age, 150
years after Baha'u'llah's, is proving his adage again,
with the inevitable forces of globalism bringing the
human family together -- for good and bad. The
retrogressive forces of tribalism and narrow notions of
culture and religion are reacting violently to this
inevitable trend, but the coming together of the planet as
one community cannot be stopped. The planet itself is
our real nation, and we are all members of that larger
society. The enlightened have put the interests of
humankind and the natural world before the interests of
individual communities. This is the demand of our time.
[55]

Finally, one more quote from Teasdale, this time from our own
Christian tradition:

Teresa of Avila was given the extraordinary gift of union
with God. She was granted God's love to an ultimate
degree...This divine love is incomprehensible to us,
because it so overflows our capacity to love and so to
understand it. We humans have an infinite capacity for
love but only a finite experience. When we are given
awareness of God's love for us, all we can do is receive
its power in awe and respond to it with as much love as
we are capable. Human beings -- for most of their lives -
- only know this love through faith, conviction,
theological speculation, or guesses. In mystical
experience, we know it directly, and it changes us
forever. [56]

These are just three pages, there are another 362 more. Get the book, you'll enjoy reading his commentaries and you will learn much that can help you on your spiritual journey. You can still get one used on Amazon for 47 cents. I used to read a page from this book every morning just before my Centering Prayer sessions. You might prefer reading these instead of Fr. Rohr's Daily Meditations.

Another book that I have found helpful is *All Saints: Daily Reflections on Saints, Prophets, and Witnesses for our Time* by Robert Ellsberg. It, too, is divided into 365 entries of one or two pages for each day of the year. As the title states, many of the entries are on Christian saints, describing their encounters with God on their spiritual journeys. But it also has entries on prophets and witnesses for our time.

One such witness for our time is the novelist, Walker Percy Ellsberg starts off his story with a quote from Percy:

"The search is what anyone would undertake if he were not sunk in the everydayness of his own life...To become aware of the possibility of the search is to be onto something. Not to be onto something is to be in despair."

Ellsberg then continues:

Walker Percy was born in Birmingham, Alabama, on May 28, 1916, to a distinguished Southern family. After college, he went north and studied medicine at Columbia. In 1942, during a residency in pathology, he contracted tuberculosis and had to spend the next five years confined to bed in a series of sanitaria. While all the world was plunged in war, Percy lay on his back, reading and thinking intensively about the paradoxes and absurdities of the modern world. He read everything he could get his hands on by Kierkegaard, as well as novelists like Dostoevsky, Kafka, and Tolstoy...In 1946, after his release from the sanitarium, he became a Catholic.

This left many questions about what to do with his life. The one thing he was sure of, was that he had no interest in practicing medicine. Fortunately, an inheritance spared him the immediate necessity of earning a living. Instead he married and settled in New Orleans and continued to devote himself to serious reading. As his children were born and went on to school it became something of an embarrassment to explain what their father did. He read. But his reading was directed to a purpose. He was, as he later wrote of one of his characters, "onto something."

In 1954 Percy began to publish his first writings, dense philosophical essays in obscure professional journals. But he began to think about the possibility of writing about his ideas in a more popular form. The result was his first novel, The Moviegoer, which appeared in 1961 when he was 44. It won the national book award. A massively entertaining story of a young man, Binx Bolling, and his difficulty in deciding what to do with his life. The Moviegoer dealt with themes that would surface in all his subsequent novels. In particular, it explored the difficult human challenge of remaining fully alive while avoiding the lure of everydayness, routine, and despair.

Percy saw the greatest danger of our times to be "the devaluation of human life." Human beings, as he wished to show, were far from angels. They were, nonetheless, endowed with a sacred identity and destiny as "pilgrims, wayfarers on a journey."

Percy died of cancer on May 10, 1990. [57]

Another entry of Ellsberg's that I found very interesting was the 19th century autobiography of The Pilgrim. He starts off his story with a quote from The Pilgrim:

"By the grace of God I am a Christian man, by my actions a great sinner, and by calling a homeless wonderer of the humblest birth who roams from place to place. My worldly goods are a knapsack with some dried bread in it and in my breast-pocket a Bible. And that is all."

Ellsberg then continues:

So begins *The Way of a Pilgrim*, the extraordinary narrative of a religious seeker, which was published in Moscow in 1884 and appeared in English in 1930. The identity of the pilgrim is never disclosed, and apart from his own account, apparently written sometime in the mid-1800s, nothing is otherwise known of his life...

One day in church he was struck by the reading from Scripture: "Pray without ceasing." Troubled by these words, he became obsessed with discovering their meaning. In his quest, he sought spiritual advice from many quarters. Finally, he encountered a holy monk who introduced him to the ancient Byzantine tradition of *hesychia* (stillness or rest in God) and to the Jesus Prayer that lies at the heart of this spirituality. He was instructed to repeat the words, "Lord Jesus Christ, have mercy on me." The monk also introduced him to a collection of writings on hesychasm by the Greek fathers, the *Philokalia* ("Love of Beauty"). This, along with the Bible, became the focus of his daily meditation and reflection.

The pilgrim began by reciting the Jesus prayer 3000 times a day. At first this required considerable effort. But within weeks he had increased this to 6000 and then 12,000 times a day...The prayer became his constant companion as he performed his daily routines and continued on his solitary way. Eventually he had the impression that the prayer had passed from his lips to his heart. He had no further need to repeat the words; they now coincided with the rhythm of his own breathing and the beating of his heart.

The rest of his book describes his wanderings and his encounters with a rich assortment of Russian characters – soldiers, peasants, criminals, beggars, and holy monks.

Sometimes he encounters ill-treatment, as when he is accosted by robbers who refuse to believe that he carries no money. Other times he is received with pious reverence as a messenger of God. For the Pilgrim, good fortune and bad are alike...Not only does he feel that he is the happiest person on earth, "but the whole outside world also seemed to me full of charm and delight. Everything drew me to love and thank God; people, trees, plants, animals..." By the end of his book the Pilgrim is still on his way, his destination unknown, his ultimate fate untold. [58]

These are just two stories of Ellsberg's Saints, Prophets, and Witnesses for our time. He has 363 more on people like Thomas Merton, Dorothy Day, Teilhard de Chardin, Albert Schweitzer, and St. Teresa of Avila. If you do undertake the spiritual journey, you will find much in their stories to inspire and motivate you. At the end of each story, Ellsberg suggests one or two books you may want to read either about his subject or books written by his subject. This will provide you with an almost endless list of suggested readings for your journey. I bought a couple of Percy's books and also bought *The Way of a Pilgrim* and *The Pilgrim Continues His Way*. You can get a used copy of Ellsberg's book on Amazon for one cent.

A second ritual I started several years ago to remind myself to wake up and remember that I was on a contemplative journey is to go for a walk every mid-afternoon. I consider it a meditative walk. I start off the walk the same way I start off my CP sessions. I state clearly that I now intend to stay aware of the presence of God throughout my walk and not get hooked on thoughts that would have me work on problems and worries for most of the walk. When I finish with my walk, I do manage to stay awake and aware as Anthony for a while longer before I slipped back again into doing stuff in my usual consensus trance.

There you have it, my typical day on my contemplative journey since around 2008. My three rituals – the morning CP sit, the mid-morning green tea, and the mid-afternoon walk, give me three opportunities to wake-up and get hooked on an awareness of God being there with me all the time, helping me love all I meet along the way that day. Even though I feel that progress is happening, I do stay alert for more rituals or practices that could help me progress even faster.

My next brilliant idea for a new ritual came to me one day while doing my centering prayer. I knew that I should just let it go and gently go back to my sacred word but at first I just couldn't do it. I reasoned that this might be a key insight slipped into my thought stream by God, in an effort to help me progress faster on my way. But then Father Keating's training kicked in. He taught that even great insights should be let go while in centering prayer. If the insight was truly that great, it would come back to me later, after the centering prayer session was over and I could ponder it then for as long as I wished. And for the rest of that centering prayer session, I was able to let it go, several times actually. And it did come back to me after the session was over.

Here is the brilliant idea: I should take a vow of obedience to someone. Now why would such an idea have occurred to me? I had never, ever, even considered a vow of obedience before, but I had read a little about it in Thomas Merton's journals where he described some of his struggles with his vow of obedience to his Abbot. Why do monks take a vow of obedience to their Abbot? I guess there are several reasons having to do with power and control, assuming that someone has to be in charge of the monastery. But my insight concentrated on how wonderful it would be for helping me drop some of my automatic habit patterns that no longer serve me well, if I wanted to progress on my contemplative journey. One of my ego-subpersonalities may be having me doing something and the abbot can come along and say, "I want you to do something else right now". Without the vow of obedience, I might be wanting to argue that call, but if I want to be true to my vow, I will simply say, "Okay, sure". Giving someone that much power and control over my activities may be very hard, but wouldn't that be helpful. I could use that encounter to wake-up and realize that I was in ego-subpersonality mode, operating automatically. Then, just like I let go of thoughts while meditating, I could try to let go of whatever it was I was doing. It would be a little more dying to my old self so that my new Self could now live and grow.

Isn't this a great idea? I hope you can understand why it was so hard for me to let it go in my centering prayer session. So, I decided that for my next ritual I would take a vow of obedience to my wife, Susan. Who better qualified to tell me how to live my life than Susan, who already had some practice and experience in trying to set my priorities for me? It worked. And I think it did help me progress faster on my contemplative journey. It worked somewhat like what I was already doing with Susan in trying to wake-up and quickly switch subpersonalities whenever she wanted something done that was other than what I was doing. But then I was doing it out of love for her and sometimes the love was not enough to change my activity to suit her and an argument would ensue. But now with my vow of obedience, it wasn't just a question of love, it now had the force of God also wanting me to honor my vow and to change whatever it was that I was doing.

You might want to give this a try also. In addition to reminding you to wake-up more frequently, it will also score you some unpredictability and flexibility points. Your chosen Abbot will love it.

Working with the vow of obedience, got me to thinking about the Monk's vow of poverty. Pretty soon I started worrying that maybe someday soon I would also want to take a vow of poverty.

There is a story in the Bible, in which a rich young man comes up to Jesus, says that he likes what he hears Jesus saying, and that he would like to undertake such a contemplative journey to enter the Kingdom of Heaven. He asks Jesus what he should do. Jesus tells him the usual stuff like to love your neighbor, and not to steal, lie, or murder anyone. The young man replies that he has already been doing all these things and asked what else he could do. Jesus then tells him he could sell all that he has, give all the money away, and come follow him.

Now Jesus was not after his money. He was trying to help the rich young man. Jesus did not use words like: wake-up to your True Self, observe what you are doing, stop living automatically in a consensus trance, meditate daily, die to your old ways of living, and open yourself to new ways of living. But that is what Jesus is counseling. If he could give away all his money, that would immediately have him letting go of all his ego subpersonalities, would wake him up out of his consensus trance life, and have him start out on a brand-new life.

The Bible story ends with rich young man walking away, saying he cannot do that, that he has too many responsibilities. This may be where Jesus got the notion that it would be very hard for a rich man to enter the Kingdom of Heaven. I have never considered myself to be a rich man. My parents were very poor. I grew up poor; started working part-time after school at age 12 to help support the family. Had to work part-time and get student loans to make it through medical school. But even though I still read menus from right to left, I do now have monthly income from my social security and my pension, and I do have some savings, some property, and still even own a few stocks. By Jesus' standard, I guess I am rich and that may be why my progress to heaven has been so slow. I am still spending a lot of time worrying and managing all of my stuff. Maybe taking a vow of poverty and giving away all of my money and property would really speed up my progress. I don't want to do that just yet, but I have started to divest myself of some of my money and stuff, some to the poor, some to help the ecology and environment of the earth, and some to my sons and grandchildren. I am reasoning now that maybe doing that much, along with the waking up and self-observing with my daily rituals, will allow me to make progress on my contemplative journey without formally taking a vow of poverty. Maybe even the rich young man in the Bible, after thinking about what Jesus counseled for 20 years, was able to start out on a contemplative journey of his own.

Trying to wake up to and then staying longer in our contemplative state of mind, was just the first part of our definition of being on a spiritual journey. What about the second part that says, "while in that state, try to love all those you live with and all others you may encounter during that day."

Do we really need to be doing that? Well, if we accept that Jesus of Nazareth somehow did manage to merge his consciousness with God's Consciousness, then what Jesus counseled his followers to do, must be what God wants us to do as well. Here is how I remember that Bible story. Jesus was asked one day to summarize as succinctly as possible what is required to enter the Kingdom of Heaven. Jesus replied that he could simplify it for them in just two commandants. The first being that you should love God with your whole heart, your whole soul, your whole mind, and with your whole strength. The second was that you should love your neighbor as yourself.

There then followed, and continues to this day, a lot of speculation on just who did Jesus mean by "neighbor" and what did he mean by "as yourself". I think that God wants us to love everyone as ourselves. Recall that Jesus is also quoted to have said, "Love your enemies, bless them that curse you, do good to them that hate you, and pray for them which despitefully use you, and persecute you..." Here is Cynthia Bourgeault's input into this discussion:

> One of the most familiar of Jesus's teachings is "Love your neighbor as yourself." But we almost always hear that wrong. We hear "Love your neighbor as much as yourself". (And of course, the next logical question then becomes, "But I have to love me first, don't I, before I can love my neighbor?") If you listen closely to Jesus's teaching however, there is no "as much as" in there. It's just "Love your neighbor as yourself" – as a continuation of your very own being. It's a complete seeing that your neighbor is you. There are not two individuals out there, one seeking to better herself at the price of the other, or to extend charity to the other; there are simply two cells of the one great Life. Each of them equally precious and necessary. [59]

If you and I are "simply two cells of the one great Life," then we have a lot in common. Sure, we do have some differences and our small self sees only these. But as we learn to awaken to our True Self, we are being asked to put aside the superficial differences, and focus instead on how each one of us is alike in the consciousness of God. Seeing all we meet each day in this light will make it easier for us to love them as ourselves.

If I find it too hard to love certain people, I try at least to tolerate them, saying to myself that they, too, have a right to live here on Planet Earth. Next, thinking that they, too, probably have parents or children who love them, I try to be nice and kind to them. I'm hoping that eventually, especially if I am able to wake-up and remember that we really might just be "simply two cells of the one great Life," I will be able to love them all, as my neighbors, as myself.

Okay, that may be enough on Jesus' second commandant – to love your neighbor as yourself. But what about that first commandant – to love God with your whole heart, your whole soul, your whole mind, and with your whole strength? How are we to do that?

Recall that God is a panentheistic God, ensouling the entire material universe. God's body is the entire physical universe, including my body and your body. If we love ourselves and others, we are already loving God as well. Now let's take that up a step. The planet Earth with its entire biosphere is also a part of God's body, so love it. All of Nature, all the interactions of plants, animals, and our atmosphere, all are a part of God's body, so love it. Many traditions have emphasized the need for us to love earth, some referring to her as Mother Earth. So how can we show our love for God by loving Mother Earth? Each of us is in a unique position to do our part to keep our planet livable and lovable. Think about earth being a part of God's body when remembering that you are on your spiritual journey and do what you can that day based on your understanding of what needs to be done.

It may be that learning to love God and everyone in this way, is the main purpose for our life here on earth. If we don't learn this lesson in this lifetime, we get to try again in our next reincarnation. And we get to do this, again and again. It may be that being able to love is like a final exam for graduating from Earth School. It may be the key to getting through the narrow gate, guarding the entrance to the Kingdom of Heaven.

It may be, I don't know for sure. But I have been thinking about this for a long time. It sounds reasonable to me that it may be so. And I have been meditating and praying for a long time also.

Maybe somewhere along the way I did receive some insights, intuitions, and inspiration from God that this is the way it is.

In any case, it is enough motivation for me to keep going on my contemplative journey. To be on a contemplative journey is to be an awakening soul who is onto something...

Chapter 33
I Continue My Way

One Steppingstone in my life ended and a new Steppingstone began on March 16, 2016, the day Susan died from complications of her Parkinson Disease (PD). We found out that Susan had PD in 1999. With medications controlling her symptoms, she was able to continue her full-time practice of Pediatrics until 2004. In 2008, she had electrodes inserted into her brain in a surgery called Deep Brain Stimulation, which helped for a while, but soon that, too, failed to halt the inevitable progression of PD. Eventually she developed Parkinson Dementia, which made communications difficult and independence impossible. For many years, I took care of her here at home by myself. Then for several months I hired a caretaker to come spell me for a few hours each day. In June 2015, my sons and her sister convinced me that it would be best for all concerned to move her into a Memory Care Home, and so we did. Susan died peacefully in her sleep nine months later.

As you can imagine, the last few years were a very difficult time for me as well as for her. Susan and I had often heard Father Rohr say that you made progress on your spiritual journeys either by suffering or by praying. If you are not having to suffer much, then you must pray much. Before her PD, Susan and I had always felt that we had not suffered much in our lives, so we had better start praying more. But I consider our last few years as "suffering much" and we often commented to each other that "this" must be "suffering" and that maybe it was doing us some good. It also helped me a lot to keep thinking of Susan as my Abbot, especially whenever I was being called to do something that was very inconvenient, unpleasant, or irrational.

But now the suffering is over, so once again I think that I will have to start praying more. My objective now is to pray all the time. Not just during my Centering Prayer sessions, but all the time throughout the day.

There are a lot of people trying to do that now in one form or another. The earliest recorded tradition, called "The Jesus Prayer", is described by Abba Philimon, who lived around 600 CE, in a book called *The Philokalia*. The version of the Jesus Prayer cited by Philimon is "Lord Jesus Christ, son of God, have mercy upon me", and it is to be repeated over and over all day long. [60]

The tradition is popular in the Eastern Orthodox religion especially in Russia. I read about the Jesus Prayer in the 19th century anonymous Russian classic, *The Way of the Pilgrim*, wherein the protagonist goes about his daily chores and travels constantly repeating the Jesus Prayer. Even though the setting was 19th century Russia, that novel did give me a sense of what life might be like if I started praying ceaselessly.

Repeating "Lord Jesus Christ, son of God, have mercy on me" all day long might work for some people, but after all that I have grown through, I didn't think that it would work for me today. I started looking for a prayer or phrase that I would feel comfortable repeating ceaselessly all day long. One day while re-reading Ira Progoff's *At a Journal Workshop*, I ran across his section on Mantra/Crystals. It brought back to mind the many weekend workshops that I had attended with Progoff, either alone or with Susan, once even with my sister. In one of those workshops Progoff introduced us to a seven-syllable mantra that one could use during meditation. Although intended for use in meditation, I thought it could be continued past the time of meditation and eventually might stay with me all day long.

You may recall that I introduced you to Progoff in the chapter on Steppingstones. The main purpose of Progoff's workshops was to give us some methods and techniques that we could use to get the experiences that would move us further along in our spiritual journeys. One such method was called The Mantra/Crystal. A mantra/crystal is a seven-syllable phrase that you can repeat quietly under your breath while meditating. Here is how Progoff describes it in *At a Journal Workshop*. The italics are Progoff's:

The cycle in a unit of breathing gives us a natural criterion and measure. *Breathing in and breathing out.* In fact, that phrase itself with its seven syllables is a good indication of the length and rhythm that a Mantra/Crystal should have...

Experience indicates that a Mantra/Crystal of seven syllables carries its inherent rhythm so that, as we continue to say it under our breath in conjunction with our breathing, the rhythm establishes and maintains itself. We can each work out our own balanced rhythm of breathing in and breathing out, fitting it to the seven-syllable phrase. Thus, we can breathe in on the first three syllables, hold on the fourth, and exhale on the last three syllables...

Being not too long and not too short, the seven-syllable phrase corresponds to a full cycle of breath. Thus, it is sustained and continued at a physiological level even when it becomes very meager with respect to both its conscious and its non-conscious contents. An important consequence of this is that, at those times when the energy and the motivation of our meditation dip to a low level, the natural rhythm of the Mantra/Crystal itself can continue the meditation for us. It serves as a rider-less horse that knows where to go, continuing through the valley with only the guidance of its inner nature until it comes to the next valid phase of its journey. Many times, when the disciplines of meditation lag in a person, the momentum and rhythm of the seven-syllable Mantra/Crystal carry the process so that it does not come to halt before it contacts new energies and can re-sustain itself. In practice this is of tremendous importance. [61]

Progoff would have us create these seven syllable phrases that would serve as our Mantra/Crystals. Then he would ask us to shout out the mantra that we had created. The workshop participants came up with all sorts of seven syllable phrases -- Feeling the pain of my life, Kingdom of God receive me, Sweet love of the Universe, Doing the work of the Lord, being silent to listen, who are you, Lord, who am I? Feeling the presence of

God. None of these struck me as phrases that I might want to use in my meditation. Finally, one lady shouted out, "Are you there, Lord, do you care?" Since at that time I was still in my "Hopeful Agnostic" phase, that one hit me just right and I used it for several months. Progoff goes on to say:

> Quite often the Mantra/Crystal changes by itself in the midst of the meditation. It frequently happens that the original one is replaced by another, even as the rhythmic breathing and the process of silent meditation are continuing. The observation that has been most interesting to me in this regard is that invariably the new Mantra/Crystal that is not consciously made but simply emerges in the course of the meditation fits the criteria for making seven-syllable Mantra/Crystals, and does so without any thought or planning or editing or fixing. Most of the time, in fact, the new form and content of the Mantra/ Crystal is more appropriate to the evolving inner situation of the person than the original one that was consciously made. There is apparently a factor of inner wisdom that expresses itself at the depth of human beings whenever the circumstances are right for it. [62]

That change part actually happened to me somewhere along the way. Soon I often heard myself saying, "Here I am, Lord, help me see."

Saying the mantra throughout your meditation is quite different from the Centering Prayer version that Fr. Keating was recommending, so eventually I stopped saying the mantra. It seemed to me that just sitting during CP, not thinking, not saying anything, expectantly waiting for God to make His presence known, was more likely to have me become aware of His presence than if I sat there mumbling my mantra.

A few months ago, I started using the mantra again, reasoning this time that if God wanted to make His presence known, He would find a way to do so. And just like Progoff said, the mantra continued to evolve. I started with "Here I am, Lord, help me see," which changed slowly over time to "Knock, knock, Lord, may I come in?" The knock, knock part recalls Jesus' promise in Luke 11-9 "Knock and it shall be opened onto you," which I interpret as meaning that if we sincerely ask to have our consciousness merge with God's consciousness, that He will open that door for us.

This fits with all contemplatives' belief that we, with only our own efforts, cannot open that door, that it has to be "God's grace" that lets us in. Grace, you may recall from your Baltimore catechism days, "confers on our souls a new life, that is, a sharing in the life of God Himself." (Lesson 9, 109) Grace is not some sort of subtle energy flow from God into us. Grace is simply God opening a door, which lets us share in His life and His consciousness. So, I am asking "may I come in?"

Soon I began to wonder if it was any longer appropriate to keep begging God for things. Maybe I could just announce that I was present and waiting at one of His doors. So the mantra changed again, this time to "Knock, knock, Lord, I am here now." Many spiritual writers have counseled us to "be here now," all the way back to the 1970s when Ram Dass' published his *Be Here Now*, and more recently to Eckhart Tolle's *The Power of Now*. I think of "I am here now" as my announcement that I have awakened to a higher state of consciousness, that I am remembering that I am on a spiritual journey, and am looking out for what I could do now while still here firmly grounded on earth.

Finally, I changed the "Lord" part to "My Love" and found myself saying, "Knock, knock, My Love, I'm here now." Somehow calling God "My Love", seems more appropriate today than to keep referring to Him as "Lord", especially after all we heard about the commandment to love God and our neighbor. Don't you often call your significant other "my Love"?

So, as of January 2017, my mantra remains, "Knock, knock, My Love, I'm here now." But I am finding it hard to keep saying it throughout my meditation period, so what I'm doing now is using the mantra sort of like Fr. Keating's sacred word. I don't say it all the time. But I do start saying it again when I realize that I had gotten hooked on thinking about something. I say it for a while and soon stop again to just enjoy the quiet, the solitude, the space in-between thoughts. I firmly intend to be there, in-between thoughts, when the gong goes off on my timer, signaling the end of the meditation session. Sometimes I make it, sometimes I don't.

After the gong goes off, I firmly intend to keep saying my mantra, ceaselessly for the rest of the day. If I am saying "Knock knock, My Love, I'm here now" whenever I encounter someone, I am able to treat that person more lovingly. Whenever I come across something that needs doing, I am able to do that more enthusiastically and happily. And I am in a more receptive awareness state should God choose to show up subtly during that time.

I hope you will create such a seven-syllable mantra for yourself. Feel free to use mine if you want to, but I think that Progoff's idea is that it would be better if you create one for yourself. Start with any seven-syllable phrase of your choosing and let it evolve over time to something that will be consistent with your values and beliefs, and then let it carry you onward and upward as you continue your spiritual journey.

I think I am now moving from Act III to Act IV in my life. Recall that in Chapter 30, Steppingstones Updated, I had this to say about my Acts III & IV:

> ...during Act III I will need to reconcile the various approaches of the scientist, the philosopher, and the mystic to come up with a belief system and a set of spiritual practices with which I can live and grow...

> ...Act IV will start after I have learned to stay awake for longer periods of time, after I have integrated a little bit better all of my various subpersonalities, and after I have come up with that acceptable worldview or story, that believable set of beliefs, or at least after I have become a little more content to live with a modicum of uncertainty and doubt. By then I will have accomplished some transformation towards a life filled with more joy, love, and peace.

Yes, I think that I am ready for Act IV. I have learned to stay awake for longer periods of time, although not yet ceaselessly. I do function now as one whole integrated personality, most of the time. I do have now a worldview or story by which to live, with just a tad of healthy skepticism still remaining. And my life is now filled with an abundance of joy, love, and peace. It doesn't need to get any better than this.

I sincerely hope that the techniques, exercises, and rituals, which I have shared with you in this book will help you with struggles in your life. All you have to do is "wake up" and "remember" that you are an awakening soul, capable of functioning at a higher state of consciousness, from which you will be better able to cope with the struggles in your life.

I have started an Organization of Awakening Souls. The following is sort of an Awakening Souls manifesto. One of these days I intend to place it on our website, awakeningsouls.org, but in the meanwhile here it is. You can read it as a summary of all that I have shared with you throughout this book.

The Awakening Soul

We are souls, each of us has a body/mind, but we are souls. It is correct to say, "I have a body/mind," because it is the soul who is talking, and the soul does have a body/mind.

We do it all the time, but technically it is not correct to say, "I have a soul." It is only correct to say, "I am soul." You know this. If you understand the word, soul, you know that you are soul.

We usually act as though we were only our body/minds. We have forgotten that we are souls. Our body/minds are quite capable of functioning in the world without remembering that we are souls. Having forgotten that we are souls, our body/minds have developed an ego, a false self, a personality that functions automatically, mechanically, through habit patterns that were enculturated into us by our parents, our church, our ethnic heritage, our country, and our peers. We souls have gone to sleep.

It is time to wake up. While awake, we can observe what our body/minds are doing. We will become more aware of what is going on. We will note that our personality is actually fragmented into several sub-personalities each fighting for time to be in control of our one body/mind. As we learn to stay awake for longer periods of time, we begin to integrate these various sub-personalities into one smoothly functioning body/mind, and our lives become filled with joy, enthusiasm, and love.

When fully awake and aware, we begin to explore what it means to be human, and to ask "How do I wish to live the rest of my life?" And at the same time, we begin to explore what it means to be an awakening soul. We may get our first hints that we are a part of God's consciousness, an ever-present, loving reality, and we may get our first glimpses of what Heaven is really like.

Feel free to get in touch if you want to dialogue about any of this. The Epilogue will show you how.

Epilogue

At this time in my life, I think that the most important work I can do, is to encourage more and more people to grow up the stages of consciousness, to become awakening souls, and to help make life on this planet sustainable for human life for as long as our sun continues to shine.

I am aware of the political conflicts, the economic struggles, and the warlike mentality that pervade our planet today. The only way these conditions will improve is to have more people and more nations functioning at higher stages of consciousness. Please help me bring more peace, justice, and joy to our lives and to the lives of future generations yet to come.

You can best help me in this mission now by critiquing this book. Focus on the main ideas presented here. Were they presented clearly? Do you agree? Disagree? Are you interested in becoming an awakening soul? Do you have any questions? Do you wish to dialogue?

If you do email, you can write to me at:

anthonyfromgranger@awakeningsouls.org

If you wish to send me a letter by the postal service, address it to:
Anthony, P.O. Box 33, Granger, TX 76530

I do intend to continue my contemplative journey of praying, reading, writing, and attending conferences   I may even be moved to start a blog or newsletter someday to continue sharing what I am learning. If you don't wish to dialogue, you can follow anonymously what I am doing on my website: awakeningsouls.org. So far the site is rather primitive. I need to get better at designing and maintaining websites and/or get a helper. So, better if you get in touch. I'm looking forward to hearing from you.

Notes and References

[1] Tart, C. T. *Waking Up* (Boston: New Science Library, Shambhala, 1986) p. 196.

[2] Assagioli, Roberto, *Psychosynthesis* (New York: The Viking Press, 1965) pp. 75-76.

[3] Synthesis, Vol.1 (Redwood City, CA: The Synthesis Press, 1977) pp. 97-99.

[4] Progoff, Ira, *At a Journal Workshop* (NY: Penguin Putman Inc., 1992) pp. 77-78.

[5] de Ropp, Robert S. *The Master Game* (NY: Dell Publishing Co Inc. 1968) pp. 62-65.

[6] Tart, C. T. The dynamics of waking sleep. In J. Needleman & G. Baker (Eds.), *Gurdjieff* (New York: Continuum, 1996). p 116.

[7] Ibid., p 126.

[8] Deikman, A. J. *The Observing Self* (Boston: Beacon Press, 1982) p. 94.

[9] Ibid., p 129.

[10] Ouspensky, P.D. *In Search of the Miraculous* (NY: Harcourt Brace, 1949) pp. 120-1.

[11] Assagioli, Roberto, *The Act of Will* (Baltimore: Penguin Books, 1974) pp. 215-216.

[12] Ibid., p 217.

[13] Wilber, Ken, *A Theory of Everything* (Boston: Shambhala, 2000) pp.21-22
For further details on the stages of consciousness, see Beck, Don and Cowan, C.C *Spiral Dynamics* (Malden, MA: Blackwell Publishers Inc. 2000) and Graves, C.W. *Levels in Human Existence, (2004)* or *The Never Ending Quest. (2005)*

[14] Assagioli, Roberto, *Psychosynthesis* (New York: The Viking Press, 1965) pp. 17-18.

[15] Wade, Jenny, *Changes of Mind* (Albany: SUNY Press, 1996) pp. 158.

[16] Ibid., pp. 159-163.

[17] Ibid., p 164.

[18] Maslow, A.H. *Motivation and Personality* (NY: Harper & Row, 1970) pp. 173-174.

[19] Maslow, A.H. *Toward a Psychology of Being* (NY: Van Nostrand Rhld, 1968) p. 104.

[20] Ibid., p. 105.

[21] Ibid., p. 106.

[22] Ibid., p. 106.

[23] Ibid., p. 107.

[24] Wilber, Ken, *Integral Psychology* quoted from *The Collected Works of Ken Wilber* (Boston: Shambhala, 1999) pp. 483-484.

[25] Targ, Russell, *Limitless Mind: A Guide to Remote Viewing and Transformation of Consciousness* (2004)

[26] Dossey, Larry, *Prayer Is Good Medicine: How to Reap the Healing Benefits of Prayer* (1997)

[27] Assagioli, Roberto, *Psychosynthesis* (New York: The Viking Press, 1965) pp. 86-87.

[28] Monroe, R.A. *Journeys out of the Body* (NY: Broadway Books, 1977) pp. 27-28.

[29] Ibid., p. 29.

[30] Ibid., pp. 46-48.

[31] Murphy, Michael, *The Future of the Body: Explorations Into the Further Evolution of Human Nature* (NY: Jeremy P. Tarcher/Putman, 1992) p. 112.

[32] Ibid., p. 113.

[33] Ibid., p. 115.

[34] Bailey, L.W. and Yates, Jenny, Editors *The Near-Death Experience: A Reader* (NY:Routledge, 1996) p. 7.

[35] Moody, R.A. *Life After Life* (San Francisco: Harper, 2001) pp. 167-168.

[36] Cressy, Judith, *The Near-Death Experience* (Hardcover – March, 1994)

[37] Ring, Kenneth, *Lessons from the Light* (NY: Insight Books, 1998)

[38] Weiss, B.L. *Many Lives, Many Masters* (NY: Simon & Schuster, 1988) pp. 24-25.

[39] Ibid., p. 28.

[40] Ibid., pp. 28-29.

[41] Ibid., p. 35.

[42] Ibid., p. 40.

[43] Weiss, B.L. *Only Love is Real* (NY: Warner Books, 1997) p. 150.

[44] Ibid., pp. 151-152.

[45] Ibid., pp. 152-153.

[46] Wilber, Ken, *Sex, Ecology, Spirituality: The Spirit of Evolution* (Boston: Shambhala, 1995) p. vii.

[47] Mitchell, Edgar, *The Way of the Explorer* (NY: G.P. Putnam's Sons, 1996) pp. 3-4.

[48] Ibid., pp. 143-144.

[49] Assagioli, Roberto, *Psychosynthesis* (New York: The Viking Press, 1965) p. 87.

[50] Wilber, Ken, *Sex, Ecology, Spirituality: The Spirit of Evolution* (Boston: Shambhala, 1995) pp. 264-265.

[51] Starr, Mirabai, *God of Love* (New York: Monkfish Book Publishing Co., 2012) p. 8.

[52] Ibid., p. 70.

[53] Ibid., p. 104.

[54] Teasdale, Wayne, *The Mystic Hours* (Novato, CA: New World Library, 2004) p. 174.

[55] Ibid., p. 178.

[56] Ibid., p. 115.

[57] Ellsberg, Robert, *All Saints: Daily Reflections on Saints, Prophets, and Witnesses for Our Time* (New York: Crossroad Publishing Co., 2001) pp. 233-235.

[58] Ibid., pp. 429-430.

[59] Bourgeault, Cynthia, *The Wisdom Jesus* (Boston: Shambhala, 2008) pp. 31-32.
    See also Cynthia's latest book *Heart of Centering Prayer: Nondual Christianity in Theory and Practice* (Boulder: Shambhala, 2016).

[60] I got this historical information by looking up "The Jesus Prayer" on Wikipedia.

[61] Progoff, Ira, *At a Journal Workshop* (NY: Penguin Putman Inc., 1992) pp. 332-333.

[62] Ibid., p. 333.

Made in the USA
San Bernardino, CA
03 July 2017